TWENTY-FIRST CENTURY
CHICAGO

Revised Second Edition

For April,
Welcome to Chicago
& Elmhurst College!
Connie

Edited by
Dick Simpson
Constance A. Mixon
and Melissa Mouritsen

University of Illinois at Chicago, Elmhurst College, and College of DuPage

cognella®
academic publishing

Bassim Hamadeh, CEO and Publisher
Angela Schultz, Senior Field Acquisitions Editor
Jamie Giganti, Senior Managing Editor
Jess Estrella, Senior Graphic Designer
Natalie Lakosil, Senior Licensing Coordinator
Christian Berk, Production Editor

Printed in the United States of America

ISBN: 978-1-5165-1160-0 (pbk) / 978-1-5165-1161-7 (br)

www.cognella.com   800-200-3908

Contents

PART III: CHICAGO POLITICS

PART IV: CHICAGO GOVERNMENT

PART V: GLOBAL CHICAGO

PART VI: METROPOLITAN CHICAGO

PART VII: A NEW CHICAGO

To the next generation of Chicagoans who will create a better future

Acknowledgments

This book is completely new, but draws upon the work of the writers and editors of the earlier *Chicago's Future in a Time of Change* books published since 1976 by Stipes Publishing. With this book we build upon that foundation.

We are especially grateful for Dorothy Storck, who helped to polish our words in the introductions. And Robin Kastengren, who helped with our final edits to this edition.

Finally, Cognella's staff: Angela Schultz, Senior Field Acquisitions Editor; Jamie Giganti, Senior Managing Editor; Natalie Lakosil, Senior Licensing Coordinator; Jess Estrella, Senior Graphic Designer; Dani Skeen, Marketing Assistant; and Christian Berk, Production Editor. Each helped to make the book you hold in your hands possible.

PART I

Choosing Chicago's Future

By Dick Simpson and Constance A. Mixon

Introduction

Chicago was born more than one hundred and fifty years ago. Some of our older suburbs are over a century old. We are the third-largest city in the United States with a population of just under 3 million people. Over 9.5 million people live in the metropolitan region. Metropolitan Chicago is larger in population and has greater wealth than most nations in the world.

During the last several decades, we have been transformed into a "global city." At the same time, population, jobs, and housing stock have been declining for the first time in the history of the city, since the Great Chicago Fire of 1871 and the Great Depression of the 1930s. We are also still recovering from the "Great Recession" of 2008. The "political machine," which has governed the city since the Chicago Fire and, more firmly since its reorganization under Mayor Cermak in 1931, was transformed under former Mayor Richard M. Daley. Daley's twenty-two-year reign brought Chicago into the global economy and reoriented political power. Today, Chicago is governed by a new political boss, Mayor Rahm Emanuel.

In this book, we explore many of the fundamental dimensions and conditions of Chicago's metropolitan life. While some of the articles in the book will stress the region's shortcomings, we want to emphasize that Chicago has many possibilities for a positive future. We have some of the best businesses on the planet. We have a population that represents nearly every segment of the world and speaks nearly all of its languages. We have a positive history of reform efforts (as well as a history of scandals and rogues). By our decisions and our actions, we will collectively determine the future of Chicago in the twenty-first century.

ECONOMIC CONDITIONS

Throughout the 1970s and early 1980s, the city of Chicago lost manufacturing jobs at a rate of 25,000 a year, for a total loss of more than 250,000 jobs. This dramatic downturn in manufacturing left Chicago with an uncertain future as the capital of the Rust Belt. Because of deindustrialization, white flight, and decreasing federal aid, the city of Chicago also lost an average of 12,500 units of housing and 60,000 residents a year during the 1970s. Our total city population has dropped from 3.6 million in 1950 to just 2.7 million today. If this continues, Chicago may drop from the third largest to the fourth largest U.S. city behind New York, Los Angeles, and Houston by 2025.[1] Over the last sixty years, the city itself has lost nearly a million people—despite the pretty new buildings in the South and West Loop and the new condominiums popping up in increasingly gentrified neighborhoods. To put this population loss in context, since the 1950s, Chicago "has lost more people than currently live in all of San Francisco, Boston, or D.C."[2] Without our fairly recent gains in Latino population, the total population loss in Chicago would have been much greater. Today, the older manufacturing base of Chicago's regional economy has mostly been replaced—first by the service economy, and now by the global economy.

The new knowledge and service economies of Chicago, created by global forces, employ fewer people than the economies of yesteryear. Furthermore, most of the region's high-growth industries, like financial services and high-tech firms, are concentrated downtown. An economic restructuring and reorganization of the Chicago labor market has resulted in significant social and economic inequalities. While manufacturing jobs once paid the equivalent of at least $50,000 a year, plus full health benefits and good pensions, today's two-tiered global economy has produced a large segment of service jobs paying an average of only $15,000 a year, with few or no benefits. These wage inequalities are integrally related to our city's entrenched patterns of poverty and segregation and became a major issue in both the 2015 city elections and in the 2016 presidential elections nationally.

By the turn of the twenty-first century, Chicago had shed its title of being the Rust Belt capital and is now the Midwest capital of the global economy. This means Chicago's fate is now directly connected to the fate of the international economy of which it is a part. As part of the global economy, international conditions and the role of transnational corporations directly affect our region in ways we no longer control. Decisions like the merger of our banks, the closure of manufacturing plants like Motorola, collapse of major service companies like Arthur Andersen, and bankruptcies of major companies like United Airlines and the *Chicago Tribune* all occur without input from the city, suburban, or state governments. Local corporations—and certainly local communities—have little to no voice in determining what will be done. These decisions are made elsewhere. There are few restraints on global businesses.

As a result of the 2008 global recession, the Chicago region lost more than 264,000 jobs from 2008–2010.[3] In the wake of the recession, the city of Chicago faced a 400-million-dollar deficit in 2010. The city partially closed that deficit by selling off the city's parking meters to a private firm. It faced an additional $654.5 million deficit in the 2011 budget, which led to more employee furloughs and to cutting more city jobs. In 2015, with a deficit of $297 million, the city, public schools, and park district all had their bond ratings downgraded to "junk" status. Chicago Public Schools (CPS) in 2015 failed to extend teacher contracts for another year, citing a looming 1.5-billion-dollar deficit. The Chicago Transit Authority (CTA) also found itself facing a 1-billion-dollar deficit and significant reductions in state aid in 2015. Dismal city finances have produced an economic environment where taxpayers are continually squeezed for more revenue, while more and more services are cut and employees are laid off.

By 2016, the Chicago city government budget problem became so bad that Mayor Emanuel and the city council had to levy an additional $755 million in taxes and borrow an additional $1 billion to pay the city's bills. Finally, in July, 2016 the state of Illinois was able to pass a stop-gap budget for 2015 through December 2016, but many areas like higher education and social services were left severely underfunded. Local governments are facing the need to raise taxes once again. Pension deficits at state and local governments have now become unsustainable. Chicago city government, the Chicago Public Schools, and the state face the worst budget crisis in recent history. The state's bond ratings are the lowest now of any state in the nation. Only California has had a lower rating among the large states, and it has recovered since its low point.

Despite a regional unemployment rate of 6.4 percent in 2015, unemployment can be as high as 60 percent of households in the poorest Chicago neighborhoods and suburbs. Twenty-five percent of African Americans in Chicago are jobless, and "Chicago has the highest black unemployment rate among the nation's five most populous cities."[4] Part of the reason for this racial disparity, according to Michael Dawson, a professor at the University of Chicago, is our city's "extreme segregation" that "deprives many residents of the predominantly black South and West Sides of adequate public transit and job networks."[5]

As the articles in this book will detail, the major economic challenge in the Chicago metropolitan region over the last four decades has been the loss of manufacturing jobs and our switch first to the service and now to the global economy. With this new global economy, we face the problem of making sure that the benefits of globalization do not create a new richer class and leave a much poorer, more desperate class behind. We must also find ways to attract and expand our shrinking middle class while finding ways to have a more equitable distribution of the wealth generated by the new global economy.

The principal social problem of metropolitan Chicago is not found in any one system that doesn't work, such as the public schools, the health care system, or the criminal justice system. Rather, the major social problem in Chicago is the connection between race and poverty. This problem of race and poverty underlies and penetrates each challenge we face, in education, health care, criminal justice, and all the rest. The challenge of poverty and race in Chicago has resulted in a permanent underclass.

While the Chicago metropolitan area is extremely diverse, we remain one of the most segregated regions in North America. Most Chicagoans live in racially and economically homogeneous neighborhoods, as reflected by our high segregation index of more than 72 percent. This means that for each Chicago neighborhood and suburb to have a racial mix equal to the metropolitan region as a whole, 72 percent of the people would have to move. Most of us currently live in segregated neighborhoods.[6]

The city of Chicago is approximately 33 percent black, 32 percent white, 29 percent Latino, and 6 percent Asian and other. Since 2000, there has been a noteworthy decline in the African American population, while the Latino population has been growing. From 2000 to 2010, 72 census tracts in the metropolitan region of 1,821 census tracts switched from white to Hispanic and 22 from white to black. The clearest change is that whites are no longer the majority in the city, where they had been dominant since 1833. While whites remain the majority in the metropolitan region, population changes are occurring rapidly in every part of the region. Latino immigrants, for example, are increasingly likely to skip the city and move directly into suburbs, following jobs and affordable housing.

Many minorities—especially African Americans—live in the poorest communities, as race and poverty go together in Chicagoland. Yet, to paraphrase Lincoln, we know that Chicago cannot exist half slave and half free, half black and half white, half poor and half rich. Being black and poor must no longer be synonymous. Neither should being poor and Asian or Latino.

Unfortunately, there is a racial or "color gap" in metropolitan Chicago. Income inequality has continued to rise since the 1960s, despite national policies such as civil rights laws and the "war on poverty" that attempted to eliminate discrimination and poverty. The concentration of misery and high crime in the racial ghettos of Chicago and Chicago's segregated suburbs is not just. The same division of poverty and wealth that occurs so obviously in the city occurs in the entire metropolitan region. Suburbs like Harvey and Markham are black and poor; communities like Oak Park and Evanston are managing to handle their racial and economic disparities; while some communities on the North Shore and in the western suburbs remain all white, segregated, very wealthy, and very smug.

The most telling study of segregation in Chicago was originally done in 1965 by demographer Pierre deVise. He examined 250 Chicago community areas with more than 2,500 people in them. He measured median family income, median value of homes, and assessed real estate valuations per resident or median rent, and ranked each community from 1 to 250.

The ten richest communities were in the suburbs. They were nearly all white, mostly far north or west of the city like Kennilworth, Winnetka, and Hinsdale. The ten poorest communities were within the city limits, on the South and West Sides, and were nearly all black. Later studies up to the present day have confirmed this basic pattern of geographical and racial segregation, but have added the city neighborhoods of the Loop and Lincoln Park to the list of wealthiest communities and expanded the list of poorest communities beyond the city to southern suburbs like Harvey and Robbins.

In an attempt to solve the ghetto problem in Chicago, the city and federal government tore down high-rise Chicago Housing Authority (CHA) projects like Cabrini-Green and the Robert Taylor Homes, which were "synonymous with high crime rates and urban decay."[7] The original plan for transformation was to scatter CHA residents into newly built mixed-income housing. But new public housing, for which existing CHA residents had to reapply and qualify, was not built as quickly as the high-rise buildings were coming down. Chicago's attempt at transforming public housing is still unfinished and has left tens of thousands of families displaced. Throughout the metropolitan region, we have too little affordable housing for poor and working-class families, which perpetuates existing patterns of racial and economic segregation.

One of the problems of residential segregation is that poor minority communities also have the worst schools, the highest level of crime, the fewest jobs, and the fewest ways out of poverty. It leads to a permanent underclass in which families are trapped in poverty for generations.

POLITICAL CONDITIONS

An elite class of businesspeople, politicians, and heads of major institutions have ruled the city of Chicago for the last hundred and fifty years. An aristocracy of local businesspeople, along with politicians have similarly run most suburbs.

Political machines first ruled the city after the Great Chicago Fire of 1871. The first political boss was Michael Cassius McDonald, a gambler-saloonkeeper who noticed the common bonds between criminals and politicians and introduced them to each other. The first machines served the rapidly growing ethnic communities in Chicago during the latter part of the nineteenth century and the first part of the twentieth century.

The machines of Chicago have been both Republican and Democratic, suburban and inner-city. To understand them, we need to define our terms. As political scientists, we use the term *political machine* to mean a permanent political organization or political party that is characterized by patronage, favoritism, loyalty, and precinct work. They spawn patronage, corruption, and inefficient costly governments. Machines provide certain payoffs for supporters at all levels. They provide patronage jobs for their precinct workers, local government services as favors to those voting for the party slate of candidates, and lucrative, overpriced contracts for businesspeople who give large campaign contributions.

In the suburbs, Republican machines have recently been successfully challenged by Democrats. There is an overall pattern of greater penetration by Democrats into the previously controlled Republican parts of the metropolitan region. DuPage County, once the most Republican county in the United States, voted Democratic for president in 2008 and 2012. In 2012 and 2014, the county elected and reelected several Democratic congressional and state legislative candidates. The Republican advantage in counties like DuPage previously rested on the assumption that these suburban growth centers were filling up with prosperous upper- and middle-class professionals, who cared most about low taxes and being left alone to raise their kids. This is changing.

At the same time political change is occurring in the suburbs, the Chicago political system is also evolving. The Richard M. Daley regime, which combined remnants of the old machine and elements of a new political machine, ended in 2011 with the election of Mayor Rahm Emanuel. The first election of Rahm Emanuel in 2011 ushered in a new political era for Chicago. During his first term in office, Mayor Emanuel successfully pushed a neoliberal policy agenda through a very compliant rubber-stamp city council. This policy agenda earned him the label "Mayor 1%." Emanuel's critics argue that his policies have overwhelmingly benefited his friends in the business world while ignoring the needs of average city residents. As detailed later in this book, public policies in Chicago have spawned a long list of mutually beneficial relationships for the mayor and his top campaign contributors.

As he "was forced to fight for his political life in the city's first mayoral runoff" in 2015, Emanuel did, however, shift "his policies slightly to the left on issues like a city minimum-wage increase and affordable housing requirements."[8] As he sought his second term as mayor of Chicago, Emanuel argued he had made progress in "tackling underfunded worker pensions, establishing a longer school day, cutting wasteful spending, slashing red tape and finding the money to revitalize public transit."[9] His argument did not, however, persuade most Chicagoans, who failed to give him a majority of their votes in the February 2015 election. Forced into a humbling runoff election against Cook County Commissioner Jesus "Chuy" Garcia, Emanuel did eventually win the April 2015 runoff election, with 56 percent of the vote to Garcia's 44 percent.

Mayor Emanuel had only a few months to enjoy his second victory until protests broke out. With the release of the Laquan McDonald police shooting videotape in December 2015, "Black Lives Matter" protests came to Chicago. Demonstrations have continued since over the high crime and murder rates in African American communities of the city. Crime has also spilled over into white and Latino communities and even onto the expressways. Police abuse and corruption with proven cases of white police officers caught on social media killing unarmed blacks have fueled the discontent in Chicago and throughout the nation. These crises have caused the firing of the Chicago police superintendent and the head of Independent Police Review Authority (the police investigative unit); a scathing city task force report; and a full investigation by the United States Department of Justice. Thus far, the "reforms" that have been adopted have been inadequate to solve our high crime rates, instances of police abuse, corruption, and brutality. Overall, Mayor Emanuel's clout and popularity have plummeted as a result.

Mayor Emanuel has continued to rely on some of the same components of the Daley machine models, but he has even more campaign contributions from the global economy, including significant amounts from outside of Chicago. Due to his previous positions in the White House, Congress, and Wall Street, he has a major national network of campaign contributors, unmatched by any previous contenders for the office. In 2015, Mayor Emanuel and his PAC (Chicago Forward), spent more than $30 million in the preliminary and runoff elections. By contrast, his challenger in the runoff election, Jesus "Chuy" Garcia, and his union allies spent only $4.6 million, far behind Emanuel.[10]

While previous Chicago machines relied on ward organizations and patronage armies to help win elections, Mayor Emanuel has yet to fully establish this basis of support. His political power comes from his ability to raise money and distribute the spoils to his backers.

Mayor Rahm Emanuel has continued Mayor Richard M. Daley's policies of catering to the affluent winners in a globalized economy. Some of the most recent amenities designed for Chicago's wealthy residents living in gentrified neighborhoods include: a bike-share program; farmers' markets; a river walk; and the 606 elevated trail. Urban amenities like sushi restaurants and bike and hiking paths are also important to Chicago's global businesses, seeking to attract young, innovative, and talented employees, who increasingly want to live and work in the city.

Although the transformation began before Emanuel became mayor, Chicago has become two cities: one for wealthy residents and tourists, with a gleaming downtown; and one for the poor, with neglected and isolated neighborhoods. Chicago's 2015 mayoral election was an election of these two Chicagos. Emanuel's runoff challenger, Jesus "Chuy" Garcia, repeatedly accused the mayor of turning his back on the city's neighborhoods and ignoring the working class and the poor residents of the city. While Garcia "was constantly seeking ways to introduce himself to the electorate, Emanuel was recreating himself as a gentler person that was learning to listen to people's concerns and defining Chuy through negative commercials as not prepared for the job."[11] In the end, Emanuel—and money—won.

GOVERNMENTAL CONDITIONS

The major governmental problem in the Chicago metropolitan region is that our governments are fragmented, inefficient, and inequitable in their delivery of services to citizens. They are a nineteenth-century set of governments trying to cope with twenty-first century problems.

In Cook County, there are 540 separate units of government with the power to tax. There are 1,200 separate units of government dispersed throughout the metropolitan region. Chicagoans pay property taxes to 7 governments, while suburbanites pay property taxes to as many as 17 separate government agencies. Strong political machines and strong bosses like Richard J. Daley were originally needed to make this cumbersome governmental machinery work at all. Today's plethora of governments continues to inhibit accountability, efficiency, effectiveness, and coordination.

The legislative branch of Chicago city government, the Chicago City Council, remains a rubber stamp, although there have been sparks of independence. A study of voting records released by the University of Illinois– at Chicago in 2014 (and detailed in this book) found that 38 of the 50 aldermen voted with Emanuel 90 percent or more of the time. The progressive caucus of the council, which had eight aldermen identifying with them during Mayor Emanuel's first term, only voted 67 percent of the time with the mayor. At the end of the 2015 runoff elections, the progressive caucus achieved a net gain of three members, bringing the total number of progressives in the council up to eleven.[12]

As a result of the elections and other political pressures, the Chicago City Council is becoming slightly more independent. During the first ten months of the second Emanuel term, the number of aldermen voting more than 90 percent of the time with the mayor on critical divided roll call votes decreased to 28 (56 percent), while those aldermen opposing the mayor and voting less than 80 percent of the time has increased to 13 (26 percent). There is "still a rubber-stamp council but it is a weaker, less reliable rubber stamp than Emanuel had in his first four years in office."[13] Aldermen are also offering more of their own legislative proposals without first clearing them with the mayor.

Four things have shaken up the old order and led to some increased independence among aldermen:

1. In April 2015, Rahm Emanuel was forced into a runoff election with Chuy Garcia, demonstrating that the mayor had less political clout than when he won outright in 2011.
2. The city's budget problems, which were building for years, caused the mayor to propose $755 million in tax increases, including a property tax hike of $543 million and a new garbage collection tax, all of which were unpopular with citizens and aldermen.
3. The public release of the Laquan McDonald shooting videotape ignited a revolt in the African American community followed by months of major protest demonstrations, which led to the firing of the police superintendent and the head of Independent Police Review Authority (the police abuse investigative agency).
4. Emanuel's public approval rating plummeted to the lowest level for any mayor since Michael Bilandic, who lost his subsequent election. According to the latest *New York Times* poll, only 25 percent of the public approves of the job Mayor Emanuel is doing, and only 8 percent of blacks believe the mayor "cares a lot about people like them."

Because Mayor Emanuel has become politically weaker, aldermen are now less willing to follow him blindly, especially on hard votes like raising taxes; and aldermen don't want to go against the clear wishes of their constituents on such issues. However, it must be noted that Mayor Emanuel has still won every vote in the council and hasn't had to use his veto power to do so.

Suburbs also need to improve and reform their local town and village councils. Many suburban town councils vote unanimously on all legislation without any meaningful debate or dissent. Virtually none of the 540 governments within Cook County boasts a really strong and vital legislative branch that functions well. This must change if local governments in the metropolitan region are to work well and democratically in the twenty-first century.

In addition to rampant political corruption, patronage, and waste, our crazy quilt of governments with taxing authority creates duplication and inefficiency. This is a fractured, multilayered government that has grown up haphazardly over the last one hundred fifty years. The 540 governments within Cook County include: the county itself, which is the nineteenth-largest government in the United States; 129 municipalities; 30 townships; and 380 special districts, such as the school, park, and library districts. Other districts include large regional sectors like the Metropolitan Water Reclamation District of Greater Chicago and the Regional Transportation Authority.

Our multiple local governments don't have the ability, scope, or political will necessary for comprehensive planning in the metropolitan region, and these overlapping governments create inefficiencies. Any proposal to reduce inequalities, disparities, and inefficiencies by creating a metropolitan government fails because there are almost no "metropolitan citizens" who identify with the metropolitan region. Proposals for metropolitan government are blocked by powerful political interests, racial tensions, and the suburban fear of being governed by the Chicago machine.

One small improvement has been made in regional governance. NIPC (the Northeast Illinois Planning Commission) and CATS (the Chicago Area Transportation System) have been merged into a single regional agency with a single staff, authority, and a larger budget. The new agency is called CMAP, the Chicago Metropolitan Agency for Planning. However, this new agency has too few powers to compel compliance with its plans by all the separate governments. Without real money or power, it is not very effective in constructing a system of governance in the metropolitan region.

The Chicagoland Mayor's Caucus, while allowing for some coordination and cooperation between Chicago and suburban towns, is forced to avoid contentious issues like expansion of O'Hare Field or a new third regional airport. Like CMAP, the Mayor's Caucus depends on voluntary cooperation between multiple separate units of government that jealously guard their powers.

Looming over all other governmental crises has been the budget and pension impasse in state government. As of June 2016, the state of Illinois had gone a year without a budget and has at least a $10 billion dollar structural deficit—. And the state has a pension deficit of more than $100 billion dollars. All local governments have had similar problems, causing them to cut services, raise taxes, and confront pension debts they don't have the ability to pay.

During this time of crisis, the Illinois state government has been operating on the previous 2015 budget (despite a cut in income tax revenue) for those programs and services that are required to be paid by court order, or in a few cases like public schools, which the governor and the legislature have agreed to fund to prevent major crises like closing schools altogether.

One example that illustrates the effects of the budget impasse can be found in higher education. The Illinois General Assembly in its proposed 2015–2016 budget, proposed an 8 percent cut in state funding to state universities, while the governor proposed a 32 percent cut. Since neither budget was approved, nothing was paid to the state universities and community colleges for ten months, until a stopgap measure was finally passed providing only 30 percent funding (a 70 percent cut). Even that was done only to keep several state universities like Chicago State University from closing their doors altogether. The new stop-gap budget for 2016-2017 funds most state universities only at 82% of the 2015 budget. Social services, doctors, pharmacies, other businesses, and even state highway repair are in similar situations. Many non-profits, governmental agencies, and businesses are at the brink of bankruptcy because of financial uncertainty in Illinois and drastic cutbacks in programs.

We are currently in the midst of the worst financial crisis in Illinois since the Great Depression. This limits the potential and future of Chicago and the state of Illinois.

CONCLUSION

In the new global economy and changing society, we face many challenges. While Mayor Rahm Emanuel has promised changes and recorded some progress, significant challenges remain. Certainly, the budget and financial crises are critical. In addition, there are perennial problems—like racial segregation and income inequality—to be confronted. However, the Chicago metropolitan region also has great strengths as the seventh most important global city in the world and as one of the wealthiest economic regions. For us to have a more positive future, we must begin by understanding our past and collectively adopting a plan to implement our vision for the future. We, as citizens, can choose a more positive future for our metropolitan region.

NOTES

1. Strahler, Steven. 2016. *Crain's Chicago Business*, March 23.
2. Hertz, Daniel Kay. 2015. "Unnecessary population loss on the north side is a Problem for the whole city." *City Notes*, March 16.
   http://danielkayhertz.com/2015/03/16/unnecessary-population-loss-on-the-north-side-is-a-problem-for-the-whole-city/
3. Merrion, Paul. 2014. "Which way is Chicago's economy going?" *Cain's Chicago Business*, January 4.
4. Emmanuel, Adeshina. 2014. "Chicago's black unemployment rate higher than other large metro areas." *Chicago Reporter*, November 16.
5. Ibid.

6. Ihejirika, Maudlyne. "Studies: Chicago Among the Most Segregated Cities," *Chicago Sun-Times*, March 3, 2016, p. 18; and Brandon Campbell, "Decades After Civil Rights Act Study Shows Chicago Making Progress But Still Segregated," *Inside-Booster*, March 16–22, 2016, pp. 1 and 6.

7. Anderson, Bendix. 2013. "Transforming Chicago's Public Housing." *Urban Land Magazine*, September 23.

8. Dardick, Hal, and John Byrne. 2015. "New Chicago City Council still driven by Emanuel agenda." *Chicago Tribune*, May 17.

9. Hinz, Greg, and Thomas A. Corfman. 2014. "Here's What the Numbers Say About Rahm Emanuel." *Crain's Chicago Business*, November 8.

10. Pearson, Rick, and Hal Dardick. 2015. "Emanuel, allies spent at least $22.8 million to win." *Chicago Tribune*, April 16.

11. Richardson, Shelby. 2015. "Chicago's mayoral election: A tale of two cities." *People's World*, April 10. http://peoplesworld.org/chicago-s-mayoral-election-a-tale-of-two-cities/

12. Dardick, Hal, and John Byrne. 2015. "New Chicago City Council Still Driven by Emanuel Agenda." *Chicago Tribune*, May 17.

13. Simpson, Dick, et al. "A More Active City Council: Chicago City Council Report #8," Chicago: University of Illinois at Chicago Department of Political Science, March 23, 2016; http://tinyurl.com/AMoreActiveCouncil. See also Fran Spielman, "New Study Shows Traces of Spine in Chicago City Council," *Chicago Sun-Times*, May 23, 2016, pp. 1 and 4; and Ted Cox, "Weak Rahm Means Gutsier City Council But Rubber Stamp Remains: Study," *DNA Info*, May 23, 2016.

Re-Election Victory Speech

By Rahm Emanuel

A five-candidate field in the February 2015 mayoral election forced Chicago Mayor Rahm Emanuel into a humbling runoff. This speech was delivered by Mayor Emanuel on the evening of April 7, 2015, after he won re-election to a second term against Cook County Commissioner Jesus "Chuy" Garcia. He won the runoff with 56 percent of the vote to Garcia's 44 percent.

April 7, 2015

Thank you Chicago!

I want to thank my wonderful friend, my dearest friend, my greatest ally, my wife Amy... she voted this morning with Zach [Mayor Emanuel's son], who got a chance to vote for the first time ever in an election. They were undecided until this morning, but they broke.

While a lot of people describe Chicago a lot of ways, all of us describe it as home. To the second city that voted for a second term, and a second chance: I have had the good fortune to serve two presidents. I've had the fortune of being elected to Congress. Being mayor of the City of Chicago is the greatest job I've ever had and the greatest job in the world...I am humbled at the opportunity to continue to serve you, the greatest city, with the greatest people, for the next four years.

I want to congratulate Chuy Garcia for running an excellent race. I want to also congratulate him, he is a good man who clearly loves the City of Chicago and clearly loves his family. As an immigrant, he represents the promise of Chicago and I want everybody to hear this loud and clear across this great country: you just saw an election between both the grandson of an immigrant and an immigrant, which is why we are the greatest city in America. And don't let anybody ever tell you, around the world, there is no other city that an immigrant from Mexico, and the grandson of an immigrant from Moldova can both run for the highest office of this great city. That is why we are the greatest city. Because here in Chicago, here in Chicago, we're immigrants who come for the promise, the promise of Chicago.

* * *

And to all the voters, I want to thank you for putting me through my paces…I will be a better mayor because of that. I will carry your voices, your concerns into…the mayor's office. I hear you on the importance of neighborhood high schools and better choices. I hear you on the importance of raising minimum wage so that no family that works, ever raises a child in poverty ever again. Not in the City of Chicago.

* * *

I also want to be clear, I hear you about the importance of finding jobs for our ex-offenders, who made a different choice in life, and they too, want to become whole. And I hear you about the importance of building a new Chicago, where everybody gets the chance to participate in building this great city. From our roads, our waterways, our airports, our schools, our community colleges, our parks and our playgrounds—everybody has a chance to participate in that great exercise called building a new Chicago. These are the north stars that I hear from our grocery stores, to our el stops, to our front stoops. Chicago I hear you. I'm proud of what we've accomplished in these past four years, but I understand the challenges we face will require me to approach them differently. And work in a different fashion. The only way to meet these challenges is to bridge the gap that divided us, and start focusing on the things that unite us and bring us together.

We are the city that works…and that means it has to work for everyone, in every neighborhood, in every part of the City of Chicago. And in the era of hard choices, I can't promise that everybody will be pleased with every decision. But the challenges we face, we face together, as one community, one city, one voice, where every voice counts. Make no mistake, the challenges we face were not campaign talking points. The decisions we make over the next four years will determine what Chicago will look like in the next 40 years.

* * *

Now I want to offer a couple special thanks here. One, to the thousands of volunteers who went door to door and made the phone calls. I want to thank you. I want to thank my co-chairs Susanna Mendoza, Jesse White, Luis Gutierrez, Bobby Rush… And specifically, I want to thank also my friends in organized labor, the business community, and the community groups who contributed their time and their resources for this campaign. To my hard working campaign staff, who I've put through the paces, who went beyond the call of duty, and met the challenge of this runoff. And my staff at City Hall, that work day in and day out to live up to the expectations of all Chicagoans. To my wife Amy, to my children Zachariah, Alana and Leah, and my brothers Ezekiel and Ari that are here, and to my parents who I want to thank for teaching all of us to not only have our convictions, but the courage to fight for them, to fight for what we believe in, to fight for what we think is right. They are a testament.

And to all the people of Chicago, who have given me this incredible privilege to serve as your mayor for another four years, thank you, god bless you, and god bless Chicago.

PART II

Race and Class

Photograph by Rick Kohnen. From the author's collection.

Introduction

Class and racial discrimination and stratification are found in most of our nation's metropolitan areas. Chicago is no exception. As discussed in this section's articles, race and class are intertwined. Although no longer the most segregated city in the United States, ten of Chicago's poorest fifteen neighborhoods are at least 94% African American.[1]

Residential segregation, all too common throughout the Chicagoland area, leaves citizens, mostly minorities, confined to ghettos with underperforming schools and few job opportunities. As early as the 1960s, demographer Pierre de Vise and sociologist William Julius Wilson studied the connection between the race and poverty. De Vise found that the ten poorest communities in the 1960s were all in the inner city and all black. The ten richest were all suburban, mostly north suburban, and all white communities. Two decades later, in 1980, sociologist William Julius Wilson found patterns of poverty and segregation in Chicago had remained unchanged since the 1960s. Updating Wilson's work to the 2010 censuses finds poverty is moving further south and west from the original ghettos, and becoming slightly less concentrated. Still today, the basic patterns of segregation, poverty, and wealth in metropolitan Chicago remain essentially the same as when de Vise and Wilson first studied them.

The problem of spatial racism in Chicago was addressed by Chicago's Archbishop Cardinal Francis George in 2001, who argued that,

> The face of racism looks different today than it did thirty years ago. Overt racism is easily condemned, but the sin is often with us in more subtle forms ... Spatial racism refers to patterns of metropolitan development in which some affluent whites create racially and economically segregated suburbs or gentrified areas of cities, leaving the poor—mainly African Americans, Hispanics and some newly arrived immigrants—isolated in deteriorating areas of the cities and older suburbs.[2]

Reporter Steve Bogira recently examined "some of the quality-of-life indicators" we would have "hoped would improve for black Americans" in Chicago since the 1960s.[3] Detailed below, Bogira found in Chicago there was little progress and little improvement. Neighborhood segregation, poverty, and inequality, commonplace in the civil rights era, has persisted from generation to generation in Chicago.

CHICAGO THEN & NOW

SEGREGATED NEIGHBORHOODS		POVERTY RATE	
1960	2011	1960	2011
69% of African-Americans lived in community areas that were 94 percent black	63% of African-Americans lived in community areas that were 95 percent black	29.7% for African-Americans	34.1% for African-Americans
		7.4% for whites	10.9% for whites

MEDIAN INCOME		UNEMPLOYMENT RATE	
1960	2010	1968	2012
$4,800 for African-American families	$29,371 for African-American households	7.6% for African-Americans	19.5% for African-Americans
$7,700 for white families	$58,752 for white households	2.3% for whites	8.1% for whites

Source: Steve Borgira/Chicago Reader, "Chicago Then & Now." Copyright © 2013 by *The Chicago Reader*.

Chicago's racial and economic disparities limit access to opportunity. This was compounded by the 2008 recession, which hit the poor, the young, the uneducated and minorities the hardest. In 2000, 19.6% of Chicagoans had incomes below the federal poverty level.[4] By 2013, poverty had increased to 23% in the city, with 10% of our residents living in extreme poverty. In some neighborhoods on Chicago's south and west sides, over 60% of residents live below the poverty level.[5] Even more troublesome, in our world class global city, is the fact that over 30% of our children, regardless of race, are living in poverty. Yet, race matters. Detailed in the image below, there is a growing racial gap in child poverty. In 2011, over 36% of Latino and over 50% of black children in Chicago were living in poverty. These percentages have increased from 2000, when about 25% of Latino and 40% of black children were considered to be poverty.[6]

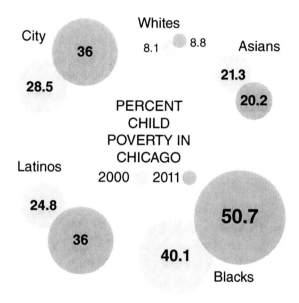

The racial divide in Chicago and its suburbs is paralleled by an income and wealth divide. The Voorhees Center at the University of Illinois at Chicago has documented there are now three Chicago's: 1) High-income Chicago is concentrated on the north side of the city and just west and south of the loop; 2) poor Chicago is concentrated on the south and west sides of the city, where the housing projects and Black ghettoes existed; and 3) a shrinking middle-income Chicago is sandwiched on the far northwest and southwest sides. Today, middle-income Chicago only includes 16% of the city's census tracks. This becomes ever more stark, as income inequality between the rich and the poor in the Chicago metropolitan region has doubled between 1970 and 2010. In Chicago, the rich are very rich, and the poor very poor.

In the three Chicago's documented by the Voorhees Center, affordable housing is quickly disappearing for both the squeezed out and shrinking middle class, and those living in and at the margins of poverty. In Chicago, the "median rent for a one-bedroom apartment in the city tops $1,600."[7] The Chicago Housing Authority (CHA) provides apartments in public housing and housing vouchers to eligible low-income families. While demand has always exceeded supply at CHA, the gap has become more pronounced during Mayor Rahm Emanuel's tenure, who has been criticized for the underutilization of CHA resources and sitting on a CHA surplus of $440 million dollars.[8] Prior to Emanuel taking office,

> ...the CHA delivered an average of 843 affordable units of housing each year, either in new construction or as rehabbed units. ... That number dropped by almost half in the first year of Emanuel's administration, to 424. The following year, that number was down again by almost three-fourths, to a paltry 112—even as the CHA's stockpiles of unspent cash continued to skyrocket. In 2013, the CHA constructed or rehabbed only 88 housing units, and the agency was on track for 2014 to meet a goal of 40 new units—less than 10% of the annual production rate the year before Emanuel took office.[9]

In 2014, the CHA opened its public housing wait list for the first time since 2010; and its voucher wait list for the first time since 2008.[10] More than 280,000 households applied for these coveted spots on the CHA wait list. Yet, those who did get spots on the 2014 CHA wait list, are unlikely to receive help from the CHA anytime soon. In 2012, *The Chicago Reporter* "found that CHA was cashing federal rent checks worth millions for empty apartments while a record number of families sat on a wait list hoping for a unit to open up."[11] In Chicago, the average wait time for CHA rent subsidies is ten years, in contrast to the national wait time average of 12-24 months.[12]

According to the CHA, "ninety-seven percent of the people receiving housing assistance are black or Latino, and 85 percent are women... Some 15,000 families on the list are homeless."[13] Mayor Emanuel's 2015 runoff challenger, Jesus "Chuy" Garcia repetitively criticized the Mayor and the CHA during the campaign. A few weeks before the April 7th election, Garcia argued, "Mayor Emanuel controls the CHA - and for four years now he's shortchanged low-wage workers, seniors on fixed incomes and children in poverty of critically needed affordable housing."[14]

No longer simply a white and black city, one of the biggest changes in recent decades has been the increasing Latino and Asian population in Chicago. Metropolitan Chicago hosts the eighth largest Asian American population in the United States, as they now number 450,000 or 5.4% of the total population. Latinos now comprise about 30% of the city's population and an ever-increasing proportion in our suburbs. While the increasing presence of Latino and Asian American populations has transformed the Chicago metropolitan region into a more multi-cultural, multi-racial, and multi-ethnic city, it has not been an easy transformation. Rather, as discussed in the articles that follow, it has been hampered by polarized political debates centered on immigration status.

NOTES

1. *Segregation in Chicago.* 2006. Center for Urban Research and Learning at Loyola University Chicago Loyola University. Chicago, IL http://www.luc.edu/curl/cfm40/data/minisynthesis.pdf
2. George, Cardinal Francis. 2001. "Dwell in My Love: A Pastoral Letter on Racism," April 4.
3. Bogira, Steve. 2013. "A Dream Unrealized for African-Americans in Chicago." *Chicago Reader.* August 21. http://www.chicagoreader.com/chicago/african-american-percentage-poverty-unemployment-schools-segregation/Content?oid=10703562
4. *Social IMPACT Research Center's analysis of the U.S. Census Bureau's 2000 Decennial Census and 2007-2011 5-year American Community Survey.* 2013. January 9. http://www.ilpovertyreport.org/sites/default/files/uploads/Chicago_Neighborhood_Indicators_00-11_130109.pdf
5. "Poverty Rate Data - Information about poor and low income residents." U.S. Census, 2013. http://www.city-data.com/poverty/poverty-Chicago-Illinois.html#ixzz1BFpArK8f
6. Bogira, Steve. 2012. "Chicago's growing racial gap in child poverty." *Chicago Reader.* October 4. http://www.chicagoreader.com/Bleader/archives/2012/10/04/chicagos-growing-racial-gap-in-child-poverty
7. KaiElz. 2015. "Garcia: Misuse of CHA funds shows Emanuel's wrong priorities for affordable housing." *Chicago Defender.* March 22. http://chicagodefender.com/2015/03/22/garcia-misuse-of-cha-funds-shows-emanuels-wrong-priorities-for-affordable-housing/
8. Newman, Jonah. 2014. "CHA wait list exposes Chicago's affordable housing crisis" *Chicago Reporter.* November 26. http://chicagoreporter.com/cha-wait-list-exposes-chicagos-affordable-housing-crisis/
9. KaiElz. 2015. "Garcia: Misuse of CHA funds shows Emanuel's wrong priorities for affordable housing." *Chicago Defender.* March 22. http://chicagodefender.com/2015/03/22/garcia-misuse-of-cha-funds-shows-emanuels-wrong-priorities-for-affordable-housing
10. Newman, Jonah. 2014. "CHA wait list exposes Chicago's affordable housing crisis" *Chicago Reporter.* November 26. http://chicagoreporter.com/cha-wait-list-exposes-chicagos-affordable-housing-crisis/
11. Newman, Jonah. 2014. "CHA wait list exposes Chicago's affordable housing crisis" *Chicago Reporter.* November 26. http://chicagoreporter.com/cha-wait-list-exposes-chicagos-affordable-housing-crisis/
12. KaiElz. 2015. "Garcia: Misuse of CHA funds shows Emanuel's wrong priorities for affordable housing." *Chicago Defender.* March 22. http://chicagodefender.com/2015/03/22/garcia-misuse-of-cha-funds-shows-emanuels-wrong-priorities-for-affordable-housing/
13. Grim, Ryan, Arthur Delaney and Kim Bellwar. 2015. "Rahm Emanuel's Housing Agency Sitting On Hundreds Of Millions Of Dollars With Massive Waitlist." *Huffington Post.* March 18.
14. KaiElz. 2015. "Garcia: Misuse of CHA funds shows Emanuel's wrong priorities for affordable housing." *Chicago Defender.* March 22. http://chicagodefender.com/2015/03/22/garcia-misuse-of-cha-funds-shows-emanuels-wrong-priorities-for-affordable-housing/

The Halsted Street Saga

By Jane Addams, Florence Scala, Studs Terkel, and Dick Simpson

The saga of the Halsted Street neighborhood was started a hundred years ago with Jane Addams' Hull House trying to offer an alternative to the cycles of immigrant poverty. It continues with the story of how the present day university has now gobbled up the old neighborhood. In between, Florence Scala tells us how it happened that a neighborhood, rich in tradition and heritage, was replaced by a university with an urban mission.

The three vignettes presented here trace a hundred years of struggle as neighborhoods are destroyed and rebuilt in a different twenty-first century city.

1900–1920 BY JANE ADDAMS

Twenty Years at Hull House

Jane Addams and the settlement house she founded early in the twentieth century were major forces in American history. She was an important leader in the settlement house movement, the progressive movement in American politics, the fight by suffragettes for women's right to vote, and the peace movement. She and her colleagues at the Hull House Settlement helped to expose many of the problems of the inner-city poor of her day and to pass laws and to change government policies in ways that benefited the poor. This is her description of the neighborhood in which she worked and lived in the early decades of the twentieth century.

Halsted street has grown so familiar during 20 years of residence that it is difficult to recall its gradual changes—the withdrawal of the more prosperous Irish and Germans, and the slow substitution of Russian Jews, Italians and Greeks.

Halsted street is 32 miles long, and one of the great thoroughfares of Chicago; Polk Street crosses it midway between the stockyards to the south and the shipbuilding yards on the north branch of the Chicago River. For the six miles between these two industries the street is lined with shops of butchers and grocers, with dingy and gorgeous saloons, and pretentious establishments for the sale of ready-made clothing. …

Hull House once stood in the suburbs, but the city has steadily grown up around it and its site now has corners on three or four foreign colonies. Between Halsted street and the [Chicago River] live about ten thousand Italians—Neapolitans, Sicilians, and Calabrians, with an occasional Lombard or Venetion. To the south on Twelfth Street are many Germans, and side streets are given over almost entirely to Polish and Russian Jews. Still farther south, these Jewish colonies merge into a huge Bohemian colony, so vast that Chicago ranks as the third Bohemian city in the world. To the northwest are many Canadian-French, clannish in spite of their long residence in America, and to the north are Irish and first-generation Americans. On the streets directly west and farther north are well-to-do English-speaking families, many of whom own their houses and have lived in the neighborhood for years; one man is still living in his old farmhouse.

The policy of the public authorities of never taking an initiative, and always waiting to be urged to do their duty, is obviously fatal in a neighborhood where there is little initiative among the citizens. The idea underlying our self government breaks down in such a ward. The streets are inexpressibly dirty, the number of schools inadequate, sanitary legislation is unenforced, the street lighting is bad, the paving miserable and altogether lacking in the alleys and smaller streets, and the stables foul beyond description. Hundreds of houses are unconnected with the street sewer. The older and richer inhabitants seem anxious to move away as rapidly as they can afford it. They make room for the newly arrived immigrants who are densely ignorant of civic duties. The substitution of the older inhabitants is accomplished industrially also, in the south and east quarters of the ward. The Jews and Italians for the finishing of the great clothing manufacturers, formerly done by American, Irish, and Germans, who refused to submit to the extremely low prices to which the sweating system, has reduced their successors. As the design of the sweating system is the elimination of rent from the manufacture of clothing, the "outside work" is begun after the clothing leaves the cutter. An unscrupulous contractor regards no basement as too dark, no stable loft too foul, no rear shanty too provisional, no tenement room too small for his workroom, as these conditions imply low rental. Hence these shops abound in the worst of the foreign districts where the sweater easily finds his cheap basement and his home finishers.

The houses of the ward, for the most part wooden, were originally built for one family and are now occupied by several. They are after the type of the inconvenient frame cottages found in the poorer suburbs twenty years ago. Many of them were built where they now stand; others were brought thither on rollers, because their previous sites had been taken for factories. The fewer brick tenement buildings which are three or four stories high are comparatively new, and there are few large tenements. The little wooden houses have a temporary aspect, and for this reason, perhaps, the tenement-house legislation in Chicago is totally inadequate. Rear tenements flourish; many houses have no water supply save the faucet in the back yard, there are no fire escapes, the garbage and ashes are placed in wooden boxes which are fastened to the street pavements.

One of the most discouraging features about the present system of tenement houses is that many are owned by sordid and ignorant immigrants. The theory that wealth brings responsibility, that possession entails at length education and refinement, in these cases fails utterly. The children of an Italian immigrant owner may "shine" shoes in the streets and his wife may pick rags from the street gutter, laboriously sorting them in a dingy court. Wealth may do something for her self-complacency and feeling of consequence; it certainly does nothing for her comfort or her children's improvement nor for the cleanliness of anyone concerned. Another thing that prevents better houses in Chicago is the tentative attitude of the real estate men. Many unsavory conditions are allowed to continue which would be regarded with horror if they were considered permanent. Meanwhile, the wretched conditions persist until at least two generations of children have been born and raised in them.

In every neighborhood where poorer people live, because rents are supposed to be cheaper, there is an element which, although uncertain in the individual, in the aggregate can be counted upon. It is composed of people of former education and opportunity who have cherished ambitions and prospects but who are caricatures of what they meant to be —"hollow ghosts which blame the living men." There are times in many lives when there is a cessation of energy and loss of power. Men and women of education and refinement come to live in a cheaper neighborhood because they lack the ability to make money, because of ill health, because of an unfortunate marriage, or for other reasons which do not imply criminality or stupidity. Among them are those who in spite of untoward circumstances, keep up some sort of an intellectual life; those who are "Great for books," as their neighbors say. To such the Settlement may be a genuine refuge. ...

From the first it seemed understood that we were ready to perform the humblest neighborhood services: We were asked to wash the newborn babies, and prepare the dead for burial, to nurse the sick, and to "mind the children." Occasionally these neighborly offices unexpectedly uncovered ugly human traits. For six weeks after an operation we kept in one of our three bedrooms a forlorn little baby who, because he was born with a cleft palate, was most unwelcome to his mother, and we were horrified when he died of neglect a week after he was returned to his home; a little Italian bride of fifteen sought shelter with us one November evening, to escape her husband who had beaten her every night for a week when he returned home from work, because she had lost her wedding ring; two of us had officiated quite alone at the birth of an illegitimate child because the doctor was late in arriving, and none of the Irish matrons would "touch the likes of her"; we ministered at the deathbed of a young man who during a long illness of tuberculosis had received so many bottles of whisky through the mistaken kindness of his friends, that the cumulative effect produced wild periods of exultation, in one of which he died.

We were also early impressed with the curious isolation of many of the immigrants; an Italian woman once expressed her pleasure in the red roses that she saw at one of our receptions in surprise that they had been "brought all the way from Italy." She would not believe for an instant that they had been grown in America. She said that she had lived in Chicago for six years and had never seen any roses, whereas in Italy she had seen them every summer in great profusion. During all that time, of course, the woman had lived within ten blocks of a florist's window; she had not been more than a five-cent car ride away from public parks; but she had never dreamed of faring forth herself, and no one had taken her. Her conception of America had been the untidy street in which she lived and had made her long struggle to adapt herself to American ways. ...

The Settlement, then is an experimental effort to aid in the solution of the social and industrial problems which are engendered by the modem conditions of life in a great city. It insists that these problems are not confined to any portion of a city. It is an attempt to relieve, at the same time, the overaccumulation at one end of society and the destitution at the other; but it assumes that this overaccumulation and destitution is most sorely felt in the things that pertain to social and educational privileges. From its very nature it can stand for no political or social propaganda. It must, in a sense, give the warm welcome of an inn to all such propaganda, if perchance one of them be found an angel. The one thing to be dreaded in the Settlement is that it loses its flexibility, its power of quick adaptation, its readiness to change its methods as its environment may demand. It must be open to conviction and must have a deep and abiding sense of tolerance. It must be hospitable and ready for experiment. It should demand from its residents a scientific patience in the accumulation of facts and the steady holding of their sympathies as one of the best instruments for that accumulation. It must be grounded in a philosophy whose foundation is on the solidarity of the human race, a philosophy which will not waver when the race happens to be represented by a drunken woman or an idiot boy. Its residents must be emptied of all conceit of opinion and self-assertion, and ready to arouse and interpret the public opinion of their neighborhood. They must be content to live quietly side by side with their neighbors, until they grow into a sense of relationship and mutual interests. Their neighbors are held apart by differences of race and language which the residents can more easily overcome. They are bound to see the needs of their neighborhood as a whole, to furnish data for legislation, and to use their influence to secure it. In short, residents are pledged to devote themselves to the duties of good citizenship and to the arousing of the social energies which too largely lie dormant in every neighborhood given over to industrialism. They are bound to regard the entire life of their city as organic, to make an effort to unify it, and to protest against its overdifferentiation.

1940–1967 STUDS TERKEL INTERVIEW OF FLORENCE SCALA

Excerpts from: *Prologue: Florence Scala*

Decades after Jane Addams founded Hull House, Florence Scala, an Italian housewife and later businesswoman and aldermanic candidate, describes the fight between the Halsted/Maxwell Street neighborhood and city hall. It is a fight the neighborhood, like many urban neighborhoods, lost. Even the Hull House board of directors betrayed the neighborhood.

I was born in Chicago, and I've always loved the city. I'm not sure any more. I love it and I hate it every day. What I hate is that so much of it is ugly, you see? And you really can't do very much about it. I hate the fact that so much of it is inhuman in the way we don't pay attention to each other. And we can do very little about making it human ourselves.

What I love is the excitement of the city. There are things happening in the city every day that make you feel dependent on your neighbor. But there's detachment, too. You don't really feel part of Chicago today, 1965. Any more, I don't feel any [attachment].

I grew up around Hull House, one of the oldest sections of the city. In those early days I wore blinders. I wasn't hurt by anything very much. When you become involved, you begin to feel the hurt, the anger. You begin to think of people like Jane Addams and Jessie Binford and you realize why they were able to live on. They understood how weak we really are and how we could strive for something better if we understood the way.

My father was a tailor, and we were just getting along in a very poor neighborhood. He never had money to send us to school; but we were not impoverished. When one of the teachers suggested that our mother send us to Hull House, life began to open up. At the time, the neighborhood was dominated by gangsters and hoodlums. They were men from the old country, who lorded it over the people in the area. It was the day of moonshine. The influence of Hull House saved the neighborhood. It never really purified it, you know what I mean? I don't think Hull House intended to do that. But it gave us ... well, for the first time my mother left that damn old shop to attend Mother's Club once a week. She was very shy, I remember. Hull House gave you a little insight into another world. There was something else to life besides sewing and pressing. ...

I always remember the neighborhood as a place that was alive. I wouldn't want to see it back again, but I'd like to retain the being together that we felt in those days.

There were Negroes living in the neighborhood even then, but there was not the tension. I've read about those riots in Chicago in the twenties—the race riots. But in our neighborhood it never did come to any kind of crisis. We used to treat each other as neighbors then. Now we look at each other differently. I think it's good and bad in a way. What we're doing is not understanding, some of us, what it was like then. I think that the American-born—the first generation, the second generation—has not hung on to what his mother and father had. Accepting someone naturally as a man. We don't do that today.

I think that the man who came over from Europe, the southern European especially, who was poor, could understand and see the same kind of struggle and have immediate sympathy for it. He accepted the Negro in the community as a man who is just trying to make a way for himself, to make a living. He didn't look upon him as a threat. I think it was the understanding that both were striving. Not out of some great cause, but just in a human way. I'm convinced that the first and second generation hasn't any concern about the other person's situation. I think money and position are hard to come by today and mean an awful lot, and now they see the Negro as a threat. Though they may say he's inferior, they know damn well he's not. He's as clever as we are and does many things better than we can. The American-born won't accept this, the first and second generation family, especially among the Italians and Poles, and the Irish, too. …

Through my teens I had been a volunteer at Hull House. After the War, Eri Hulbert, Jane Addams's nephew, told me of a dream he had. The Near West Side, our area, could become the kind of place people would *want* to live in, close to the city. Did I think this was possible? I said no, people didn't care enough about the neighborhood to rebuild it. But he introduced me to the idea of city planning. He felt the only hope for big cities, in these communities that were in danger of being bulldozed, was to sit down and look and say we have a responsibility here. He convinced me that you could have a tree on the West Side, see?

That's where my life changed. I became involved with a real idea and talking to people like the banker, the social worker, and the Board of Trustees at Hull House. But I suddenly realized my inadequacy. I simply couldn't understand their language, you know? I had to go back to school.

This is where I began to lose the feeling of idolatry you have about people. I think that's bad. I idolized the people that were involved in Hull House. I thought they could never make a mistake. I was later to find out they were the ones who could hurt me the most. I feel that people have to be prepared always for imperfections in everyone, and we have to feel equal, really, to everyone. This is one of the things lots of slum kids, people who came out of poor areas, don't have. Not to be afraid to say something even though it may be way off base. I did this many times and I'd be embarrassed, realizing I had said something that had nothing to do with what they were talking about. But Eri Hulbert kept saying it makes no difference, just keep at it. You're as good as they are …

In those days it was a new idea. You had to fight the politician who saw clearance and change as a threat to his power, his clout. He likes the kind of situation now around Maxwell Street, full of policy and hot goods being sold on the market and this kind of stuff that could go on and on without too much interference from authority because it's so oppressed. The rotten housing and no enforcement of codes and all that business. We had a tough time selling the Catholic Church, too. From '47 to '56 were rough years. It was tough selling people on the idea that they could do it for themselves, that it was the only way it could be done. Their immediate reaction was: You're crazy, you know? Do you really think this neighborhood is worth saving?

All the meetings we had were so much frustration. Eri Hulbert was trying to lead us in a democratic way of doing something about our city. The misunderstandings never came from the neighborhood people. It arose out of the Hull House Board's unwillingness to understand. He couldn't get his point across.

Eri Hulbert committed suicide before our plan was accepted by the city. His death, more than anything else, opened a door which I never dreamed could open. You know, there's a real kind of ugliness among nice people. You know, the dirty stuff that you think only hoodlums pull off. They can really destroy you, the nice people. I think this is what happened to Eri, the way he was deserted by his own. I think it really broke his heart. What disturbs me is that I was a grown woman, close to thirty, before I could see. Sometimes I want to defend the rotten politicians in my neighborhood. I sometimes want to defend even gangsters. They don't pretend to be anything but what they are. You can see what they are. They're not fooling anybody, see? But nice people fool you.

I'm talking about the [Hull House] Board of Trustees, the people who control the money. Downtown bankers, factory owners, architects, people in the stock market. The jet set, too. The young people, grandchildren of old-timers on the Board, who were not really like their elders, if you know what I mean. They were not with us. There were also some very good people, those from the old days. But they didn't count so much any more. This new crowd, this new tough kind of board members, who didn't mind being on such a board for the prestige it gave them, dominated. These were the people closely aligned to the city government, in real estate and planning. And some very fine families, old Chicago families. (Laughs.) The nicest people in Chicago.

* * *

In the early Sixties, the city realized it had to have a campus, a Chicago branch of the University of Illinois. (There was a makeshift one at the pier out on the lake.) There were several excellent areas to choose from, where people were not living: a railroad site, an industrial island near the river, an airport used by businessmen, a park, a golf course. But there was no give. The mayor [Richard J. Daley] looked for advice. One of his advisors suggested our neighborhood as the ideal site for the campus. We were dispensable. [This advisor] was a member of the Hull House Board. It was a strange thing, a very strange thing. Our alderman, he's not what I'd call a good man—even he tried to convince the Mayor this was wrong. But the Mayor was hearing other voices. The nice people.

The alderman alerted us to the danger. Nobody believed it. The priest himself didn't believe it. They had just opened the parish, a new church, a new school. Late in the summer of 1960 the community could have been touched off. But the people were in the dark. When the announcement came in 1961, it was a bombshell. What shocked us was the amount of land they decided to take. They were out to demolish the entire community.

I didn't react in any belligerent way until little kids came knocking at the door, asking me to attend a meeting. That's where the thing got off the ground. It was exciting to see that meeting, the way people felt and the way they talked and the way—they hurt—to hear our Italian priest, who had just become an American. This was in February, we had just celebrated Lincoln's birthday. He had just become a citizen, he couldn't understand.

Though we called the Mayor our enemy, we didn't know he was serving others. It was a faceless thing. I think he'd just as soon have had the university elsewhere. But the pressures were on. We felt it as soon as our protests began. …

I shall never forget one board meeting. It hurt Miss Binford [a colleague of Jane Addams who had lived and worked at Hull House from 1906 until its destruction in 1965] more than all the others. That afternoon, we came with a committee, five of us, and with a plea. We reminded them of the past, what we meant to each other. From the moment we entered the room to the time we left, not one board member said a word to us. No one got up to greet Miss Binford nor to speak to her. No one asked her a question. The chairman came forward, he was a gentleman, and showed us where to sit.

Miss Binford was in her late eighties, you know. Small birdlike in appearance. She sat there listening to our plea and then she reminded them of what Hull House meant. She went back and talked, not in a sentimental way, about principles that must never waver. No one answered her. Or acknowledged her. Or in any way showed any recognition of what she was talking about. It's as though we were talking to a stone wall, a mountain.

It was pouring rain and we walked out of the room the way people walk out who feel defeat. I mean we walked out trying to appear secure, but we didn't have much to say to each other. Miss Binford could hardly speak at all. The shock of not being able to have any conversation with the board members never really left her. She felt completely rejected. She knew then there would be no help anywhere. In the past, whenever there was a serious problem in the juvenile courts, she could walk into the Mayor's office and have a talk with him, whoever he was. Kelly, for instance, or Kennelly, or Cermak. And never fail to get a commitment from him. Never. But she knew after this meeting, she'd never find that kind of response again. And sure enough, to test herself, she made the rounds. Of all the people who had any influence in town, with whom she had real contact, not one responded. They expressed sympathy, but it was hands off. Something was crushed inside her. The Chicago she knew had died.

I don't think we realized the stakes involved in this whole urban renewal system. The money it brings in, the clout necessary to condemn land … a new Catholic Church was demolished, too. It had opened in '59, built near Hull House with the city's approval. The Church was encouraged to go ahead and build, so as to form the nucleus for the new environment, see? It cost the people of the area a half million dollars. The Archdiocese lends the parish money, but the parish has to repay. It's a real business arrangement.

Now the people of the area have learned a good deal, but it was a bitter education. The politicians' actions didn't bother us as much. We hated it, we argued about it, we screamed about it out loud. Daley gave the orders and the alderman followed it. This kind of thing we could understand. But we could never understand the silence of the others. A group wanted to picket the Archdiocese, but I felt it was wrong, because we were put into a position of fighting education, the University being built, you know. …

In an area like ours, the uprooting is of another kind. I lived on the same block for over forty-five years; my father was there before me. It takes away a kind of stability big cities need. Lots of the people have moved into housing no better than the kind they lived in. Some have moved into public housing. The old people have really had it worse: Some have moved into "nicer" neighborhoods, but they're terribly unhappy, those I've spoken with. Here, downtown in the Loop, everything is clearing and building and going up. And the social workers in this town, boy! I can hardly look at them with respect any more. The way they've knuckled down to the system themselves, because everybody wants a Federal grant or something. They don't want to be counted out. I'm sick of the whole mess and I don't know which way to go.

There are the little blessings that come out of struggle. I never knew Jessie Binford as a kid at Hull House. I used to see her walking through the rooms. She had such dignity, she just strode through the rooms and we were all kind of scared of her. In the past four or five years, we became close friends. I really knew the woman. It meant something to her, too. She began to know the people in the way she knew them when she first came to Hull House as a young girl. It really gave her life, this fight. It made clear to her that all the things she really believed in, she believed in all the more. Honor among people and honor between government and people. All that the teacher tells the kids in school. And beauty.

There was a Japanese elm in the courtyard that came up to Miss Binford's window. It used to blossom in the springtime. They were destroying that tree, the wrecking crew. We saw it together. She asked the man whether it could be saved. No, he had a job to do and was doing it. I screamed and cried out. The old janitor, Joe, was standing out there crying to himself. Those trees were beautiful trees that had shaded the courtyard and sheltered the birds. At night the sparrows used to roost in those trees and it was something to hear, the singing of those sparrows. All that was soft and beautiful was destroyed. You saw no meaning in anything any more.

There's a college campus on the site now. It will perform a needed function in our life. Yet there is nothing quite beautiful about the thing. They'll plant trees there, sure, but it's walled off from the community. You can't get in. The kids, the students, will have to make a big effort to leave the campus and walk down the streets of the area. Another kind of walling off. …

To keep us out. To keep the kids out who might be vandals. I don't see that as such a problem, you know. It wasn't the way Jane Addams saw it, either. She believed in a neighborhood with all kinds of people, who lived together with some little hostility, sure, but nevertheless lived together. In peace. She wondered if this couldn't be extended to the world. Either Jane Addams brought something to Chicago and the world or she didn't.

2000–2011 BY DICK SIMPSON

Watch Out for the Good Guys

The story of the Halsted Street neighborhood didn't end with the creation of the University of Illinois at Chicago in the 1960s. It continued in the twenty-first century when university expansion, with the help of Chicago city government, destroyed the commercial market place and the last of the neighborhood's history. Some call the new student housing and private market upscale condominiums progress. Others decry the wanton destruction of neighborhoods in the constant rebuilding of the city.

The University of Illinois at Chicago has torn down the remaining buildings of the old Halsted/Maxwell Market. Yes, a couple of buildings like the police station—which served as the set for the Hill Street Blues television program—survived the wrecking ball. Yes, some building facades (with the silhouettes of people drawn in the windows) are glued to new structures like the mammoth parking garage. And a few more statues of children playing ball have been erected. And yes, in one old building there may be a museum open to document a past that not only doesn't exist, but which my university helped destroy.

Some call this progress. Others say it's inevitable. The cynical say it is just the way for real estate developers with political connections to make a buck on the backs of the poor. New housing and upscale shops have been built. The university has expanded its facilities to house more students and to provide better facilities for some departments. There is a new "Forum" building to hold local and international conferences and more university faculty and young couples now live in the new condos.

Certainly teaching the students of Chicago, the suburbs, and the world is a good service that we at the university provide. No one can be against better education. But the university, the mayor, and local politicians have conspired to expand university facilities in the worst way possible.

Today's policy of destruction began nearly 40 years ago when the university began at its Halsted site. At the time Florence Scala, who led the fight against destroying the Italian/ Greek neighborhood which had been on the near West Side for more than 100 years.

Now more than 40 years later, the collusion between the local ward politicians, the university, and Mayor Richard M. Daley is even more blatant. The former 1st Ward Alderman and the city's department of Streets and Sanitation cut off city services to the Halsted/

Maxwell Street Market. Rather than reorganize the old market with vendor licenses and fees and having the city clean up after each Sunday open-air market, they let the filth accumulate. A cleaned up and sealed off Maxwell Street Market has been moved a few blocks east to make way for more university expansion. Many fewer Chicagoans go there now. Many more visited the Maxwell Street Market of the last century. This Mayor Daley, like his father, readily agreed to the closing of the market and the university's expansion plan because it would get rid of this historic eyesore for him and the developers.

Once the Mayor decided to ram the plan through, all creative alternatives and efforts at compromise with the vendors, the preservationists, and the university were crushed. The fix was in: this was now a done deal.

So we will get a prettier Halsted/Maxwell area. The market has already been moved and downscaled. It probably will be completely eradicated over time. What is being lost? Bluesman Jimmie Lee Robinson, who like so many other Bluesmen and women, learned the Blues and perfected their craft performing on Maxwell street, puts it this way in his guest column in *Streetwise*: "Maxwell Street was a holy place. It was sanctified by the Jewish people and many Blues and Gospel musicians and preachers of every religion. …[T]hese old buildings remaining on Maxwell and on Halsted Street are the temples of the Souls of Chicago Past. The aura of the past is still in these buildings."

Poor people aren't able to buy cheap goods at the market any more. Street peddlers who have risen to business prominence from humble Maxwell Street beginnings will not do so in the bright new twenty-first century. And a university which claims to value its urban mission has managed to kill yet another urban institution rather than creatively revitalizing it.

There is always in a city, a tearing down to build up. A new University Village has been born. New residents have moved in and are attempting to build a new neighborhood. But the neighborhood of Addams, Scala, and new immigrants is forever gone. The destruction which the university and the city began over 40 years ago is completed. Shame on us. We failed our urban mission. Florence Scala was right. You expect Chicago politicians to sell the people out—but at least they are honest about what they do. It's the good people you have to watch out for.

Two Who Stood Up Against Racial Segregation in Chicago

By Kenan Heise

Racial segregation has existed in Chicago since its founding in the 19th century. But as long as it has existed, there have been Chicagoans who have fought to end it. This article is based on a conversation between Leon Despres, a white former alderman and life long civil rights advocate, and his friend Timuel Black, an African-American civil rights leader who unsuccessfully campaigned against the Chicago political machine on many occasions. Despres, age 99, and Black, age 88, discuss their experience with racism and segregation and how it has changed throughout the years.

Timuel Black at 88 years old and Leon Despres at 99 years of age have witnessed enormous racial changes during their generational spans in Chicago. Over these years, they also personally attacked the mired-in-prejudice status quo and worked for change.

The two sat down to lunch recently in a Hyde Park restaurant. Leon is white, the former alderman of the neighborhood and a long-time civil rights activist. Tim is African-American, a professor, a four-time political candidate and an oral historian of Chicago's black community. They could not have eaten here together when they were young. The restaurant's predecessor at that time did not serve "coloreds."

Times have changed. Many around them wore dashikis and other Western African garb that proudly proclaimed their heritage.

Leon's life has spanned ten decades in the city long known as "the most segregated in the North." Tim's has done so for almost nine decades. Each man had found a unique and significant way to respond to segregation and racial bias.

This writer took notes on their conversation as it focused on what had occurred during their lifetimes, is happening today and yet can and needs to change in the future.

Tim has compiled the first two volumes of a three-volume Chicago African-American oral history, *Bridges of Memory: Chicago's First Wave of Black Migration* (Northwestern University Press, 2007).

On four separate occasions, he [Timuel Black] ran for political office in Chicago against patronage-laden candidates backed by the late Mayor Richard J. Daley. He lost each time.

Tim understood the system that he was up against and coined the term, "plantation politics" to describe a political environment in which African-American office holders were and still often are beholden to a white political boss and machine.

As alderman of the 5th Ward from 1955 to 1975, Leon earned a reputation as the city's unrelenting conscience on civil rights. Although he is white, a December 1966 Negro Digest article called him: "the lone Negro spokesman in the Chicago city council." There were, at the time, six black Chicago aldermen.

The Negro Digest's description of him echoed one by noted black novelist Ronald Fair. Both Fair and the article's author maintained that no African-American alderman deserved the title of "Negro spokesman." Each was too occupied with refusing to speak out or act on the deep rooted racial issues affecting not only the black community but also themselves and their own families. These aldermen's allegiances, the two writers maintained, were not to their constituents but rather to Mayor [Richard J.] Daley. They argued this fact clearly demonstrated that the black aldermen took their stances because they were not beholden to the voters but to political patronage and the various favors Daley dispensed. Leon and Tim took the occasion of their luncheon to share memories of the past and to look to the future.

Leon recalled the shock he had felt in 1930 when *The Chicago Defender's* founder, Robert Abbott, told him what he believed would happen if he, as a black man, walked into the Palmer House, attempted to get on an elevator and the man operating it shot him dead. The operator, Abbott said, would be neither convicted nor even arrested.

"He said it with certainty and I believed him," Leon recalled. "But I was stunned."

Tim responded that like any other African-American growing up in Chicago, he had experienced far too many instances of blatant prejudice to be able to record them. He spoke about early in his career being assigned to teach at a Chicago public high school. Once the principal saw the color of his skin, the young teacher was told that the position had been filled.

He added stories from his oral history volumes, citing one in which a man felt he had to put down "American" under the category "race" in order to get hired.

Things are far better now, especially legally, the two agreed. "At my age, I rejoice that Chicago has come as far as it has in regard to race," Leon said. "But people are still imprisoned by racial segregation in this city. Often—as in the past—it is an imprisonment based on where they are forced to live—in neighborhoods where there are no jobs, few opportunities, no good schools, no health facilities, no stores, no decent housing, no personal safety and limited public transportation." The dominant group here continues to use prejudice to label a people inferior. As a result, the segregationist himself pays a big price for his attitude in terms of the problems in his community that his actions and his mentality helped create. The victims, however, have to pay an even higher price.

"It is all more subtle now than it was in the past," Tim added. "It no longer seems as deliberate and as visible as it was, but it is very visible when you see where people live, many involuntarily." Both men agreed involuntary segregation continues to be an enormous problem for Chicago because it inevitably leads to an inequality of resources and opportunity. Among their combined suggestions:

1. Get the establishment to confront the problem in its entirety.
2. End housing segregation by race and class.
3. Find ways to help people with poor educational backgrounds get training to help their children learn.
4. Do something about the problem facing the black community of youth going to jail for drug-related offenses and then being released into the community with the consequent crippling effects.

"We need a massive effort in which people are given voices with which to speak and the tools with which to live," Leon added. "We especially must see people with prestige, influence and standing assume an active role against segregation, period. We need them to be forthright champions of racial equality, raise questions and speak up.

"By such people, I start with Mayor Richard M. Daley. You never hear him speak directly about segregation in Chicago. If you asked him if he is against it, he would say, 'Oh, yes.' But he must bring up the question. We all need to hear him do it. Neither do we hear the governor [Rod Blagojevich] or the president [George W. Bush] speak to segregation in this state or country. They have lines in their speeches, but that is a far different thing than speaking up for change.

"Segregation is deep-seated in our society and in our city. People who have influence have to contribute to the opposition to it." Tim added that real change can come if the different ethnic and racial groups—especially African-Americans, Latinos and Asian Americans—get together to see their common needs and unite around them.

"We need alliances, coalitions of these groups to work together, especially through their schools, churches and organizations. They need to map out what they can do socially as well as economically to bring about real change."

These comments are not the words of Sunday morning talk show guests. Rather, these were two community elders speaking about what they had fought for and intend to continue to fight for even when they have become what people consider "very, very old."

The Case for Reparations

By Ta-Nehisi Coates

Born in 1923 near Clarksdale, Mississippi, Clyde Ross saw his family slowly robbed of their farm, their livestock and eventually their livelihood by the white Southern 'kleptocracy.' He served in the Army during World War II where he experienced freedom from the rigid Southern establishment, only to find nothing changed. He moved to Chicago during the Second Great Migration hoping for something better, yet what he found was more of the same.

…Clyde Ross…came to Chicago in 1947 and took a job as a taster at Campbell's Soup. He made a stable wage. He married. He had children. His paycheck was his own. No Klansmen stripped him of the vote. When he walked down the street, he did not have to move because a white man was walking past. He did not have to take off his hat or avert his gaze. His journey from peonage to full citizenship seemed near-complete. Only one item was missing—a home, that final badge of entry into the sacred order of the American middle class of the Eisenhower years.

In 1961, Ross and his wife bought a house in North Lawndale, a bustling community on Chicago's West Side. North Lawndale had long been a predominantly Jewish neighborhood, but a handful of middle-class African Americans had lived there starting in the '40s. The community was anchored by the sprawling Sears, Roebuck headquarters. North Lawndale's Jewish People's Institute actively encouraged blacks to move into the neighborhood, seeking to make it a "pilot community for interracial living." In the battle for integration then being fought around the country, North Lawndale seemed to offer promising terrain. But out in the tall grass, highwaymen, nefarious as any Clarksdale kleptocrat, were lying in wait.

Three months after Clyde Ross moved into his house, the boiler blew out. This would normally be a homeowner's responsibility, but in fact, Ross was not really a homeowner. His payments were made to the seller, not the bank. And Ross had not signed a normal mortgage. He'd bought "on contract": a predatory agreement that combined all the responsibilities of homeownership with all the disadvantages of renting—while offering the benefits of neither. Ross had bought his house for $27,500. The seller, not the previous homeowner but a new kind of middleman, had bought it for only $12,000 six months before selling it to Ross. In a contract sale, the seller kept the deed until the contract was paid in full—and, unlike with a normal mortgage, Ross would acquire no equity in the meantime. If he missed a single payment, he would immediately forfeit his $1,000 down payment, all his monthly payments, and the property itself.

The men who peddled contracts in North Lawndale would sell homes at inflated prices and then evict families who could not pay—taking their down payment and their monthly installments as profit. Then they'd bring in another black family, rinse, and repeat. "He loads them up with payments they can't meet," an office secretary told The Chicago Daily News of her boss, the speculator Lou Fushanis, in 1963. "Then he takes the property away from them. He's sold some of the buildings three or four times."

Ross had tried to get a legitimate mortgage in another neighborhood, but was told by a loan officer that there was no financing available. The truth was that there was no financing for people like Clyde Ross. From the 1930s through the 1960s, black people across the country were largely cut out of the legitimate home-mortgage market through means both legal and extralegal. Chicago whites employed every measure, from "restrictive covenants" to bombings, to keep their neighborhoods segregated.

* * *

In Chicago and across the country, whites looking to achieve the American dream could rely on a legitimate credit system backed by the government. Blacks were herded into the sights of unscrupulous lenders who took them for money and for sport. "It was like people who like to go out and shoot lions in Africa. It was the same thrill," a housing attorney told the historian Beryl Satter in her 2009 book, Family Properties. "The thrill of the chase and the kill."

The kill was profitable. At the time of his death, Lou Fushanis owned more than 600 properties, many of them in North Lawndale, and his estate was estimated to be worth $3 million. He'd made much of this money by exploiting the frustrated hopes of black migrants like Clyde Ross. During this period, according to one estimate, 85 percent of all black home buyers who bought in Chicago bought on contract. "If anybody who is well established in this business in Chicago doesn't earn $100,000 a year," a contract seller told The Saturday Evening Post in 1962, "he is loafing."

Contract sellers became rich. North Lawndale became a ghetto.

Clyde Ross still lives there. He still owns his home. He is 91, and the emblems of survival are all around him—awards for service in his community, pictures of his children in cap and gown. But when I asked him about his home in North Lawndale, I heard only anarchy.

"We were ashamed. We did not want anyone to know that we were that ignorant," Ross told me. He was sitting at his dining-room table. His glasses were as thick as his Clarksdale drawl. "I'd come out of Mississippi where there was one mess, and come up here and got in another mess. So how dumb am I? I didn't want anyone to know how dumb I was.

"When I found myself caught up in it, I said, 'How? I just left this mess. I just left no laws. And no regard. And then I come here and get cheated wide open.' I would probably want to do some harm to some people, you know, if I had been violent like some of us. I thought, 'Man, I got caught up in this stuff. I can't even take care of my kids.' I didn't have enough for my kids. You could fall through the cracks easy fighting these white people. And no law."

But fight Clyde Ross did. In 1968 he joined the newly formed Contract Buyers League—a collection of black homeowners on Chicago's South and West Sides, all of whom had been locked into the same system of predation. There was Howell Collins, whose contract called for him to pay $25,500 for a house that a speculator had bought for $14,500. There was Ruth Wells, who'd managed to pay out half her contract, expecting a mortgage, only to suddenly see an insurance bill materialize out of thin air—a requirement the seller had added without Wells's knowledge. Contract sellers used every tool at their disposal to pilfer from their clients. They scared white residents into selling low. They lied about properties' compliance with building codes, then left the buyer responsible when city inspectors arrived. They presented themselves as real-estate brokers, when in fact they were the owners. They guided their clients to lawyers who were in on the scheme.

The Contract Buyers League fought back. Members—who would eventually number more than 500—went out to the posh suburbs where the speculators lived and embarrassed them by knocking on their neighbors' doors and informing them of the details of the contract-lending trade. They refused to pay their installments, instead holding monthly payments in an escrow account. Then they brought a suit against the contract sellers, accusing them of buying properties and reselling in such a manner "to reap from members of the Negro race large and unjust profits."

In return for the "deprivations of their rights and privileges under the Thirteenth and Fourteenth Amendments," the league demanded "prayers for relief"—payback of all moneys paid on contracts and all moneys paid for structural improvement of properties, at 6 percent interest minus a "fair, non-discriminatory" rental price for time of occupation. Moreover, the league asked the court to adjudge that the defendants had "acted willfully and maliciously and that malice is the gist of this action."

Ross and the Contract Buyers League were no longer appealing to the government simply for equality. They were no longer fleeing in hopes of a better deal elsewhere. They were charging society with a crime against their community. They wanted the crime publicly ruled as such. They wanted the crime's executors declared to be offensive to society. And they wanted restitution for the great injury brought upon them by said offenders. In 1968, Clyde Ross and the Contract Buyers League were no longer simply seeking the protection of the law. They were seeking reparations.

According to the most-recent statistics, North Lawndale is now on the wrong end of virtually every socioeconomic indicator. In 1930 its population was 112,000. Today it is 36,000. The halcyon talk of "interracial living" is dead. The neighborhood is 92 percent black. Its homicide rate is 45 per 100,000—triple the rate of the city as a whole. The infant-mortality rate is 14 per 1,000—more than twice the national average. Forty-three percent of the people in North Lawndale live below the poverty line—double Chicago's overall rate. Forty-five percent of all households are on food stamps—nearly three times the rate of the city at large. Sears, Roebuck left the neighborhood in 1987, taking 1,800 jobs with it. Kids in North Lawndale need not be confused about their prospects: Cook County's Juvenile Temporary Detention Center sits directly adjacent to the neighborhood.

North Lawndale is an extreme portrait of the trends that ail black Chicago. Such is the magnitude of these ailments that it can be said that blacks and whites do not inhabit the same city. The average per capita income of Chicago's white neighborhoods is almost three times that of its black neighborhoods. When the Harvard sociologist Robert J. Sampson examined incarceration rates in Chicago in his 2012 book, Great American City, he found that a black neighborhood with one of the highest incarceration rates (West Garfield Park) had a rate more than 40 times as high as the white neighborhood with the highest rate (Clearing). "This is a staggering differential, even for community-level comparisons," Sampson writes. "A difference of kind, not degree."

In other words, Chicago's impoverished black neighborhoods—characterized by high unemployment and households headed by single parents—are not simply poor; they are "ecologically distinct." This "is not simply the same thing as low economic status," writes Sampson. "In this pattern Chicago is not alone."

The lives of black Americans are better than they were half a century ago. The humiliation of Whites Only signs are gone. Rates of black poverty have decreased. Black teen-pregnancy rates are at record lows—and the gap between black and white teen-pregnancy rates has shrunk significantly. But such progress rests on a shaky foundation, and fault lines are everywhere. The income gap between black and white households is roughly the same today as it was in 1970. Patrick Sharkey, a sociologist at New York University, studied children born from 1955 through 1970 and found that 4 percent of whites and 62 percent of blacks across America had been raised in poor neighborhoods. A generation later, the same study showed, virtually nothing had changed. And whereas whites born into affluent neighborhoods tended to remain in affluent neighborhoods, blacks tended to fall out of them.

This is not surprising. Black families, regardless of income, are significantly less wealthy than white families. The Pew Research Center estimates that white households are worth roughly 20 times as much as black households, and that whereas only 15 percent of whites have zero or negative wealth, more than a third of blacks do. Effectively, the black family in America is working without a safety net. When financial calamity strikes—a medical emergency, divorce, job loss—the fall is precipitous.

And just as black families of all incomes remain handicapped by a lack of wealth, so too do they remain handicapped by their restricted choice of neighborhood. Black people with upper-middle-class incomes do not generally live in upper-middle-class neighborhoods. Sharkey's research shows that black families making $100,000 typically live in the kinds of neighborhoods inhabited by white families making $30,000. "Blacks and whites inhabit such different neighborhoods," Sharkey writes, "that it is not possible to compare the economic outcomes of black and white children."

The implications are chilling. As a rule, poor black people do not work their way out of the ghetto—and those who do often face the horror of watching their children and grandchildren tumble back.

Even seeming evidence of progress withers under harsh light. In 2012, the Manhattan Institute cheerily noted that segregation had declined since the 1960s. And yet African Americans still remained—by far—the most segregated ethnic group in the country.

With segregation, with the isolation of the injured and the robbed, comes the concentration of disadvantage. An unsegregated America might see poverty, and all its effects, spread across the country with no particular bias toward skin color. Instead, the concentration of poverty has been paired with a concentration of melanin…

…The Contract Buyers League's suit brought by Clyde Ross…was rooted in Chicago's long history of segregation, which had created two housing markets—one legitimate and backed by the government, the other lawless and patrolled by predators. The suit dragged on until 1976, when the league lost a jury trial. Securing the equal protection of the law proved hard; securing reparations proved impossible. If there were any doubts about the mood of the jury, the foreman removed them by saying, when asked about the verdict, that he hoped it would help end "the mess Earl Warren made with Brown v. Board of Education and all that nonsense." …

Latino Immigrant Civic Engagement in the Chicago Region

By Magda Banda and Martha Zurita

As discussed in the following article, politics occur not only at the level of voting but also by participation in neighborhood and civic organizations. This participation has led to significant victories by Latinos in the Chicago region. Chicago is no longer just a black–white city but has become a multi-racial city. Thus, the incorporation of Latinos into the political fabric of the city is important.

At the very core of our society is the active participation of its members. It is a concept as old as our country. However, not all members of our society, particularly immigrants, have access to our more official form of participation, namely voting. As such, it is important that everyone have access to various forms of participation so that their voices can be heard and needs be met. This paper examines the civic participation of Latino immigrants in the metropolitan Chicago region, as well as the role of community-based organizations as facilitators for many Latino immigrants' civic engagement.

INTRODUCTION

In the metropolitan Chicago region, as with other parts of the country, the growth of the Latino population is significant and truly noteworthy. From 1990 through 2004 the population of Latinos in the region grew by 95 percent, to comprise 20 percent of the region's total population. During the same time period, the region's non-Latino growth rate was only four percent.[1] In 2004 one in five Chicagoland residents was Latino and Chicago had the third largest Latino population in the nation, after Los Angeles and New York. Most of the growth of the Latino population in the state was experienced in the six-county Chicago region. Ninety-two percent of the state's Latinos were concentrated in metropolitan Chicago, compared to 62 percent of non-Latino Illinoisans who resided there, according to the 2000 Census.

Today, we know that the large majority (79 percent) of the region's Latinos are of Mexican descent.[2] Latinos of Puerto Rican origin comprise eight percent and South Americans four percent. Central Americans make up three percent of the region's Latinos. Cubans account for one percent of the region's Latinos and Latinos of other origins make up five percent.[3]

The growth of the Latino population cannot be discussed without examining the impact of immigration; a significant portion of the Latino growth from 1990 to 2004 was due to immigration, primarily Mexican immigration. In 2000, almost half (47 percent) of the Latino population in the six counties was foreign born.[4] In DuPage, Lake, and Kane Counties, the majority of their Latino populations were born outside of the United States (51 percent, 53 percent, and 52 percent, respectively). The city of Chicago has rates similar to the region; 47 percent of the Latinos residing in Chicago were born outside of the United States.

LATINO VOTING RATES IN ILLINOIS

Although the Latino population is booming in terms of growth rates, they have low number of voters, which translates into limited impact on policy. Using voter registration and voting as one important measure of civic participation, we see that in Illinois, Latinos show significantly lower participation than Whites and African Americans. In the November 2004 election, less than 60 percent of Latinos in Illinois were citizens, which clearly lowered the number of Latinos who could vote.[5] (See Figure 1.)

This was quite the opposite for Whites and Blacks whose majorities were citizens (98 percent and 99 percent, respectively). With less than 60 percent of the Latino population being citizens, it was not a surprise that only one-third (33 percent) of all Latinos in Illinois were registered to vote, whereas 75 percent of Whites and 72 percent of Blacks were registered. In terms of those that actually went to the polls, less than 30 percent of Latinos in Illinois voted, compared with 66 percent of Whites and 67 percent of Blacks. It is important to note that Latinos have voting rates similar to other groups; 86 percent of all Latino registered voters voted during the November 2004 election, compared to 88 percent of Whites and 93 percent of Blacks. Due to their citizenship status, however, many Latinos do not qualify to vote; less than one-third of Latinos in Illinois have their voices heard through voting. As such, it is imperative that Latinos, particularly immigrants, have their voices heard through other forms of civic participation.

Figure 1. Reported Voting and Registration for Voting-Age Population for Metropolitan Chicago, 2004.

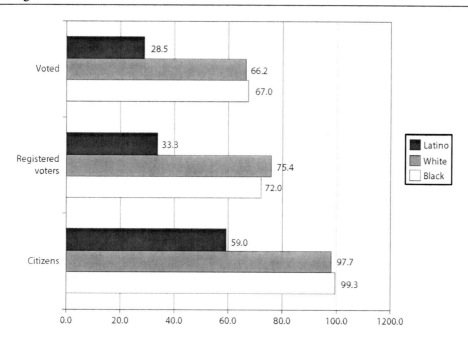

LATINO IMMIGRANT PARTICIPATION IN CHICAGO REGION

In the summer of 2003, the Institute for Latino Studies conducted an unprecedented survey of 1,500 Latino households in the Chicago region. This rich dataset examined many facets of their lives and will create a richer understanding of this population, which will then enable policymakers and social service agencies to serve them better. One area examined in the household survey was householders' level of civic participation. The sample in the study was representative of the Latino population. More than half (53%) of the survey respondents were foreign-born, who were the focus of this analysis. There were many types of civic involvement that the survey measures, such as membership in block clubs, Parent Teacher Associations, hometown associations, and religious organizations. Overall, the involvement in these types of activities was relatively low. The participants' involvement was lower than Latinos nationally.[6] However, similar to national trends, Chicagoland Latino immigrants participate at higher rates in religious (12 percent) and school-related organizations (7 percent).

The percentage of foreign-born participants who were registered to vote was also low. Less than 30% of participants were registered to vote where they lived. When examining the levels of immigrants registered to vote by age group, we see that the older age cohorts, 50–64 and 65+ had higher rates of voter registration, 61% and 66%, respectively. However, the voter registration levels of the younger cohorts were significantly less. This is particularly true for those 18–24 and 26–35 years of age whose levels were 8% and 11%, respectively.

Figure 2. Foreign-born Latino Participation in Groups by Type.

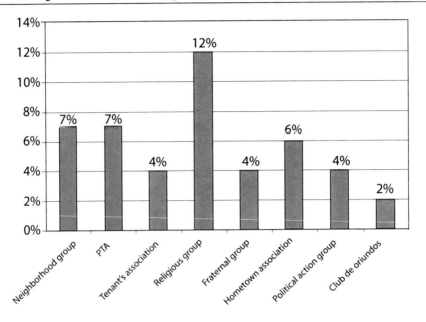

Figure 3. Foreign-Born Latino Registered Voters and Citizens by Age Group.

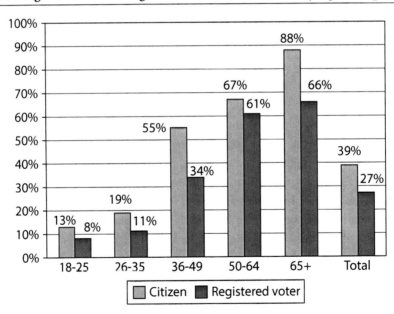

In Figure 3, we see that the younger age cohorts have the lowest rates of citizenship, which is to be expected. As such, it is understandable that they have the lowest rates of voter registration. However, the largest disparities between citizenship and voter registration are in the 36–49 and 65+ age cohorts.

A significant relationship was found amongst the views of immigrant respondents and their levels of participation in activities. There was a significant relationship, for example, amongst those who have worked with neighbors on neighborhood issues and those who felt that people like them could make their community a better place to live (r = .16). [7]

There was also a relationship between people's interest in politics and their memberships in specific types of groups, such as clubs de oriundos or clubs de paisanos (r = .12). Similarly, a relationship existed between people's interest in politics and their working with their neighbors on neighborhood issues (r = .12). Furthermore, the more people believed that public officials cared about people like them thought, the more likely they were to work with their neighbors on neighborhood issues (r = .12).

REASONS FOR LOW CIVIC PARTICIPATION

As with any population, there are various reasons for low levels of civic participation. Through a study conducted by the Institute for Latino Studies in the summer of 2004 on the development of Latino leadership, researchers identified specific challenges to Latino immigrant civic participation. These reasons were the following: Latinos' lack of trust and fear of being exposed; political indifference; lack of resources and time; limited English proficiency; and lower levels of formal educational attainment.

Since many of the communities in which these groups work include recent newcomers who are not familiar with U.S. systems, there is a need to gain their trust, in order for them to work with the organizations and take on issues of importance to them. This lack of trust is even more present for those who immigrated without proper documentation. Undocumented immigrants are more fearful of being exposed, due to the threat of being deported. As such, they are less likely to challenge the status quo or injustices, because they do not want attention brought to themselves or their status.

Some immigrants from Latin American countries, particularly Mexico, bring with them a viewpoint of political indifference deriving from experiences with local and federal governments in their home countries. During the Latino leadership study in the summer of 2004, many interviewees mentioned "political apathy" as a challenge to Latino immigrant participation.

Due to limited finances, immigrants may have to work more than one job in order to make ends meet. In the metro region, for example, the median income for foreign-born Mexican householders in 1999 was $40,700.[8] This was much less than the median income of non-Latino Whites in the region, which was $60,128.[9] As a result, many people face time constraints to participate in outside activities, particularly if these activities do not provide financial resources to the family or immediate returns or wins. Limited financial resources then act as a hurdle to civic engagement for some.

Another major reason some Latino immigrants do not participate civically is limited proficiency in English. People's comfort level with English, particularly conversational

English, can affect their participation levels. From the interviewee's perspective, if one cannot speak English fluently, one might not feel comfortable or confident expressing oneself in front of an audience or policymaker.

Civic participation rates are higher among individuals with higher educational attainment levels.[10] However, 66% of Mexican immigrants in the metro region have less than 12 years of schooling.[11] The low level of formal education among Latino immigrants has been identified as a challenge by many interviewees from the ILS leadership study.

> I only had a high school education, but felt that I had more sense than [policymakers]. I was still intimidated to face better educated people.
>
> —Magdalena, 50-year-old leader, Mother of 6

IMMIGRANT STORIES

Mrs. Sandra Martinez. Mother of 2, Mexican, 31 years old

Sandra moved into a new neighborhood on Chicago's south side five years ago. Although she has lived in the U.S. for ten years, she only recently became engaged in community organizing trainings and movements approximately three years ago, when organizers invited her. She had many doubts as to what services were available and how to participate in community activities. Through the organization's trainings, Sandra became involved in the New Americans Initiative and the efforts for driver's licenses for undocumented immigrants. Prior to her involvement in the organization, Sandra was unhappy in her neighborhood and planned to move out …

Ms. Alejandra Gomez, Single, Mexican, 19 years old

Alejandra has lived in the U.S. for five years. She has been involved with a community-based organization for approximately one year. A speaker came to her high school and talked about a leadership program targeting undocumented student issues. There were a few reasons that moved Alejandra to become involved. First of all, the issues facing undocumented students directly affected Alejandra. Secondly, her major was justice studies because she likes to "fight for people's rights."

Before becoming involved with the organization, Alejandra was not aware of the issues affecting her. "I knew I was undocumented but I didn't know what it was … the Dream Act, the Student Adjustment Act. [Then] I found out." Being part of the leadership trainings allowed Alejandra to see not only that she was not alone as an undocumented student, but that she could push for legislation. "I got to see I wasn't the only one affected. I got to see others like myself and it inspired me. I felt that I was not alone as an undocumented student. … I also developed leadership skills because I was shy before. Also, my English skills improved. I learned about U.S. government systems. I met people working in politics.

I got to be on TV and was even interviewed. … Most importantly, I'm informed now and know what's going on with the Dream Act and similar policies."

Alejandra feels more ready to help others. The program has had an exponential result in terms of how it touches people indirectly. She was able to reach out to people in two ways: she shared her enthusiasm for organization with people close to her and was also able to put what she learned into practice through her participation in public events and speaking with politicians about issues. "Of course, I always recommended it because of things I learned—to be activist, develop as leader, reach out to other people, and network. It's great … for students who are interested in fields dealing with government. … I recommend it to friends and family." Alejandra believes that she helps improve her community, particularly by educating policymakers on issues affecting her community. "I'm helping my community behind the scenes… I've spoken with Alderman Manny Lopez and told him about my situation as an undocumented student. I've talked with [then State Senator] Miguel del Valle. I went to Springfield. I've spoken with Congressman] Luis Gutierrez."

SIGNIFICANT VICTORIES

Through their civic engagement, Latino immigrants, as well as others, have had significant impact on their communities and the state of Illinois, which will benefit families today and in the years to come. One such example was the 2004 passing of *Illinois House Bill 60*, which extends in-state college tuition for undocumented students who have attended Illinois high schools for a minimum of three years. Also, in 2004, was the passing of the *Illinois New Americans Initiative*. It is a $9 million, three-year citizenship acquisition program aimed at immigrants in the state. Additionally, the *Illinois Family Care program* was passed in 2004. This program is another major accomplishment that benefits 80,000 uninsured families.

It is through the work of non-profit agencies, some local and others not, that Latino immigrants' participation in civic life is facilitated. There were various ways in which organizations engaged community members. One way was by working on specific campaigns or issues impacting the community, such as driver's licenses for undocumented drivers or in-state college tuition for undocumented students. Another way was involving community members in specific local projects, such as increasing Local School Council nominations for local schools. Other organizations sponsored residents to attend traditional community organizing workshops, such as with the Industrial Areas Foundation (IAF).

PARTING THOUGHTS: NEED FOR FACILITATING ORGANIZATIONS

Clearly, in order for Latino immigrants' voices to be heard, there is a need for alternative forms of civic participation. As stated earlier, less than 60 percent in Illinois are citizens and only one-third of all Latinos over age 18 are registered to vote. Yet, the data from the Institute for Latino Studies' household survey in the summer of 2003 show that Latino immigrant householders are not involved at high rates. The Institute study on Latino leadership during the summer of 2004 found that there is a need for organizations to facilitate the civic engagement process. This need exists for various reasons: Latino immigrants' lack of trust and fear of being exposed; political indifference; lack of resources and time; limited English proficiency; and lower levels of formal educational attainment. In the end, the Latino leadership study found that engaged community residents, along with facilitating organizations, have significant impacts on their communities and society, just as our nation's forefathers had envisioned.

NOTES

1. U.S. Census Bureau, American Community Survey, 2005 and http://www.nd.edu/~chifacts/.
2. U.S. Census Bureau, American Community Survey, 2005.
3. "Other" category includes people identified only as "Hispanic" or "Latino."
4. Paral, T. Ready, S. Chun, and W. Sun. 2004. *Latino Demographic Growth in Metropolitan Chicago.* Research Reports v 2004.2. Institute for Latino Studies, University of Notre Dame.
5. U.S. Census Bureau, Current Population Survey, November 2004.
6. Boraas. 2003. *Volunteerism in the United States.* Monthly Labor Review (August 2003).
7. The Pearson's Correlation Coefficient (r = .16) was calculated using respondents' feeling that people like them could have an impact in making their community a better place to live and if they and their neighbors worked on neighborhood issues together in the last two years. This relationship was significant at the 0.01 level. A perfect positive linear correlation would be 1.00, whereas a perfect negative linear correlation would be –1.00.4
8. Paral, R. & T. Ready. (2005). *The Economic Progress of US- and Foreign-Born Mexicans in Metro Chicago: Indications from the United States Census.* University of Notre Dame, Institute for Latino Studies.
9. Paral, R., Ready, T., Chun, S., & W. Sun. (2004). *Latino Demographic Growth in Metropolitan Chicago.* University of Notre Dame, Institute for Latino Studies.
10. Boraas, S. (2003). *Volunteerism in the United States.* Monthly Labor Review.
11. Paral, R. & T. Ready. (2005). *The Economic Progress of US- and Foreign-Born Mexicans in Metro Chicago: Indications from the United States Census.* University of Notre Dame, Institute for Latino Studies.

Chicago's Burgeoning, Diverse Asian-American Community Faces Challenges

By Dahleen Glanton and Michael Holtz

An often forgotten minority group, Asian-Americans in Chicago are experiencing increasing poverty and joblessness. Despite the stereotype of Asians as "model minorities," many find the road to success hindered by a stagnant economy and their lack of proficiency in English. Improving the economic and social status of Asian-Americans in Chicago will be determined, in part, by their active participation in the political process.

Devon Avenue on Chicago's North Side is vastly different from the coastal city in India that Sam Varghese left two years ago. Yet, in this growing population of old and new Asian-American immigrants, he has found his life's work registering them to vote.

Though Varghese, who came to the United States on a family visa, has not been here long enough to obtain his own voter's card, he can draw from an ample pool. In the past decade, the Chicago area has seen an explosion of new residents from India, the Philippines, China and other Asian countries, part of a national surge that pushed Asian-Americans ahead of Latinos as the fastest-growing immigrant group in country, according to the 2010 census.

The Asian-American population in the six-county metro area grew 39 percent from 2000 to 2010, creating a burgeoning community of more than 580,000 that increasingly has migrated away from its hub on Devon to the suburbs. But along with the rapid growth has come a barrage of social and economic issues that set the Midwest apart from other regions with higher concentrations of Asian-Americans.

Contrary to their stereotype as "model minorities," many Asian-Americans in the Chicago area—home to 87 percent of Asian-Americans in Illinois—live in poverty and lack education, problems that are exacerbated by inadequate language and job skills, according to a study released [Thursday, September 6, 2012] at a national conference of Asian-American organizations meeting in Chicago.

In such a diverse community of more than 25 ethnic groups, needs and interests differ considerably, making it difficult for community organizers such as Varghese to get people to coalesce around a common cause. As a result, the community, while swelling in numbers, is splintered and has struggled to build the political muscle needed to demand attention. "I tell people it's their right, privilege and responsibility," said Varghese, a 34-year-old community organizer for the Asian American Institute, an advocacy group in Chicago. "People don't think their vote matters, but (voting) is an important way to get our voices heard."

The report, compiled by the Asian American Institute and the Washington-based Asian American Justice Center, is the first of its kind to analyze 2010 census data to determine the economic and social status of Asian-Americans in the Midwest. It is the focal point of the two-day civil rights and social justice conference that brought together hundreds of professionals, community activists and others to discuss issues affecting Asian-Americans and Pacific Islanders.

The study paints a dismal picture in the aftermath of the recession. In contrast to more established communities in California and New York, where Asian-Americans are more likely to be among the highest-income and best-educated immigrants, Chicago's Asian-American community saw a 40 percent increase in the number living in poverty — a growth rate higher than all other racial groups, according to researchers.

One in 3 Asian-Americans have difficulty speaking English, and adults 25 and older are less likely than whites to have a high school diploma. Asian-Americans also suffered because of the stagnant job market. From 2007 to 2010, their number of unemployed in Illinois grew by 200 percent, the study found.

"A lot of people, when they think of Asian-Americans—if they think of them at all—think of the model-minority myth. It's the idea that Asian-Americans, as a recent minority group, are well-educated and therefore doing fine in terms of finances," said Marita Etcubanez, program director for the Asian American Justice Center. "But if you disaggregate the data, you see that while some segments are doing well, there are some that are definitely struggling and need help."

The Chicago area has become increasingly attractive to immigrants because of its diverse businesses and large corporations that have a global outlook. But it also has become a relocation area, drawing immigrants from other parts of the country looking for opportunities. Although the largest concentration of Asian-Americans are in Cook, DuPage and Lake counties, Kane, McHenry and Will counties saw their numbers more than double.

Advocates have long pushed for political and legislative changes that would give Asian-Americans a stronger voice in choosing legislators and other elected officials. Asian-Americans also have a huge stake in issues such as affirmative action and immigration policy, said Tuyet Le, executive director of the Asian American Institute.

That makes voter outreach efforts crucial, particularly during the presidential election year, she said, adding that voter registration among Asian-Americans in Illinois increased 53 percent from 2000 to 2008.

"There is a large number of Asian-Americans who are undocumented. Sometimes we're not as vocal, and we're hoping someone else will fight that fight," said Le. "But we have to realize that it's important to stand up and voice our concerns because when policies come down, (policymakers) may write things in a particular way that doesn't benefit us."

Redistricting has been a particularly difficult issue in the community, Le said, because of population patterns. But last year, Chicago's first Asian-American alderman, Ameya Pawar, an Indian, was elected, in the 47th Ward. "The redistricting process is difficult in terms of the way our communities are dispersed, which impacts the fact that there aren't districts that have large numbers of Asian-Americans," Le said. "But there is potential and things are beginning to happen now. Ald. Pawar won in an area that did not have a large number of Asian-Americans."

This year [2012], Illinois was the first state to be required by the U.S. Justice Department to offer ballots printed in Hindi because of its population surge of South Asians. Poll workers who speak Hindi, Gujarati and Urdu also must be on hand in some polling places. Indian-Americans represent the largest ethnic group among Asian-Americans in the Chicago area, with a population of more than 180,000. "One thing that's unique about Illinois is that South Asians are so prominent and comprise a large part of the Asian-American population. That's not true in all parts of the country," said Ami Gandi, executive director of the South Asian American Policy and Research Institute in Chicago. "That's why it's so important to have South Asians at the table when issues concerning Asian-Americans are being discussed."

Asian-Americans have suffered from home foreclosures as well as social issues such as domestic violence, substance abuse and crime among young people, according to Kiran Siddiqui, executive director of the Hamdard Center, a social services agency in the Devon Avenue area. Over the past two years, the agency has seen a 25 percent increase in families applying for public benefits such as food stamps and cash grants, she said. Many are moving into joint-family living arrangements because they can't afford to live on their own. "Things are very bad for them if they come and ask for help, especially from the government. ... Asking for a hand is a dishonor to them and their families," Siddiqui said. "But unfortunately they are faced with not being able to pay rent or buy groceries."

Five years ago, Asian-Americans owned more than 59,000 businesses throughout Illinois, employing more than 100,000 people, the study found. But during the recession, many businesses, such as Korean-owned dry cleaners and beauty supply stores, shut down. "About 40 percent of our clients that have small businesses have maintained them, but the other 60 percent have not been able to maintain it, and closed shop," Siddiqui said. "They're not trying to stay one step head. They're actually just trying to keep their head afloat."

In many ways, 63-year-old Carmelita Dagmante considers herself lucky since arriving in Chicago from the Philippines 12 years ago. A manager at a laundry on West Devon Avenue, she works a 14-hour shift six days a week, earning money to send back home to her family. With three grandchildren in school in the Philippines, including one in college, Dagmante said she sends about half her paycheck home to cover their tuition and other expenses. She keeps enough to cover her rent, utilities and groceries but little else. "That is my life here," she said, tears trickling down her face. "I'm happy doing it. I'm working for them."

Varghese, the outreach worker from India, also has dreams. In Kerala, India, he said, he earned three master's degrees, in sociology, anthropology and religious studies. His long-term goal, he said, is to work hard at his contract job as an outreach worker and gain more responsibility. "This is our country," Varghese said, armed with voter registration forms and informational fliers that he hands out along Devon. "We're not aliens. We need to participate in this process so our government pays attention to us."

A Deepening Divide

Income Inequality Grows Spatially in Chicago

By Lauren Nolan

In this article, The Voorhees Center at the University of Illinois at Chicago details the polarizing spatial patterns of growing wealth, growing poverty and the shrinking middle class in Chicago.

A recent study completed by the Brookings Institution ranks Chicago 8th in income inequality among the nation's largest cities. Yet, there is more to Chicago's inequality story. Research completed by The Voorhees Center at the University of Illinois at Chicago, in partnership with Cities Centre at the University of Toronto, reveals that not only has inequality in Chicago been growing over the last 40 years, it also exhibits strong spatial patterns. Chicago is now a highly-polarized city absent of middle class households that in 1970 made up nearly half the city. By 2010, the number of wealthy census tracts had increased nearly four-fold with a visible concentration on Chicago's North Side, while tracts that are very low-income and with high rates of poverty expanded on the South and far West sides.

UNDERSTANDING CHANGE: THE "THREE CITIES" METHODOLOGY

Using methodology developed by the University of Toronto's Cities Centre, Census tracts in Chicago were classified into one of three categories based on income change from 1970 to 2010. These categories tell a story of three distinct 'cities' within a city, each with different experiences over the past forty years. "City #1" (indicated in blue on the map below) is a predominately high-income area of Chicago where incomes have risen relative to the region's average. In 2010, City #1 is concentrated largely on the North and near West sides. By contrast, City #3 (indicated in red) represents largely low-income areas of Chicago, where neighborhood incomes have fallen over the past few decades compared to the regional average. City #3 comprises much of Chicago's South and far West sides. In between City #1 and City #3 is City #2, where incomes have remained fairly similar to the regional average since 1970. These City #2 areas (indicated below in white) are sandwiched between City #1 and City #3, with small concentrations in the far northwest and southwest corners.

Neighborhood Income Change, City of Chicago 1970–2010

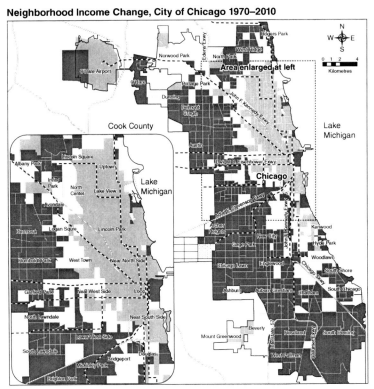

Change in census tract average individual income compared to the Chicago MSA average, 2010 versus 1970

Increase 20% to 254% (167 CTs; 21% of the City)
Increase or Decreases is Less than 20% (210 CTs; 26% of the City)

Decreases 20% to 114% (417 CTs; 53% of the City)

Income Definition: Census tract average individual income for persons age 15 and older. Data Sources: 1970–2000 Decennial Census, 2008–2012 Five-Year American Community Survey.

Image produced by Cities Centre, University of Toronto.

Census Tract Income Distribution

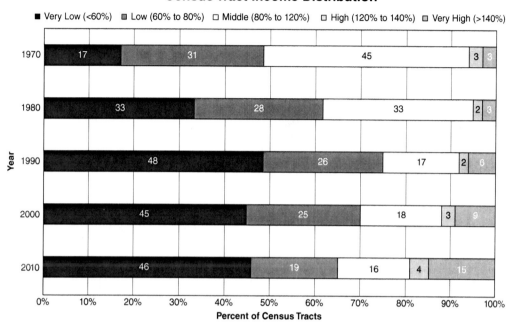

■ Very Low (<60%) ▨ Low (60% to 80%) ☐ Middle (80% to 120%) ☐ High (120% to 140%) ▨ Very High (>140%)

Income Definition: Census Tract average individual income for persons age 15 and over. Income is measured relative to the metropolitan area average each year using tract boundaries as they existed each census year. Data Sources: Decennial US Census. 1970–2000, 2008–2012 Five-Year American Communit Survey.

In 1970, the majority (46%) of Census tracts in Chicago were middle-income, meaning their average individual income fell within 80% to 120% of the regional average. Very high income tracts (over 140% of regional average income) comprised only 4% of the city, while very low income tracts (those with individual incomes averaging 60% or less of the regional average) comprised 17% of the city. By 2010, middle income tracts shrunk to only 16% of the city. Very high income tracts grew to 15% and very low income tracts swelled to almost half (46%) of the city. Chicago's high-income residents are increasingly concentrated on the city's North side, while large swaths of the South and far West sides house most of Chicago's low-income residents.

City of Chicago Average Individual Income

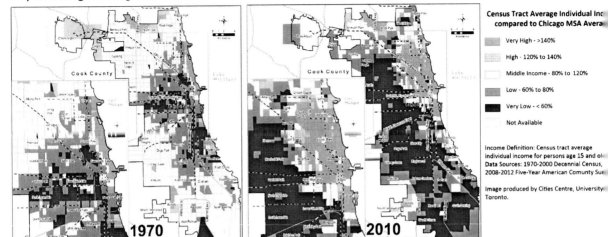

GROWTH IN CHICAGO'S GINI COEFFICIENT

In addition to spatial patterns of wealth and poverty, Chicago's wealth has become more concentrated. The Gini coefficient (or Gini index) is a commonly used index of wealth concentration. The closer a country or city's coefficient is to 0, the more equally distributed its income. The closer the Gini coefficient to 1, the more unequal its income distribution. In Chicago, Gini coefficients increased across the board for the city, its suburbs, and the metropolitan area as a whole since 1970, reflecting growing income inequality throughout the region. Figures for the city of Chicago more than doubled, increasing from 0.163 in 1970 to 0.328 by 2010. (Note that the Gini Coefficient for the US in 2010 was .411 according to the World Bank). The greatest jumps in coefficient values occurred from 1980 to 1990 for all geographies, and from 2000 to 2010 for the city of Chicago.

Chicago Gini Coefficient, 1970-2010

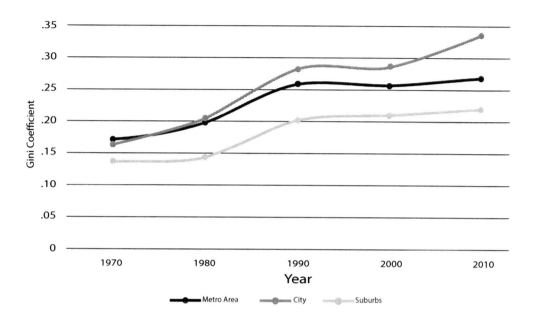

WHY DOES THIS MATTER?

It has long been held that a 'healthy' level of inequality is needed to encourage growth and progress. But how much inequality is too much? Various academics and policy researchers including former Secretary of Labor Robert Reich and economist Thomas Piketty have triggered debates about whether the U.S. has become too unequal. A recent study from the Organisation for Economic Co-operation and Development (OECD) suggests that growing income inequality may be dampening rather than helping growth, particularly when income inequality is associated with unequal educational opportunities. Inequality has figured prominently into recent public discourse. President Obama has declared it "the defining challenge of our time," and mayors such as New York's Bill de Blasio have addressed the theme in successful campaigns. As trends continue, leaders and policy makers will have to increasingly consider what growing inequality means not only for individual and family well-being, but for the health of cities, communities, and the nation as a whole.

PART III

Chicago Politics

Photographer unknown. From the author's collection.

Introduction

An examination of the political history of the city of Chicago reveals eight different political eras, each with unique and defining characteristics:

1. 1833–1860: **Booster Regime** of businessmen as mayor and aldermen. Very few partisan divisions.
2. 1860–1871: **Civic Wars of the Partisan Regime** during the Civil War. Tensions and political divisions were so great, the city council couldn't meet for four months during 1862 and1863.
3. 1871–1931: **First Political Machines and the Council of the Grey Wolves.**
4. 1931–1983: **Urban Growth Machine and Rubber-Stamp City Council** begun under Mayor Cermak. Perfected under Mayor Richard J. Daley.
5. 1983–1987: **Council Wars and Progressive Regime** under Mayor Harold Washington.

6. 1987–1989: **Chaos, Fragmented City Council, and Weak Mayor** period under Mayor Eugene Sawyer.
7. 1989–2011: **New Machine and Return of the Rubber-Stamp City Council** under Mayor Richard M. Daley.
8. 2011–Present: **Post-Daley Era** of Chicago politics.

The political machine grew up with the city after the Great Chicago Fire. The first political boss was Michael McDonald, a gambler-saloonkeeper who noticed the common bonds between the criminals and politicians and introduced them to each other. McDonald's occupation of saloonkeeper was not that unusual for the time. Saloons are closely associated with the history of machine politics in Chicago and in most other industrial cities of the United States. Saloons provided politicians with the means to contact and organize voters, and the political machine protected saloons from raids by the police. By the latter part of the nineteenth century, one of the most common occupations of Chicago committeemen and aldermen was that of saloonkeeper.

More than spawning corruption, the machine also served the rapidly growing immigrant and ethnic communities of Chicago during the latter part of the nineteenth and the early part of the twentieth centuries. In some ways, the Chicago political machine acted as a social welfare service for the poor and immigrant populations. A "precinct captain" ran blocks and neighborhoods within the wards of Chicago. Immigrants depended on their precinct captain for services, jobs, and advice. On Election Day, precinct captains expected their services and favors to be repaid through votes. In 1900, there were 35 wards within the boundaries of Chicago, with 15 to 20 precincts in each ward. Today, the number of precincts in each of Chicago's 50 wards varies from a low of 24 to a high of 74.[1]

Originally, there were multiple political machines in Chicago, entrenched by patronage and corruption. The City Council of Grey Wolves (1890s) was run by cliques of machine aldermen in a constant struggle with Progressive Era reformers. Then, in 1931, Anton Cermak created a single Democratic machine, which was continued after his death by Mayor Ed Kelly and party boss Pat Nash. After a brief interlude under Mayor Martin Kennelly, Richard J. Daley came to power and perfected the Democratic Party machine in Chicago.

The political machines of Chicago have been both Republican and Democratic, suburban and inner city. Even today, the Republican machine of DuPage County is nearly a mirror image of the Democratic machine of Chicago. These political machines have been defined as a permanent political organization or political party that is characterized by patronage, favoritism, loyalty, and precinct work. An inevitable side effect of machine politics, as detailed in the articles that follow in this section, is corruption, scandals, and inefficient government service delivery.

The Richard J. Daley machine, however, had a distinctive set of features that refined the machine politics that had governed most of the larger East Coast and Midwest cities. As shown in Figure 1, it was an economic exchange within the framework of the political party and an economic growth machine that married the political party to big businesses in public-private partnerships.

Figure 1: Richard J. Daley Machine

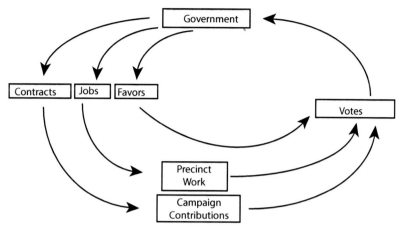

Source: Created by Dick Simpson, based on course lectures by Milton Rakove.

Patronage jobs at city hall begat patronage precinct captains who contacted voters and persuaded them to trade their votes for machine candidates for favors and city services. Government contracts from city hall convinced otherwise Republican businessmen to give the campaign contributions necessary to fund campaign literature, walking-around money, and bribes. These contributions of precinct work, money, and votes won elections for the Daley machine. With Richard J. Daley controlling both city and county governments, he was able to distribute the spoils necessary to keep the machine running.

Mayor Richard M. Daley continued many of the same practices as his father but also modernized the Chicago machine and city government (see Figure 2).

Figure 2: Richard M. Daley Machine

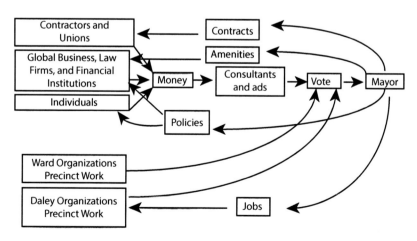

Source: Created by Dick Simpson.

Despite superficial similarities, such as having a Mayor Daley in charge of the city of Chicago, several aspects of the second Daley machine differed significantly from his father's political machine. Patronage/precinct organizations were supplemented with media-based, synthetic campaigns. Campaigns were centered on the candidate more than the party, and ward organizations were supplemented by special Daley political organizations. As shown in Figure 2, old-style patronage and corruption coexisted with multimillion-dollar campaign contributions from global corporations, high-tech public opinion polling, and media manipulation in the Richard M. Daley machine. The ward organizations—especially organizations like the Hispanic Democratic Organization (HDO)—worked the precincts. City contractors and construction labor unions contributed money to the mayor's campaigns and to the aldermanic campaigns he supported.

In a major change from past regimes, rich individuals, global businesses, law firms, and financial institutions contributed millions of dollars to hire national political consultants to do public opinion polling, direct mail, and slick TV ads during the second Daley's reign as mayor. In both the 2003 and 2007 elections, Richard M. Daley raised nearly $4 million per election.

The payoffs in the Richard M. Daley machine were also different. There were still some patronage jobs given to precinct workers and contracts flowed to contributing businesses, just like under the Richard J. Daley machine. But at the end of the twentieth century and the beginning of the twenty-first, urban amenities like flowers in the parkways, wrought-iron fences, Millennium Park, the museum campus, and, most importantly, a tax structure favorable to the new global economy were added. Keith Koeneman concludes in his article about Richard M. Daley, included in this section, that "it is likely that history's judgment will be that [Richard M.] Daley's achievements outweigh his mistakes. It is a reasonable bet that the 'one line of history' for Rich Daley is that he was the leader who helped transform Chicago into a global city."

THE RAHM EMANUEL MONEY MACHINE

The 2011 mayoral election ushered in a new era of Chicago politics. A defining characteristic of this new era is the mayor's seemingly endless ability to raise money. In 2011, Mayor Rahm Emanuel raised more than $12 million to win the mayor's office, more than three times the amount Mayor Richard M. Daley raised in his last election. In 2015, Mayor Emanuel more than doubled his own record-breaking fund-raising totals, raising over $30 million for his own campaign committee and the coffers of his super-PAC, Chicago Forward.[2] The *Chicago Tribune* reported in 2015 that Emanuel benefited from the "elite corps of roughly 100 donors … Those donors, consisting of individuals, couples, business partners and firms, are responsible for more than $14 million of the $30.5 million he has raised since fall 2010." The *Tribune* further revealed, "more than half of those loyal donors have received a tangible benefit from the mayor or his administration, ranging from city contracts to help with regulators."[3]

While previous Chicago machines relied on ward organizations and patronage armies to win elections, Mayor Emanuel has yet to fully establish this basis of support. His political power comes from his ability to raise money. As detailed in Figure 3, Mayor Emanuel's Money Machine operates by:

1. Awarding **city contracts** to building trade contractors and unions, along with Direct Voucher Payments (DVPs) to downtown global businesses;
2. Pursuing global and corporate-centered **public policies**; and
3. Providing **urban amenities**, desired by Chicago's wealthy individuals and corporate elite.

Figure 3. The Rahm Emanuel Money Machine

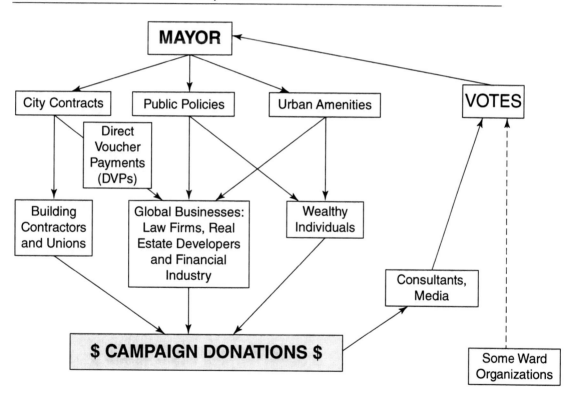

Source: Created by Constance A. Mixon and Dick Simpson

City Contracts and DVPs

Chicago is considered a "labor town," with a long history and tradition of unionization. During Mayor Emanuel's tenure, the Chicago Teachers Union (CTU) and American Federation of State, County and Municipal Employees (AFSCME) have vigorously and publicly fought his proposals for school and pension reform. In 2012, the Chicago teachers' strike put the mayor's rocky relationship with public-sector unions on the national stage.

In the 2015 mayoral election, labor did not, however, speak with one voice. Building contractors and their unions lined up in support of Mayor Emanuel. Although the Chicago Federation of Labor (CFL) did not make an official endorsement in the 2015 mayoral election, Mayor Emanuel appeared with CFL president Jorge Ramirez and nine other Chicago union leaders from the hospitality and building trades just one month prior to the February election. This joint appearance announced support for increased trade show promotion and business in the city. At that event, Mayor Emanuel said, "labor has been a partner in implementing the reforms that allow us to attract more conventions and tradeshows, and all of the resources that come with them, to Chicago."[4] In the 2015 runoff election, Emanuel was backed by more than fifteen mostly building trade unions (carpenters, painters, laborers, pipe fitters, and plumbers). These building trade unions control an increasing number of jobs in real estate development and public infrastructure projects in Chicago.[5] When questioned about union support for Emanuel, labor leader Jim Sweeney of the International Union of Operating Engineers said, "For us, the discussion just came back to: The economy is doing good in the city, and the mayor's done the right things."[6]

In Rahm Emanuel's Money Machine, there is a heavy reliance on mutually beneficial deals between the mayor and his top campaign contributors. Direct Voucher Payments (DVPs) are representative of these mutually beneficial relationships and are a key component of the new Chicago Money Machine. DVPs have provided lucrative payments to businesses contributing to Mayor Emanuel. These contributions have come from the businesses directly and from their top employees. Under Illinois procurement law, municipalities are allowed to avoid traditional government contract requirements through the DVP process. DVPs do not require any type of bids or public documentation. The firms receiving the payments do not have to demonstrate qualifications or document the services they provide. Lacking any sort of formal government contract process, it is nearly impossible to determine what the city gets in exchange for payments.[7]

The *International Business Times* (*IBT*) in 2015 examined data from Chicago's DVP system. While questioning the lack of transparency, *IBT* found that Mayor Emanuel's administration used DVPs in a "no-bid process, where there is not even a contract, just a payout ... firms that have received tens of millions of dollars' worth of shadowy [DVPs] ... have given more than $775,000 worth of campaign contributions to the mayor's political organizations."[8] Scott Waguespack, who serves as alderman of the 32nd Ward, said, "the mayor is paying back his campaign contributors using the DVP process ... He talks a lot about his commitment to ethics reform. But his own practices show that he has no commitment to ethics reform."[9]

Public Policies

Rahm Emanuel has been labeled "Mayor 1%," implying that his policies overwhelmingly benefit his friends in the business world while ignoring the needs of average city residents. As with city contracts and DVPs, public policies in Chicago have spawned a long list of mutually beneficial relationships for the mayor and his top campaign contributors. For example, Winston & Strawn, the law firm that drew up the city's infamous parking meter deal, contributed over $100,000 to Emanuel.[10]

In 2013, Mayor Emanuel appointed a top executive from Citadel as the city's comptroller, overseeing the Department of Finance. Citadel is a Chicago-based "hedge fund with $23 billion in capital invested globally."[11] Ken Griffin, founder and chief executive of Citadel, contributed nearly $1 million to pro-Emanuel campaign committees from 2014 to 2015.[12] Using tax increment financing (TIF), in 2014 the mayor pushed through a plan to provide up to $55 million for the development of a new Marriott hotel in the South Loop.[13] Citadel is "one of the 25 largest institutional owners of Marriott stock."[14] Citadel is also an investor in the Chicago Mercantile Exchange, which Emanuel backed for state tax breaks.[15]

Kari Lydersen's article, included in this section, is taken from her book, titled *Mayor 1%*. Lydersen argues that Mayor Emanuel has taken a neoliberal, private-sector approach to politics and public policy. Emanuel's privatization approach to public policy has resulted, according to journalist Rick Perlstein, in "the transfer of the ownership or operation of resources that belong to all of us, like schools, roads and government services, to companies that use them to turn a profit."[16] Perlstein writes for *In These Times*, an independent, nonprofit magazine located in Chicago. His article, titled "How to Sell Off a City," includes a graphic (see Figure 4) of privatization under Mayor Rahm Emanuel.

Mayor Emanuel's policy solutions have also focused on public-sector reform, which has produced significant budget cuts, shuttering public schools and mental health clinics, largely in low-income minority neighborhoods. As Constance Mixon points out in her article about education in Part V of this book, private charter schools, funded by pubic dollars, have greatly expanded and benefited under the Emanuel administration.

Figure 4. Privatization Under Mayor Rahm Emanuel

Source: Rick Perlstein, "Privitization under Rahm," http://inthesetimes.com/article/17533/how_to_sell_off_a_city. Copyright © 2015 by In These Times. Reprinted with permission.[17]

Urban Amenities

Mayor Rahm Emanuel has continued Richard M. Daley's policies of catering to the affluent winners in a globalized economy. Emanuel's elite-oriented public policies have been "dubbed 'gentry liberalism': increased spending on amenities and subsidies targeted at the elite, accompanied by painful cuts in basic public services for the poor and middle class."[18]

As the list of urban amenities for wealthy individuals and global businesses continues to expand under Mayor Emanuel, violent crime in the city's poorest neighborhoods is increasing; public schools have closed under the guise of cost savings; and social services have been slashed. When asked about her experiences living in Chicago under Mayor Rahm Emanuel, Trish Kahle, a resident of the Pilsen neighborhood, said, "No one I know could afford to live overlooking Millennium Park. So it's like there are two Chicagos: one for Rahm and his friends and one for the rest of us. The new Chicago glitters from the skyscrapers, but it's still dirty and broken down for the rest of us."[19]

AN ELECTION OF TWO CHICAGOS[20]

As Trish Kahle points out, Chicago has become two cities: one for wealthy residents and tourists, with a gleaming downtown; and one for the poor, with neglected and isolated neighborhoods. Chicago's 2015 mayoral election was an election of these two Chicagos. Jesus "Chuy" Garcia, who forced Emanuel into a humbling 2015 runoff, repeatedly accused the mayor of turning his back on the city's neighborhoods. When the final votes were tallied, however, 56 percent voted for Emanuel. It was a racially and economically divided election. Whites voted overwhelmingly for Emanuel. Blacks gave him a bare majority of support, while Latinos voted overwhelmingly for Garcia. As more whites registered and voted than Latinos, Emanuel won. Chicago wards with an average income over $60,000 voted 62 percent for Emanuel. In poorer minority wards in which the average income was under $60,000, Garcia got only 49 percent of the vote. It was not enough. However, Garcia's strong support—especially among younger and minority voters—showed that Chicago may well have a progressive Latino mayor in the future.

Although Mayor Emanuel won reelection in 2015, his city council is no longer as comfortable a rubber stamp as it has been. A number of aldermen with 100 percent voting agreement with the mayor were defeated. The progressive bloc of aldermen who typically oppose the mayor almost doubled. These progressive aldermanic victories happened in spite of the nearly $2 million spent by the mayor's PAC to defeat them.

The Chicago teacher strike in 2012, tax increases in 2015, and multiple police abuse scandals brought to light by a white Chicago policeman shooting and killing a black youth, Laquan McDonald, have caused Emanuel's approval ratings to plummet to only 25 percent. Chicago has also been rocked by anti-Emanuel demonstrations and an ever more independent, weaker rubber-stamp city council.

Political divisions in Chicago reflect a national debate as well. The 2016 presidential elections and the budget stalemate in Illinois state government have continued to heighten the clash between two Americas, two Chicagos, and two futures. On one side of this split vision of our future is Donald Trump, the Republican nominee for president. He has pledged to "make America great again" through pro-business, anti-immigration policies. At the other end of the political spectrum, US Senator Bernie Sanders almost became the Democratic Party nominee, running on a platform of "justice for all, not just the super-rich." He had endorsed Chuy Garcia in his race for mayor of Chicago. Garcia then endorsed Sanders for president and became a major surrogate speaker for the Sanders campaign, especially with Latino audiences.

Hillary Clinton, the eventual Democratic Party nominee, ran on the theme of "Hillary for America," declaring that she would build upon and expand President Obama's agenda.

The Republicans opposed her as representing an Obama third term. Mayor Emanuel, who has been an employee and ally of the Clintons since the 1990s, supported Hillary's candidacy.

As the 2016 elections demonstrate, Chicago and America are once more at a political crossroads. Will the wealthy, the so-called 1 percent, prevail with their pro-capitalist, individualistic agenda, or will Chicago and the country choose a more progressive agenda like those of Mayor Harold Washington, President Obama, Bernie Sanders, and Hillary Clinton? As often before in our political history, we must choose between progressive reform, moderate pragmatic politics, or modern political machine control.

NOTES

1. "Paring precincts." 2011. *Chicago Tribune*, March 18. http://articles.chicagotribune.com/2011-03-18/opinion/ct-edit-precincts-20110318_1_runoff-elections-wards-election-day

2. Ruthhard, Bill, Jeff Coen, and John Chase. 2015. "Tribune report: Emanuel's rare political reach fuels fundraising machine." *Chicago Tribune*, February 2. www.chicagotribune.com/news/local/politics/ct-rahm-emanuel-washington-connections-met-20150202-story.html#page=1

3. Ibid.

4. Chicago Federation of Labor. 2015. Press Release: "Mayor Emanuel, Labor Leaders and Choose Chicago announce $105,000 sponsorship for PCMA Convening Leaders conference," January 5. www.chicagolabor.org/news/press-releases/mayor-emanuel-labor-leaders-and-choose-chicago-announce-105000-sponsorship-for-pcma-convening-leaders-conference

5. Batley, Melanie. 2015. "Chicago's Powerful Unions Divided Over Rahm Emanuel." *Newsmax*, April 6. www.newsmax.com/US/Chicago-mayor-unions-Rahm-Emanuel/2015/04/06/id/636653

6. Davely, Monica. 2015. "In Chicago's Reshaped Politics, Unions Are Divided Over Mayoral Race." *New York Times*, April 5.

7. Cunningham-Cook, Matthew. 2014. "Rahm Emanuel: Campaign Donors Get Shadowy No-Contract Payouts From Chicago." *International Business Times*, February 10. www.ibtimes.com/rahm-emanuel-campaign-donors-get-shadowy-no-contract-payouts-chicago-1812054

8. Ibid.

9. Ibid.

10. Chase, John, Bill Ruthhart, and Jeff Coen. 2015. "Rahm Emanuel's Donors." *Chicago Tribune*, March 30. http://apps.chicagotribune.com/news/local/politics/rahm-emanuel-contributions-2015/?entity=winstonstrawn

11. "Citadel analyst made millions off info from Dell insider, FBI says." 2014. *Crain's Chicago Business*, November 25. www.chicagobusiness.com/article/20141125/NEWS01/141129888/citadel-analyst-made-millions-off-info-from-dell-insider-fbi-says

12. Korecki, Natasha. 2015. "Billionaire Ken Griffin throws in another $500,000 for Rahm re-election. *Chicago Sun-Times*, March 16. http://chicago.suntimes.com/chicago-politics/7/71/445392/billionaire-ken-griffin-throws-another-500000-rahm-re-election

13. "City Council approves subsidy for McCormick Place hotel." 2014. *Crain's Chicago Business*, March 6. www.chicagobusiness.com/realestate/20140306/CRED03/140309856/city-council-approves-subsidy-for-mccormick-place-hotel

14. Sirota, David, and Ben Joravsky. 2014. "Revealed: Rahm Emanuel's top donor bought stock in Marriott just before it was awarded huge Chicago contract." *PandoDaily*, April 8. http://pando. com/2014/04/08/revealed-rahm-emanuels-top-donor-bought-stock-in-marriott-just-before-it-was-awarded-huge-chicago-contract

15. Chase, John, Bill Ruthhart, and Jeff Coen. 2015. "Rahm Emanuel's Donors." *Chicago Tribune*, March 30. http://apps.chicagotribune.com/news/local/politics/rahm-emanuel-contributions-2015/?entity=citadel

16. Perlstein, Rick. 2015. "How To Sell Off a City." *In These Times* Magazine, January 21. http:// inthesetimes.com/article/17533/how_to_sell_off_a_city

17. Ibid.

18. Renn, Aaron. 2013. "Well-Heeled in the Windy City." *City Journal*, October 16. www.city-journal. org/2013/eon1016ar.html

19. "Chicago Under Rahm Emanuel: Readers Respond." 2015. *New York Times*, March 3. www. nytimes.com/interactive/2015/03/03/us/chicago-under-rahm-emanuel-readers-respond. html?_r=0

20. Portions of this section were previously published in Simpson, Dick. 2015. "The Elections End: Racially Divided City Sees Racially Divided Election." *Skyline*, April 15–21.

Washington's Legacy Depends on Us

By Frani O'Toole

The legacy of Chicago's first African-American Mayor, Harold Washington, often goes unrecognized. He was elected by a progressive coalition of African-Americans, Latinos, Women and White Lakefront Liberals. Washington championed reform of our city government and fought for affirmative action, community empowerment, and transparency. Mayor Washington's final legacy is in our hands. It is up to Chicagoans to continue the reforms which he began.

When Harold Washington was voted into office on April 12, 1983, Chicagoans didn't know what his election would mean. Thirty years later, we still don't have the answer. It may take some years for history books to introduce an entirely objective interpretation of the city's first African-American mayor. But when that edition is printed, when we are finally capable of reflecting without excitement or opinion, we've lost the essence of the Washington era. Whether for or against, Washington's meaning lies in the emotion he stirred: the swinging on rails at the Robert Taylor Homes with campaign posters, or the slamming of fists at city hall. So, before the heat of his "fire on the prairie" cools, let's take a look back at the life and legacy of Harold Washington.

How Washington was lured into, what his campaign organizer Jacky Grimshaw calls, "the quagmire of Chicago," we can't know for sure. That said, whatever it was that coaxed his return—perhaps pressure from black community leaders eager for a candidate, a compelling vision for Chicago, or both—it took the 1983 mayoral race by surprise. Supported by the majority of blacks, white progressives, and Latinos, Washington's coalition formed more than a campaign. Together, the three constituencies comprised a popular "movement." Laura Washington, the mayor's deputy press secretary, said that "it was really a people's campaign and a people's mayoral." With two slim victories in the Democratic primary and the general election, the "people's campaign" had made it to the polls, and "the people's mayor" had made it to City Hall.

Prior to Washington, City Hall had been the site of Machine-based politics—a factory of patronage hiring, managed by a firm city "Boss." Introduced within months of his inauguration, Washington put new emphasis on honesty and transparency within city government. The common criticism of Washington and his good-government reform was, Washington's press secretary Alton Miller said, that "people think you're a dreamer and not a doer. If you were a doer you'd be the Boss. But you're not a dreamer, you're fantasizing that democracy actually works." Now that the Machine had ceased, the "manual labor of democracy," as Miller called it, was going to be a difficult transition.

Just as George Washington and his fellow revolutionaries' declaration of democracy was met with war, so too was Harold Washington's. The Council Wars began Washington's first day in office and continued for the next four years. The strategy of the opposition was to use the City Council to form a municipal gridlock against Washington's agenda. The conflict was racially polarized; 28 of the 29 opposition aldermen were white, though politically driven. With many of Washington's stalled initiatives and appointments among the casualties of the "Council Wars," power had shifted. Don Rose, political strategist for Washington, said, "The only positive thing about Council Wars was that it in fact demonstrated that we had a strong council, weak mayor system, which not many people understood that we had because of the mayors before." Nevertheless, for a city so accustomed to being an extension of its mayor, a crippled Washington meant a crippled Chicago.

Saying that all of Chicago was crippled, however, is an overstatement. In fact, some neighborhoods and constituencies were for the first time being lifted off their feet. "His style was inclusiveness, rather than exclusiveness," said Timuel Black, civil rights leader and Washington friend. The mayor diversified city government through affirmative action and embraced voices in City Hall regardless of race, gender or sexual orientation.

Some of his strongest cries for fairness, however, came from outside City Hall. Washington's response was in delivering more money and resources to community development groups, neighborhood organizations, and grassroots agencies; Washington knew with power on the local level, local problems could be handled more effectively. Because the projects were financed through a redistribution of funds—taking money intended for city-wide use, which had been siphoned off to wealthier wards—the city's budget was balanced four years in a row. Matters like balanced budgets are significant political accomplishments and, as former alderman Dick Simpson says, so was Washington's ability to "permanently raise the floor of city government."

Even after interviewing all these people who worked closely with Washington, I can't end with a complete overview of how Harold Washington impacted the city of Chicago. His supporters might say that his philosophy on equality and neighborhood development was important then, as it is now. His critics might argue that, because of "Council Wars" and his untimely death in 1987, Washington's philosophy could only be modestly translated into legislation, and that better examples of Chicago government can be found elsewhere. That said, I don't think Washington wanted to be "unparalleled" or "unsurpassed;" he wanted his efforts to be continued. That's what makes his impact so impossible to grasp; his legacy depends on our willingness to move it forward.

Reform by Lawsuit

By Don Rose

In this article, Don Rose an independent political consultant and journalist, argues that real political reform in Chicago has come through the Courts.

Richard M. Daley will leave a schizophrenic legacy: developing and beautifying his city, boosting its economy and its arts, bringing it together socially and politically, while a cesspool of corruption, segregation and repression lingers just below the surface.

Richard M. Daley's Chicago, despite its enduring problems, is but a faint shadow of its even more corrupt and racist self. A sedulous, decades-long reform effort cleaned up the worst abuses of Richard J. Daley's Chicago, though the son at times struggled to turn back the clock. But what if I told you that the key reformers were not legislators, civic leaders or community organizers, but were in fact an unlikely combination of a moderate Republican senator and a handful of crusading lawyers?

Yes, we've elected dozens of reform-minded politicians in the past half century—including a mayor who died too soon—but the genuine, longest-lasting reforms, including some that made possible the election of other reformers, were handed down from the bench, thanks to those creative, often brilliant attorneys. This is their story.

* * *

On that fateful April night in 1955, when Richard J. Daley was elected mayor, a red-faced, beer-bellied, saloonkeeper and alderman named Mathias "Paddy" Bauler, danced a little jig and immortally proclaimed, "Chicago ain't ready for reform yet!"

Not only was it not ready for reform, but Daley would soon retool its fearsome Democratic machine into the nation's most powerful political organization—based on a new model—while the old urban machines were gasping and wheezing their last. He did it by incorporating the business and financial communities—State Street and LaSalle Street—two traditional elements of WASP-ish reform, which initially opposed his election fearing Chicago would become a "wide open town."

Their unwritten pact was first, give free reign to business and real estate development in Downtown Chicago, second, control the spread of the burgeoning black population whose second "great migration" was under way, threatening the central business district's white sanctity.

Patronage was the fuel that kept Daley's vast machine humming, along with authoritarian control of the election process, gerrymandering of the city's 50 wards, power over the courts and use of the police as a personal army.

Politics being intrinsically tied to race, Daley used every possible instrument of government, from schools, housing and employment to protective and recreational services, to suppress the African American population, creating the nation's most segregated city with the largest contiguous area of black residence outside of Africa.

It would be more than a decade before the first freshets of reform would begin the circuitous process of eroding machine politics. It took federal legislation, a potent local civil rights movement, a handful of reform politicians and most of all, that cadre of inspired young lawyers, who filed the suits that crippled the machine and began the process of bringing equal rights and equal justice to this most unequal of big towns.

Ironically, it took a Republican senator to help reform litigation succeed. Federal judges of both parties in the Northern District of Illinois were every bit the political hacks as Chicago municipal judges who typically emerged from the ranks of precinct captains and owed first loyalty to the bosses. The federal bench included Daley law partners and cronies who reliably ruled against anything resembling reform.

Elected in 1966, Charles Percy, changed the game at the urging of the Chicago Council of Lawyers, a new reform-minded bar association fed up with the Chicago Bar Association's then-obeisance to the Machine. The Council asked Percy to let it vet his nominees and recommend qualified, nonpolitical candidates for federal courts.

He did and they did. By the mid-1970s half the hacks were gone—replaced by independent-minded judges of both parties who ruled on most of the lawsuits that reined in the excesses of the political machine and called a halt to institutional racism in most operations of local government.

PATRONAGE

In 1969, a 25-year-old candidate for delegate to the Illinois Constitutional Convention filed a federal suit charging that political patronage and the use of public employees in campaigns was an unconstitutional intrusion into the election process—essentially, requiring political work by public employees was illegal.

Judge Abraham Lincoln Marovitz—a "beloved" character around town and one of Daley's closest cronies—threw the case out. Michael Shakman lost the election by some 600 votes, fewer than the number of patronage workers in his district. An appeals panel including two non-Daley Democrats reversed Marovitz and the case wound up back in District Court where rulings eventually tipped to the plaintiff.

Daley was hammered by the facts and finally agreed to a consent decree that would limit patronage abuses of employees. The decree took on the name of the plaintiff.

As the case wended its way through the courts in the 1970s, more units of government were put under its rulings. In 1979, two years after Daley's death, patronage hiring was ruled illegal.

Units of county and state government came under the hiring decree in the 1980s. A city scheme to circumvent hiring laws by using employment agencies was uncovered in 1994. Angered, Judge Wayne Andersen appointed a monitor to oversee the city's hiring practices—while a new Daley, Richard M., elected in 1989, tried to vacate the decree.

The notorious "hired truck" scandal, which exposed massive political hirings, found 40 workers guilty of rigging tests and interviews to get political workers hired. Patronage-based groups such as the Hispanic Democratic Organization were disbanded. Top aides of the younger Daley, including patronage chieftain Robert Sorich, went to jail.

"Shakman" remains the longest running reform saga in Chicago history, still making headlines. Election after election demonstrates a decrease in the Machine's strength as the grip and power of patronage continue to weaken—but does not disappear.

RIGGED ELECTIONS

Another case filed during the Illinois Constitutional Convention elections has also had a lasting impact. ACLU lawyer Bernard Weisberg, who became a federal magistrate, questioned why Illinois Secretary of State, Paul Powell, assumed the power to place candidates of his own choosing in top positions on the ballot, even though several candidates may have been in line at the same time when the filing office opened.

An unabashed Powell blustered of course he "breaks ties" himself. Otherwise, who knows, "a communist" might get the number one spot—deemed a substantial advantage. Weisberg filed a federal suit and got a quick win. A lottery system was ordered in case of "ties" at time of filing. Every jurisdiction in Illinois now uses the ballot-placement lottery to assure fairness.

Weisberg won his election and helped draft a powerful civil liberties article for the new Illinois Constitution. When Powell died, shoeboxes stuffed with $800,000 in cash were found in his office. Not because he won the lottery.

Massive vote fraud was endemic in hundreds of Chicago's 3000 precincts, largely because the election judges, appointed by party committeemen, were machine partisans—including so-called Republican judges who theoretically kept the proceedings bipartisan. Poll watchers were often ejected and results juggled while police averted their eyes.

In 1972, a reform Democratic candidate distributed poll watcher credentials to the Chicago Tribune, which exposed major vote fraud in a Pulitzer Prize-winning series. The Independent Voters of Illinois sued the election board.

Thanks to the appointment of a top Secret Service man as Election Board chairman, a consent decree permitted the watchdog group Project LEAP (Legal Elections in All Precincts) to edit and rewrite the confusing judges manual. Further, LEAP was authorized to credential and assign election judges if Republican or Democratic committeemen failed to do so by a date certain.

Honest election judges equal honest elections. Scrub, rinse, repeat.

* * *

Gerrymandery preserves incumbency. It excludes political undesirables.

Chicago's 50 wards varied widely in population well into the 1960s—the largest was five times the size of the smallest. The gadfly Sherman Skolnick sued under the 1962 one-person, one-vote Supreme Court ruling and a remapping following the 1970 census was ordered to equalize ward populations.

When the new map was drafted it became clear that equality of size did not assure fairness in racial and ethnic representation. Indeed, council cartographers cleverly used creative techniques, including dilution and concentration, to short-change African American communities of three potential black aldermen and avoid creating a Latino ward.

The concept of racial equity in political representation did not quite penetrate enough judicial minds in a 1971 suit challenging the remap, but a decade later things changed. A judge ruled for the excluded minorities but not broadly enough. The case was appealed and won. In 1986, during Mayor Harold Washington's first term, a new judge ordered seven wards redrawn with black or Latino majorities and special elections held. Victories by two black and two Latino Washington supporters finally gave the mayor a majority in the City Council.

A suit following the 1990 census eventually created the first Latino congressional district in Illinois. That and the successful earlier suits were filed by Washington's former corporation counsel Judson Miner, a founder of the Chicago Council of Lawyers, who later hired and mentored a young lawyer named Barack Obama.

POLICE SPYING

If a police state is one where the military is used for domestic political control, Daley's Police Red Squad brought us close. It began early in the century as intelligence-gathering on anarchists and other "subversives." Under Richard J. Daley, spying expanded to a vast range of community groups, civil rights and civil liberties organizations—including the ACLU and NAACP—any that ever criticized his regime. It planted undercover agents and provocateurs in neighborhood associations as well as independent political gatherings. Victims ranged from liberal aldermen to missionary nuns to actual radicals—none of whom had done anything remotely unlawful.

The Red Squad spied on meetings and marches, photographing participants and sharing files with the FBI, military intelligence agencies and the CIA. Hundreds of thousands of persons were illegally surveilled, phony charges made, negative information passed on to right-wing reporters and, in some instances, organizations were taken over by the plants and led into disruptive actions. Some of the violence at the 1968 Democratic convention was perpetrated by the squad's provocateurs.

Two similar suits were filed, one on behalf of the Alliance to End Repression network by Richard Gutman, the other by Doug Cassel and Robert Howard on behalf of several individuals and organizations with extensive Red Squad files (Disclosure: I was a plaintiff). Howard was affiliated with several public-interest law groups.

The cases were merged for trial and, after 11 years, won smashing victories against all spy agencies except the CIA. In 1985 the city was fined and subjected to a strong court order prohibiting investigations of lawful conduct.

SEGREGATION

Following passage of the 1949 National Housing Act, the City Council passed an ordinance permitting aldermen to reject public housing in their wards. Most white aldermen did, allowing only a few white projects to be built, while venal black council members wanted as many dependent African American citizens as possible in theirs. Miles of Chicago Housing Authority high-rises built during the 1950s and '60s warehoused vast numbers of blacks, setting in stone the city's pattern of racial segregation—blacks south and west, whites up north.

In 1966, the ACLU, with lead lawyer Alexander Polikoff plus now-Federal Judge Milton Shadur and Bernard Weisberg sued the CHA challenging segregation in site selection and tenant assignment under the constitution and civil rights laws. Lead plaintiff was activist Dorothy Gautreaux of the Altgeld Gardens project, where Barack Obama would years later become a community organizer.

The goal was scattered-site, integrated public housing—long a dream of early CHA idealists who were forced out for their views.

Gautreaux won in 1969. Judge Richard Austin ordered multiple scattered site developments. But the city stonewalled, resisting every inch of the way. In 1987 Judge Marvin Aspen wrested control from the recalcitrant CHA and broke the logjam. He put a savvy, progressive developer in charge and soon small, subsidized CHA developments that blended into their communities appeared throughout the city, albeit to a limited extent.

In settling a related suit, the U.S. Dept. of Housing and Urban Development created the Gautreaux program that enabled 7,500 families to move into better neighborhoods in both city and suburbs from 1977 to 1998. They lived in private dwellings, rent partially subsidized through vouchers.

Though the larger pattern of city segregation could not be broken, thousands of housing options were opened to minorities through housing mobility. By a fraction, we are no longer the nation's most segregated city.

July 4, 1965, civil rights leader Al Raby filed a well-documented complaint with the U.S. Department of Health, Education and Welfare charging Chicago schools were intentionally segregated through a multiplicity of methods including discrimination in construction of new schools, overcrowding black schools and juggling school boundary lines. It further charged discrimination in teacher assignment and unequal availability of ancillary services. Citing the 1964 Civil Rights Act, the complaint followed years of protests and boycotts, mostly aimed at the obdurate Chicago School Superintendent Benjamin Willis.

Commissioner of Education Francis Keppel cut off federal funds for Chicago schools, but Daley instantly called President Lyndon Johnson, who instantly ordered Keppel to reverse his decision.

The issue did not die. Lawsuits filed over the next 15 years, including some by the U.S. Departments of Justice and Education, were based on the same essential issues raised by Raby. Those agencies found the school system violated the U.S. Constitution and the Civil Rights Act. In 1980, the Chicago school board agreed to a detailed order to desegregate as best it could and correct the inequities.

Magnet schools and other nostrums were expanded, but the system was 85 percent minority, limiting the amount of genuine integration possible. What they proved is that separate is not equal, as the Supreme Court ruled before the first Daley was elected.

The proportion of blacks on the Chicago Police Department actually dropped between 1958 and 1968. First they were a quarter of the population and a quarter of the force; a decade later, 35 percent of the population but only 15 percent of the force. Further, the newly formed Afro-American Patrolmen's (now "Police") League documented numerous complaints about blacks being disproportionately rejected in hiring, while those on the force were discriminated against in assignments and discipline.

The Chicago Lawyers Committee for Civil Rights Under Law, working with AAPL leaders Renault Robinson and Howard Saffold, recruited several of Chicago's bluest-ribbon law firms to launch a series of suits against the police department charging discrimination in hiring, job assignment and promotions. The Department of Justice again got into the act, based on the massive amount of U.S. funds going to the police, charging the city and CPD with both race and gender discrimination.

The cases were consolidated at trial. In 1976, Judge Prentice Marshall, one of Senator Percy's appointments, ruled Chicago "knowingly discriminated against women, blacks and Hispanics in the employment of police officers and that the most effective remedy to cure that constitutional malaise is the economic sanction of withholding revenue sharing funds until [they] meet the affirmative requirements of the decree entered pursuant to this decision."

The police department had to change its ways. Minority participation is up, discrimination down—but not out. Discrimination in testing and promotions continue to generate lawsuits.

A parallel story can be told about the Chicago Fire Department. In 1973, the Department of Justice brought suit for discrimination in hiring: only about 5 percent of the department was black. A 1980 consent decree required it to be brought up to 45 percent. The city hired no firefighters for years before giving in. Minority employment, now in the thirties, rises slowly.

Even the Chicago Park District discriminated. Journalists' investigations exposed dramatic differences in the funding, maintenance, recreational services and facilities offered in black and Latino parks compared to those in white areas. Photos of disrepair in black parks were shocking. Citizen groups sued and again, the Department of Justice stepped in. The result was a consent decree against the Chicago Park District putting it under federal oversight for six years. The head of the parks at that time was Ed Kelly, a northside ward boss—later a key organizer of an unsuccessful white racist rebellion of Democrats against Washington, who had upset Jane Byrne in the 1983 mayoral primary election.

THE FUTURE

The combined force of the lawsuits that crippled patronage, made elections fairer, aided independent candidates and empowered minority populations made it possible for Harold Washington to beat the machine. But he died too soon. The 2010 Democratic primary elections saw major offices, including president of the Cook County Board, fall to black and Latino reformers. Machine bosses openly blamed their losses on the decline of patronage. Thanks again, Shakman.

Things have improved in the years from Daley to Daley, but not all things. Old problems were solved, some remained, others morphed into different shapes like the "Terminator" villain. Tax increment financing, created to save blighted areas, too often rewards the rich and robs the poor. Privatization results in corporate welfare that imposes debt on generations to come. Whole neighborhoods are left to rot while millions romp joyfully in Millenium Park.

It's time for a new cadre of inspired young lawyers who will file the suits that will bring a new wave of reform to the ills of the new century, regardless of who succeeds Richard M. Daley. Chicago may yet, be ready for reform.

Patronage from Shakman to Sorich

By Melissa Mouritsen

In 1969, Michael L. Shakman filed suit against the Democratic Organization of Cook County, in a challenge to the then-standard practice of hiring and firing government employees (who doubled as political campaign workers) based on politics, not aptitude. In 1972, the parties reached an agreement prohibiting politically motivated firings, demotions, transfers, or other punishment of government employees. A 1979 court ruling then led to a 1983 court order that made it unlawful to take any political factor into account in hiring public employees. Those decisions along with companion consent judgments—collectively called the Shakman Decrees—are binding on most city, county and statewide offices.

In an interview with the *Chicago Sun-Times* in February of 2013, Michael Shakman told reporter Mark Brown, "I have no interest in dragging this thing out."[1] This "thing" he was talking about began in 1969 when he sought to obtain a court ruling arguing that giving people city jobs based on politics and not merit is illegal. Yet decades later, even though great strides have been made, the City of Chicago and Cook County are still having trouble fully complying with the order.

THE FIRST SHAKMAN CASE

It is clear from his beginnings that Michael L. Shakman was not going to be a machine guy. Born of Jewish parents in Hyde Park, his mother was a Lithuanian immigrant and they moved several times when he was a child. His father had a variety of odd jobs including working at a music college, running a bookstore and eventually managing a bowling alley. Son Michael would eventually own the bowling alley. The Shakmans lived in various neighborhoods in Chicago and Wilmette while Michael was growing up. After completing high school and one year of college, Michael eventually settled back in Hyde Park in 1960 at the age of 18, where he has lived ever since. He graduated from the University of Chicago Law School in 1966 and clerked for Illinois Supreme Court Justice Walter Schaefer for a year. After clerking, he joined the predecessor law firm of Miller, Shakman and Beam, eventually making partner, where he remains today.[2]

Shakman returned to Hyde Park because he found the culture of the neighborhood more agreeable with his personality and interests. It was the 1960s, and the social and civil unrest at the time was having an influence on him. He was especially drawn to reform issues, helping to found the Chicago Council of Lawyers and becoming very active in the Independent Voters of Illinois where he would later become Chairman.[3] During this time and still today, Chicago and Cook County have been dominated by Democratic Party Machine Politics. Michael Shakman had no interest in joining the machine. However, dissenters and independents like him could not advance politically without machine backing.

When Shakman decided to run for the office of Delegate to the Illinois Constitutional Convention in 1969, he knew the odds were against him. But his desire to serve and bring the 1870 Illinois Constitution up to date led him run anyway. Two delegates would be elected from each state senatorial district and he believed that his district—the 24th—had enough of an independent base that he could pull off a victory. A primary election determined the top four candidates and a general election determined the two winners who would serve as state Constitutional Convention Delegates. Several well-known independents ran as well as two slated by the Democratic Party Machine. Shakman did win the primary along with Al Raby, a civil rights leader, Attie Belle McGee, wife of the postmaster of Chicago, and Odas Nicholson, one of the candidates slated by the Democratic Party. In the end, Raby and Nicholson won the general election and served as delegates.[4]

Although Raby, an independent, had won, it was clear to Shakman that Nicholson had won because the Democratic Organization had thousands of workers that did precinct work and made campaign contributions for party-backed candidates.[5] Many of these patronage workers were employees of the City of Chicago, Cook County, or held other government jobs. Shakman argued in his lawsuit that these government jobs were given as a reward for campaign work (patronage) and that many of these workers were being coerced to campaign or give contributions by whoever had gotten them their job (their sponsor).[6] These patronage workers were also doing this political work while they were on the clock, meaning that taxpayers were essentially paying their government employees to campaign for party-backed candidates. Shakman alleged that this was unconstitutional and put independent candidates running against Democratic Party backed candidates at a distinct disadvantage in election campaigns.

On October 17, 1969, Michael L. Shakman filed suit in federal court with Paul Laurie, a voter who had supported Shakman. They named the City of Chicago, the Democratic Organization of Cook County, Mayor Richard J. Daley (individually, as mayor and as Chair of the Cook County Democratic Organization), Illinois governor Richard B. Ogilvie, and Edmund J. Kucharski, (individually and as Chair of the Cook County Republican Organization) for the practice of patronage.[7] Shakman's case was initially dismissed by a federal district court that held Shakman could not prove that the defendants caused any actual harm to a person. Upon appeal, however, a majority of U.S. Appellate justices found that taxpayers were indeed harmed, stating

> The interest in an equal chance and an equal voice is allegedly impaired in the case before us by the misuse of official power over public employees so as to create a *substantial, perhaps massive,* political effort in favor of the ins and against the outs…We conclude that these interests are entitled to constitutional protection from the injury of the nature alleged, as well as from injury resulting from inequality in election procedure.[8]

Shakman responded to the ruling by saying that it "…amounts to a political emancipation proclamation for government employees who are not protected by civil service."[9] Following the ruling, representatives from the American Civil Liberties Union, the Better Government Association, the Committee for Effective City Council and the Independent Voters of Illinois joined to form the Joint Committee to End Patronage Abuse.[10]

In April of 1971, the Supreme Court of the United States upheld the U.S. Appellate court's ruling and agreed that patronage hiring violated the 14th Amendment's equal protection clause and the 1870 Civil Rights Act. The defendants, City of Chicago, the Democratic Organization of Cook County, Mayor Richard J. Daley, Illinois governor Richard B. Ogilvie, and Edmund J. Kucharski, were unsuccessful in their argument that it was a political matter that should not be subject to judicial review.[11]

PATRONAGE PACT

On October 20, 1971, fearing having to disclose their secret political party records in a drawn out courtroom proceeding, the Cook County Democratic Organization entered into a Consent Decree with Michael Shakman and Federal Judge Abraham Marovitz known as the "Patronage Pact." The Decree was an agreement not to fire or demote government employees on the basis of political work or contributions. The agreement further stipulated that government employees cannot do political work on government time.[12] The agreement did not only cover the Democratic Organization (and thus the City of Chicago and Cook County), in order to enter into the Consent Decree, Democrats insisted that Republicans also be enjoined from political firing and allowing their employees to do political work on government time. The final Pact covered all state, county and local government employees in Judge Marovitz's jurisdiction (the Northern District of Illinois).[13]

At the time, it was estimated that the Cook County Democratic Organization controlled about 50,000 jobs, mostly in the City of Chicago. In Chicago it had close to 31,000 civil service employees, over 8,000 "temporary" or patronage employees and about 1700 civil service employees on lease to temporary jobs. The *Chicago Tribune* explained the temporary patronage jobs like this:

> This last category includes those who have found patronage jobs more rewarding than civil service. A garbage man will remain a garbage man as long as he stays on civil service and picks up the garbage. But if he does some good campaigning at election time, Democrats might give him a 'temporary' job as supervisor of garbage collectors.[14]

The Decree would make temporary job "rewards" illegal, and not only level the playing field for independent candidates running for office, but free the government worker from the patronage demands of the Democratic Party.

The Patronage Pact was officially signed on May 5, 1972 and required all affected public officials to give notice to their employees of the Pact. Specifically, the defendants were enjoined from forcing employees to donate money or work for specific candidates, from being fired for refusing to do such work, and from requiring employees do political work while they were on the clock.

While this dealt a blow to the machine, it did not immediately spell the end of the machine politics. Conspicuously missing from the Pact was any sort of ban on the hiring of workers for political reasons. It also had no enforcement mechanism. If it was suspected that the order was being violated, someone would have to bring suit to the court and ask for the court to find the person or agency in contempt of court. This happened more than a few times during the remainder of Mayor Richard J. Daley's tenure.[15] As it turns out he had a hard time complying with the Pact.

THE SECOND PHASE OF SHAKMAN

Despite the Patronage Pact being signed, Michael Shakman still pursued his case in order to end government hiring on the basis of political work. According to Shakman, firing was only one part of patronage and the entire system needed to be undone. Motivated by a 1976 United States Supreme Court Case that prohibited politically motivated firing nationally, in 1977 the Democratic Party of Cook County finally admitted in court that patronage hiring occurred.[16] In 1979, two years after this admission and ten years after the initial case was filed, Judge Nicholas Bua finally ruled that patronage hiring was indeed unconstitutional.[17] Judge Bua found that patronage hiring was indeed an integral part of the way government workers got hired: not because they were qualified, but because they were "sponsored" by someone in the party or had otherwise "earned" the position by doing political work. He also found this was blatant—at times he found that people applying for these patronage posts were told by city officials that they must see first their Democratic Party Ward Committeeman. Judge Bua found that this system unfairly advantaged Democrats to win elections, disadvantaged Republicans and independents, and kept the public from having a fair electoral system.[18]

This finding of fact led to a second Consent Decree prohibiting politically motivated hiring in addition to the previous prohibitions. The combined Decrees and Pact eventually came known as the "Shakman Decree." It was up to the City of Chicago then to design its own system of hiring and firing that would not be politically motivated. Cook County Board President George Dunne did not agree with the decision and won an appeal; for a time the County was only held to the first decision.[19] Yet little by little agencies began to agree publicly that they would abide by the ruling. Two of the largest patronage havens, the Cook County Sheriff's office and the Chicago Park District, announced in 1980 that they would comply.[20]

The administrations of Mayor Michael Bilandic and Mayor Jane Byrne continued to stall the Shakman Decree by refusing to fully create and implement the new hiring system. They also continued to appeal to the United States Court of Appeals and eventually the United States Supreme Court. Harold Washington, while campaigning for the mayor's office in 1983, promised to sign the consent decree if elected. In June of 1983, one month after he was elected, Mayor Harold Washington did just that.[21] He also worked out a new personnel system for the hiring and firing of employees of the City of Chicago that was deemed acceptable by the courts and the plaintiffs. Furthermore, the parties agreed to a once per year audit by an independent agency of practices and all defendants would have to file affidavits affirming that no political hiring or firing was taking place. Years later Michael Shakman recalls Mayor Washington saying, "Patronage is dead. I know. I danced on its grave."[22]

LIVING UNDER SHAKMAN

While protecting government employees from arbitrary firings, the Shakman Decree also made it hard to remove top city administrators who actively worked against the mayor. Harold Washington found this to be especially true. Outgoing mayor and Machine loyalist Jane Byrne, who ran against Washington in the primary, had filled every position possible with her supporters before she left office.[23] Because Byrne had put her people in place, Washington would not be able to replace them with his supporters under the Shakman Decree. This was especially troubling as he sought to diversify his administration and appoint more African-Americans. Nonetheless he saw complete implementation of the decisions made in the Shakman case as an important step in bringing Chicago forward.

Harold Washington died in office in 1987, and Eugene Sawyer was chosen by the City Council to replace him. Sawyer was African-American but also a product of the Democratic organization, and once in office tried to reverse the portion of the Shakman Decree that prevented political influence in hiring.[24] He was unsuccessful and later claimed that his actions were only to avoid paying large fines stemming from the original case.[25] He argued that reversing the ruling would lessen the fines and publicly proclaimed support for Shakman. But critics claim his real aim was to have more control over hiring and firing in City Hall.

In 1989, Richard M. Daley was elected mayor. But patronage as Illinois knew it was long on its way out as the United States Supreme Court ruled in 1990 in *Rutan v. Republican Party of Illinois* that the State of Illinois also could not hire, fire, promote or transfer employees on the basis of political activity, save for a few policy making positions and those that were confidential.[26] Daley did not challenge Shakman. In fact it looked like the 1990s would be a time of final acceptance that patronage was dead. By the end of 1991, the only county or city offices not to have signed the Shakman Decree were the Cook County Board President's Office and the Office of the Cook County Assessor.[27] In 1993 the County Board President's Office would sign, and in October of 1994, so would the Assessor.[28]

PATRONAGE CONTINUES

In 2002, Mayor Richard M. Daley and the City of Chicago officially challenged the Shakman Decree in court claiming that times had evolved and patronage was no longer an issue. This challenge was in response to a decision just a few days earlier by U.S. District Court Judge Wayne Anderson finding the city in contempt of the court—meaning he had violated the Shakman Decree. According to Judge Anderson, Daley used temporary agencies and personal services contracts to hire and fire employees that circumvented the Shakman requirements, creating a way for patronage to continue. Daley defended the use of contracts and agencies calling them simply a management tool.[29]

"Democrats, Republicans, independents. I don't care who they are. We don't hire anyone on a political basis. We have never done that in the city," Daley claimed. The "we" he was referring to of course was his own administration. His father's generation did—it made sense to them because they grew up under Franklin D. Roosevelt and the New Deal and people did really owe their jobs to the Democratic Party. "One man, one party. If you read history, that was the philosophy. The Democratic Party did make a difference. People believe that and my father believed that in that generation. There's nothing wrong with that," Daley said.[30]

Aside from his belief in the non-existence of patronage, Richard M. Daley also pointed out that the enhanced hiring mechanisms in place to comply with Shakman and prove compliance to the courts had cost the city between $6 million and $9 million per year—and that taxpayers should not have to continue to carry that burden or the burden of another two million on expanding Shakman monitoring.[31] Daley proposed instead writing the specifics of the Decree into the personnel code. Daley was unsuccessful, and ultimately forced to comply with the original order and deal with the contempt citation issued by Judge Anderson.

In 2004, the Hired Truck scandal broke. It was revealed that private trucks hired to do city work were doing little or no work, had mob connections, were tied to city employees and had to pay bribes to get city contracts. The scandal also brought to light rigged hiring schemes. Shakman again took the city to court and asked a federal judge to hold Mayor Richard M. Daley personally responsible for the violations.[32] Shakman and federal prosecutors also alleged that the city had been violating Shakman for years and that a new monitoring system needed to be devised. Audits and affidavits would not suffice in the face of repeated violations of the intent of the Decree. In response, the court appointed its own monitor in 2005—just before the lid blew off the Robert Sorich scandal.

THE SORICH TRIAL

Rigged hiring, it turned out, would be one of the biggest scandals in Richard M. Daley's administration and would cause some observers to declare that patronage was alive and well. Robert Sorich was Assistant Director of the Mayor's Office of Intergovernmental Affairs (IGA) from 1993 to 2005. Federal prosecutors would eventually prove that Robert Sorich and his co-defendants, Timothy McCarthy, John Sullivan, and Patrick Slattery, used their official city positions to hand out patronage jobs to those with political sponsorship and connections—violating the Shakman Decrees.

The IGA controlled many (but not all) jobs that were protected under the Shakman Decree. The court found that campaign coordinators, union leaders and other politically connected people would nominate job candidates to Sorich and McCarthy. They would determine which politically connected job candidates should be hired and then forward lists of preselected candidates to the specific departments that did the actual hiring. So Sorich was often referred to as the "patronage chief" around City Hall.

To avoid appearing to violate the Shakman Decrees, the city posted job listings and conducted interviews with those applying. But it was all a sham—the winners had already been determined by Sorich. On July 5, 2006, Sorich, Slattery and McCarthy were all convicted of federal mail fraud in relation to the scandal. The following year, City Council approved a measure to create a $12 million fund to compensate victims.[33]

PATRONAGE TODAY

Michael Shakman did not intend for his original case in 1969 to drag out over four decades. And given the city's continued violations, it seemed unlikely that federal prosecutors would ever discharge it once and for all. But that's exactly what happened on Monday, June 17, 2014 when U.S. Magistrate Judge Schenkier officially declared an end to the Shakman Case.[34] According to the *Chicago Sun-Times*, "Schenkier said his finding of 'substantial compliance' does not mean the city has 'achieved a state of perfection.' Rather, it means that the city, 'by its actions,' no longer needs to be under the 'extraordinary restrictions' of a federal hiring monitor."[35]

Although there were city employees present who objected to the dismissal based on their experiences being denied advancement due to clout, the Judge said, "I understand the fear, given what has happened in the past. But, the idea that no one will be looking over the city's shoulder is not right."[36] The judge meant, of course, City Inspector General Joe Ferguson would be looking over the city's shoulder. And while Ferguson credits the new administration under Rahm Emanuel with making great strides in complying with Shakman, he also believes the city has a long way to go. His powers to investigate alleged patronage hiring are still few. Ferguson can investigate, but he cannot compel departments to turn over documentation. In March of 2013, the Illinois State Supreme Court affirmed that current law does not give the Inspector General the power to compel departments to turn over documentation—thus severely hampering his abilities to ensure political hiring does not occur.[37]

That the Inspector General had to go to the highest Illinois court is a sign that ethical reform is not yet complete in city hall. When Rahm Emanuel was running for mayor in 2011, he pledged to expand the power of the Inspector General. He has now been reelected to a second term, and he still has yet to do so. Instead he has created more quasi-governmental bodies such as the new Infrastructure Trust that lie beyond the control of the Inspector General because they are private-public partnerships, and not full government agencies.

Mayor Rahm Emanuel admits that a cloud still hangs over Chicago. "Our politics in the past cost the taxpayers real money. We have to earn their trust every day and prove that we ... have the people and the systems in place to actually be self-monitoring."[38] Now that Mayor Emanuel has been reelected to a second term, maybe he will fulfill campaign promises from both campaigns to end patronage at city hall and to issue in a more ethical and transparent government.

NOTES

1. Brown, Mark. "Is city ready to be free of Shakman case?" *Chicago Sun-Times*. February 6, 2013.
2. DePue, Mark. "Interview with Michael Shakman." IS-A-L-2008-009. Abraham Lincoln Presidential Library Oral History Project. February 14, 2008.
3. DePue, Mark. "Interview with Michael Shakman." IS-A-L-2008-009. Abraham Lincoln Presidential Library Oral History Project. February 14, 2008.
4. DePue, Mark. "Interview with Michael Shakman." IS-A-L-2008-009. Abraham Lincoln Presidential Library Oral History Project. February 14, 2008.
5. "2 Sue Daley for the practice of patronage." *Chicago Tribune*. October 18, 1969.
6. "Court to Hear Case: Kucharski Hails Patronage Suit Action." *Chicago Tribune*. October 25, 1970.
7. Shakman vs. The Democratic Organization of Cook County, et al. US 69 C 2145.
8. "Court to Hear Case: Kucharski Hails Patronage Suit Action." *Chicago Tribune*. October 25, 1970.
9. "Group to Aid Victims of Political Firings." *Chicago Tribune*. October 29, 1970.
10. "Group to Aid Victims of Political Firings." *Chicago Tribune*. October 29, 1970.
11. Elsasser, Glen. "Supreme Court Slaps Machine Politics Here: Top Court Hits City's Patronage." *Chicago Tribune*. April 20, 1971.

12. Enstad, Robert. "Patronage Pact Called Hogwash." *Chicago Tribune*. October 21, 1971.

13. DePue, Mark. "Interview with Michael Shakman." IS-A-L-2008-009. Abraham Lincoln Presidential Library Oral History Project. February 14, 2008.

14. Enstad, Robert. "How Does Patronage Work? Ask Vito Marzullo." *Chicago Tribune*. Sunday, November 28, 1971.

15. Jarrett, Vernon. "Last Stand in Salt Mines?" *Chicago Tribune*. January 31, 1975; "City Loses Shakman Appeal." Chicago Tribune. April 10, 1976.

16. Elrod v. Burns (1976); Ciccone, F. Richard. "Democrats will tell court political work leads to jobs." *Chicago Tribune*. February 25, 1977.

17. Branegan, Jay. "U.S. judge rules patronage jobs in Cook County illegal." *Chicago Tribune*. September 25, 1979.

18. Judge Nicholas Bua. Supplemental Findings of Fact: Shakman v. Democratic Organization of Cook County. 481 F.Supp. 1315, 1342. September 24, 1979.

19. DePue, Mark. "Interview with Michael Shakman." IS-A-L-2008-009. Abraham Lincoln Presidential Library Oral History Project. February 14, 2008.

20. Branegan, Jay. "Sheriff and park district accept Shakman Decree." *Chicago Tribune*. May 15, 1980.

21. Chandler, Christopher. "Shakman Decrees." Chicago Tribune. February 17, 2002.

22. DePue, Mark. "Interview with Michael Shakman." IS-A-L-2008-009. Abraham Lincoln Presidential Library Oral History Project. February 14, 2008.

23. Chandler, Christopher. "Shakman Decrees." *Chicago Tribune*. February 17, 2002.

24. Jarrett, Vernon. "Sawyer shows his true Shakman colors." *Chicago Sun-Times*. February 4, 1988.

25. Golden, Jr. Harry and Ray Hanania. "Shakman stand clarified." *Chicago Sun-Times*. February 8, 1988.

26. "Illinois, patronage battleground." *Chicago Sun-Times*. June 30, 1996.

27. Hanania, Ray. "Shakman covers Orr—only Hynes, Phelan out." *Chicago Sun-Times*. October 17, 1991.

28. Ortiz, Lou. "County to limit patronage hiring—Board President accepts decree." *Chicago Sun-Times*. December 3, 1993; Ortiz, Lou. "Hynes OKs Limits on Patronage Positions." *Chicago Sun-Times*. October 20, 1994.

29. Spielman, Fran. "Daley lashes out at reformer—Blasts spending more to enforce Shakman ban on political hiring." *Chicago Sun-Times*. January 18, 2002.

30. Spielman, Fran. "Daley lashes out at reformer—Blasts spending more to enforce Shakman ban on political hiring." *Chicago Sun-Times*. January 18, 2002.

31. Ibid.

32. Brown, Mark. "Shakman tries to keep it civil in city hall fight." *Chicago Sun-Times*. July 27, 2005.

33. Spielman, Fran. "Council OKs $12 million Shakman settlement—Money goes to victims of flawed process." *Chicago Sun-Times*. April 12, 2007.

34. Spielman, Fran. "Judge Releases Chicago From Shakman Political Hiring Decree." *Chicago Sun-Times*. June 17, 2014.

35. Ibid.

36. Ibid

37. Brown, Mark. "So much for Rahm the Reformer." *Chicago Sun-Times*. March 24, 2013.

38. Spielman, Fran. "Judge Releases Chicago From Shakman Political Hiring Decree." *Chicago Sun-Times*. June 17, 2014.

Daley's Legacy

By Keith Koeneman

Leaders, be they Presidents or City Mayors, will likely be remembered by their "one line of history." Richard M. Daley will be remembered as the mayor who turned Chicago into a global city. Yet, turning Chicago into a global city came at a cost, the budget deficit he left behind may also be part of how Richard M. Daley is remembered.

According to the political strategist Larry Sabato, Clare Boothe Luce—the diplomat, author and politician—used to advise American presidents "that, at most, they only got one line each in history." According to this theory, Abraham Lincoln would be remembered for emancipating slaves, George Washington for founding the United States, Richard Nixon for the Watergate scandal, and Barack Obama for becoming the country's first African-American president. Everything else would be forgotten with the passage of time. With regard to recent Chicago mayors, this "one line of history" notion appears to have some validity. Mayor Richard J. Daley was the autocratic, big-city political Boss. Michael Bilandic mishandled the snowstorm of 1979. Jane Byrne was the feisty first female mayor. Harold Washington the charismatic first black mayor.

What will future generations record as Richard M. Daley's one line in the history books? To answer that question, it is important to make judgments about his 22-year mayoral career. When Rich Daley announced his candidacy for mayor of Chicago in December 1988, the city had just suffered through 13 years of political and economic instability that verged at times on chaos. This period included five mayors, five superintendents of the Chicago Public Schools, and the black-versus-white political civil war known as the Council Wars.

During this era of decline, some members of the national media had called Chicago "Beirut on the Lake," even as the relentless deindustrialization of the Midwest had continued to drain the city of high-paying manufacturing jobs. Some believed that the once-great city of Chicago would never recover.

During Daley's press conference to announce his candidacy for mayor, his short speech acknowledged the city's needs for racial healing and revitalization of the basic services provided by municipal government. "Today, I proudly announce my candidacy for the Democratic nomination for mayor of Chicago. I do so aware of both the great challenge and the great opportunity the next mayor will find. Let's face it: We have a problem in Chicago. The name-calling and politics at City Hall are keeping us from tackling the real issues. It's time we stop fighting each other and start working together. I'm not interested in running as 'the white candidate,' or in serving as mayor of half the people. Fighting crime is not a white issue or a black issue. Good schools are not a white issue or a black issue. Protecting taxpayers against waste is not a white issue or a black issue. Working to build Chicago's economy is not a white issue or a black issue. Competent government is not a white issue or a black issue. It's time to say, 'Enough is enough.' But let's begin by recognizing how much more we can do by lowering our voices and raising our sights. It's time for a new beginning in Chicago."

Over the next two decades, Daley consistently attempted to address and solve the challenges highlighted in that speech. During this same period, race relations in Chicago stabilized and then strengthened. Daley's share of the black vote rose from 8 percent in 1989 to 61 percent in 2003. Even though the rest of his tenure as mayor would largely lack the accomplishments of his first 14 years, Daley would still go on to provide more than two decades of stability to the political and business communities. This steadiness of leadership was a stark contrast to the chaos of the 13 years that preceded his taking office.

Daley was not just a steady leader. He also took big risks to try to achieve his vision for Chicago, which included educational opportunity and a high quality of life for its citizens. In 1995, Daley agreed to take over the Chicago Public Schools, an institution whose students were 90 percent minority and lived in poverty at a rate of 85 percent. Arne Duncan, who served under Daley as CEO of Chicago Public Schools and is now President Obama's U.S. Secretary of Education, was amazed by the political courage reflected in Daley's decision. "I think his greatest accomplishment as mayor is that he had the courage to take on school reform in Chicago," Duncan says. "Politically, it was not a smart thing to do. All of his experts were telling Daley that it was going to end his career. But Daley intuitively believed that he had to do this if he wanted to help Chicago to grow and prosper and be successful, whether it was the politically astute thing to do. Daley's initial courage has now basically changed the landscape of urban education in the United States. Now, mayors all around the country are also fighting for the opportunity to reform their schools."

Whether one agrees with Duncan about the larger impact of Daley's decision to embrace school reform, it is true that Daley's position on this issue distinguished him as a leader and set the right tone for parents, educators and businesspeople in Chicago. Though today some may criticize the mixed results of Chicago's school reform efforts under Daley, these critics are missing the more important truth: Chicago's public education challenges are largely socioeconomic in nature, and therefore essentially beyond the control of one person, even the mayor. With regard to education reform in Chicago, however, Daley performed an essential task of leadership by lifting the city's vision to loftier sights and harnessing the energy of Chicagoans to focus on an important aspiration.

The story is similar with respect to public housing. An intractable problem existed that affected not only young, poor minorities but also the very social fabric of the city. By announcing his support for a Plan for Transformation in September 1999, Daley took on a big political risk to try to bring a higher quality of life to Chicagoans living in public high-rises and nearby neighborhoods. The end result was largely positive (yet not perfect). More importantly, Daley had performed a fundamental act of leadership by focusing his city on a worthy goal.

But Daley's most important accomplishment may well be his role in the transformation of Chicago into a global city. When Daley took office in 1989, the city was a mess. Chicago's population had declined by more than 837,000, or 23 percent, since 1950. More than one-third of manufacturing jobs had been lost during the same period. Race relations were poor, and the city had suffered through more than a decade of political instability. Public schools and public housing offered little hope to children.

During his decades in office, Daley physically renewed the city center and Chicago's lakefront. Out went the capital of the Rust Belt. In came an attractive and cultured global center that would become the model for many cities. Both business and culture thrived during Daley's time in power. In 2001, Boeing Corp.—a global aerospace and defense company with $51 billion in revenue—announced that it was moving its headquarters to Chicago. In 2005, *Time* magazine named Daley as one of the best big-city mayors in the United States and said he had "presided over the city's transition from graying hub to vibrant boomtown." For many, Millennium Park became known as the physical manifestation of Chicago's transformation.

In *First Son: The Biography of Richard M. Daley*, I write: "By the first decade of the 21st century, Chicago would be accepted as one of the most important global cities in the world, an urban center that combined a powerful economy with cultural sophistication. This recognition put Chicago in elite company, along with other metropolises: New York, London, Tokyo, Paris, Hong Kong and Singapore.

Chicago had a $460 billion economy, some of the best universities anywhere, and world-class dining, performing arts, cultural attractions and entertainment. Global cities such as Chicago required diverse business activity, global information exchanges, rich cultural experiences and the ability to attract talented people. Daley knew this intuitively, and the pro-business, pro-culture mayor had worked to craft policies that facilitated these goals."

Though he had important accomplishments, I write in *First Son*: "Daley was not a perfect mayor. Rather, the arc of his career was consistent with what a study of human nature would predict: a steep learning curve; a decade of disciplined work leading to mastery;

the accumulation of power; and, finally, hubris and mistakes. Unfortunately, Daley's legacy would also include a pension crisis, the midnight destruction of Meigs Field, persistent corruption within city government, high levels of crime and the mayor's financial mismanagement during his last years in office."

Two significant problems that Daley left behind for his successor are a pension crisis and a large structural budget deficit. Both were the result of a lack of discipline and represent significant leadership mistakes for Daley. Not only did Daley's final budget show a $655 million deficit, but it was the 11th consecutive deficit racked up under his leadership.

Even worse, *First Son* notes, "Unfunded pension liabilities had risen to more than $20 billion, which was equal to nearly $7,500 for every man, woman and child living in the city." Neither of these mistakes can be explained away by economic stress, since they were largely the result of decisions made long before the September 2008 bankruptcy of Lehman Brothers catapulted the U.S. economy into a financial crisis.

Another big mistake was the midnight destruction of Meigs Field airport in 2003. Though popular with some Chicagoans, this decision resembled an action by a Third World dictator rather than a step consistent with long-standing American democratic processes. "Primarily, I am appalled at the arrogant disregard of due process by whoever ordered the destruction," said Jane Byrne, the retired mayor of Chicago, in her assessment of the event. "Due process of law, the most fundamental, precious constitutional right of all citizens, even Chicagoans, was purposely ignored. I say purposely because a few hours after the destruction, the administration stated that its irrational actions had 'prevented the issue from being tied up in the courts.' We are a nation governed by laws, not individuals, and no public servant has the right to place personal opinion or convenience before the laws."

Another legitimate criticism of Daley is that he failed to directly confront entrenched public sector unions in Chicago. This mistake was obviously a contributing factor in the city's pension crisis and sizable structural budget deficit, since pensions and health care benefits for city employees have become a huge expense, and labor outlays account for approximately three-fourths of the city's corporate budget. Daley supporters may object to this criticism, saying that the mayor outsourced more municipal jobs and was less pro-union than his predecessors. This statement completely misses the more important point, however. In the competitive global economy of the 21st century, cities cannot act as if the U.S. economy is shut off from the rest of the world. The city of Chicago cannot afford to pay union workers salaries and benefits that significantly exceed those of private companies. The only way to achieve the necessary reforms of the city's cost structure is by more directly challenging public sector unions. Daley failed to do this.

Serving as mayor of a large city such as Chicago is as challenging as competing in Major League Baseball or commanding an army as a military general. It requires a high degree of skill, as well as persistence, wisdom, toughness and shrewdness. Many of the issues that cross a mayor's desk—such as crime and public education—are deeply problematical. Even a very skilled leader may have as many errors as hits.

With that in mind, it is likely that history's judgment will be that Daley's achievements outweighed his mistakes. It is also a reasonable bet that the "one line of history" for Rich Daley is that he was the leader who helped transform Chicago into a global city.

How Mayor Rahm Emanuel Awoke a Progressive Resistance in Chicago

By Kari Lydersen

If there's one thing Chicagoans have demonstrated ever since the city rose out of a swamp, it is that they will not quietly acquiesce when they sense injustice. Like the proud Chicagoans who came before them, the Chicago Teachers Union, the Mental Health Movement, and other contemporary groups are committed to questioning and shaping the meanings of democracy, leadership, power and justice.

March 4, 2012, was Chicago's 175th birthday, and the city celebrated with a public party at the Chicago History Museum. The event promised actors portraying famous Chicagoans, including Jane Addams, founder of Hull House and advocate for immigrants, children and factory workers. Little did the organizers know that the show would be stolen by a woman some viewed as a modern-day Jane Addams—more eccentric and irascible, less renowned and accomplished, but just as willing to raise her voice and speak up for the weak and vulnerable.

Mayor Rahm Emanuel grinned broadly as the Chicago Children's Choir, dressed in red, sang a lively version of "Happy Birthday."

He had reason to smile.

Ten months earlier he'd been inaugurated as leader of the nation's third most populous city, taking the reins from legendary Mayor Richard M. Daley. And while his term hadn't been a cakewalk, so far things seemed to be going well. He had inherited a nearly $700 million budget deficit and attacked it with an aggressive round of cost-cutting and layoffs. The labor unions had resisted, but ultimately Emanuel was able to strike some deals and come out on top. Meanwhile, he was moving forward with his plans to institute a longer school day, a promise that had gained him positive attention nationwide. He was already assuming Daley's mantle as the "Green Mayor": In February he had announced that the city's two coal-fired power plants would close and miles of new bike lanes were in the works.

Emanuel had even snagged two important international gatherings for Chicago: the NATO and G8 summits, to be held concurrently in May 2012—the first time both would be hosted in the same U.S. city [Ultimately, only the NATO meeting came to town, but that was still a major accomplishment].

There had been sit-ins and protests by community groups and unions related to the summits, school closings, and other issues. But Emanuel had shown a knack for avoiding and ignoring them, and so far he didn't seem to have suffered too much political fallout.

As Emanuel watched the swaying, clapping singers at the birthday party, he didn't seem to notice a crinkled orange paper banner bobbing in the crowd of revelers. It said, "History Will Judge Mayor 1 Percent Emanuel for Closing Mental Health Clinics."

He'd gotten the moniker early on in his tenure. As Occupy Wall Street–inspired protests swept the nation, it was a natural fit for a mayor known for his high-finance connections and brief but highly lucrative career as an investment banker.

A staffer did notice the banner, and told the man holding it to put it away. Matt Ginsberg-Jaeckle, a lanky longtime activist, complied, partially folding the banner and lowering it into the crowd. The song ended, and Emanuel began shaking hands with the singers and other well-wishers near a colorful, multi-tiered birthday cake.

Then a shrill, rough voice cut through the chatter, causing heads to turn as the orange banner was unfurled and raised again. "Mayor Emanuel, please don't close our clinics! We're going to die. … There's nowhere else to go. … Mayor Emanuel, please!" cried a woman with a soft, pale face, red hair peeking out from a floral head scarf and dark circles around her wide eyes that gave her an almost girlish, vulnerable expression.

It was Helen Morley, a Chicago woman who had struggled all her life with mental illness but still managed to become a vocal advocate for herself and others in the public housing project where she lived, and for Chicagoans suffering from disabilities and mental illness. For the past 15 years she'd been a regular at the city's mental health clinic in Beverly/Morgan Park, a heavily Irish and African-American, working- and middle-class area on the city's Southwest Side. It was one of six mental health clinics that Emanuel planned to close as part of sweeping cuts in his inaugural budget. He said it made perfect economic sense—it would save $3 million, and the patients could move to the remaining six public clinics. But Morley and others pleaded that he didn't understand the role these specific clinics played in their lives and the difficulty they would have traveling to other locations.

Morley's eyes were fixed unblinkingly on the mayor as she walked quickly toward him, calling out in that ragged, pleading voice, her gaze and gait intense and focused. Almost all eyes were on her—except for those of the mayor, who shook a few more hands and then pivoted quickly and disappeared through a door, studiously ignoring Morley the entire time.

"Mayor Emanuel!" she cried again as he dashed out. "Please stay here, Mayor Emanuel!"

The abruptness of the exit, the cake sitting there untouched, the lack of closing niceties, and the crowd milling around awkwardly gave the impression that the event had been cut much shorter than planned.

With the mayor gone, Ginsberg-Jaeckle and fellow activist J.R. Fleming stepped up on the stage and lifted the banner behind the cake. Morley centered herself in front of them and turned to face the remaining crowd, earnestly entreating them,

"People are dying. They aren't going to have nowhere to go!"

BENEATH THE MAYOR'S NOTICE?

Emanuel's critics and admirers have both described him as a quintessential creature of Washington and Wall Street, a brilliant strategist and fundraiser who knows just the right way to leverage his famously abrasive personality to get wealthy donors to open their wallets and to help him win races. He became a prominent fundraiser for powerful politicians in his twenties, he made some $18 million in investment banking in just two years, he played central roles in two White Houses, and he orchestrated a dramatic Democratic takeover of the House of Representatives during his six years in Congress. He clearly knows how politicking works. But being mayor is different, or at least it should be. In Washington people are often tagged as political allies or adversaries, fair game for manipulation or intimidation. In Congress, Emanuel represented his constituents, but the daily grind had a lot more to do with Beltway machinations and maneuvers. Running a city, where you are elected to directly serve people and listen to them, is supposed to be a different story. Emanuel was treating Chicago as if it were Washington. Perhaps that's why, even in his brief tenure as mayor, he has seemed to find it so easy to ignore the parents, teachers, pastors, students, patients, and others who have carried out multiple sit-ins and protests outside his fifth-floor office in City Hall.

These citizens frequently note that Daley had not been particularly accessible, sympathetic or democratic in his approach, but at least he would meet with people, acknowledge them, make perhaps token efforts to listen to their proposals and act on their concerns. Emanuel can't seem to find the time for many members of the public, they complain, even as he says he wants their input on issues like school closings.

"His response was to ignore us," said Jitu Brown, education organizer for KOCO, one of the city's oldest and most respected civil rights organizations. "We had our problems with Mayor Daley, but Mayor Daley surrounded himself with neighborhood people and he himself was a neighborhood person. This man, Rahm Emanuel, has surrounded himself with corporate people. This administration is doing the bidding of corporations and robbing us of the things our parents fought for."

If Emanuel thought primarily in terms of political and financial strategy, and the costs and benefits of how he interacted with certain people, it's understandable that he would dart away from Helen Morley. But she was clearly a woman in deep distress, both at the birthday party and at previous protests at City Hall.

"They knew who she was, she was at every sit-in," said Ginsberg-Jaeckle. "But she was never contacted by them, they never met with her, not once."

Three months later, Helen Morley would be dead. Her friends blamed the closing of the mental health center. Of course, there was no direct link between the clinic closing and the heart attack that felled Morley at age 56. But her friends are sure that the trauma of losing her anchor—the clinic and the tight-knit community there—is what pushed her ailing body past the limit. They said as much during a protest outside the city health department offices a week and a half after Morley's death, with a coffin and large photos of her in tow.

"We don't have an autopsy or a medical examiner's report. You can't show her death was related to the clinic closure," said Ginsberg-Jaeckle. "But it would be hard for anyone to say that given her heart conditions and other conditions she suffered from, that the stress and cumulative impact of everything she was going through didn't play a major role."

If Emanuel did indeed think largely in terms of adversaries, Morley was not a worthy one for him. She was impoverished, unemployed; many saw her as "crazy," as she herself sometimes said she was. Her unhappiness with the mayor and her death would cost him no political capital.

But Emanuel's attitude toward Morley and the other members of the Mental Health Movement was perhaps emblematic of a deeper issue that would haunt him in the not-too-distant future. Although he seemed adroit at manipulating the levers of power, Emanuel did not seem to understand the power of regular Chicagoans, especially Chicagoans organized into the city's rich mosaic of community groups, labor unions, progressive organizations and interfaith coalitions.

This failing would become fodder for national pundits in the fall, as the Chicago Teachers Union made headlines around the world by going on strike and filling the city streets with waves of shouting, chanting Chicagoans clad in red T-shirts. Emanuel appeared shocked and disgusted with the union's audacity, attacking them in a public relations campaign more reminiscent of a brutal electoral race than contract negotiations between two teams of public servants.

A NAFTA NEOLIBERAL

Many pundits describe Emanuel as the epitome of the modern centrist neoliberal Democrat. The North American Free Trade Agreement (NAFTA) is often viewed as a symbol of neoliberalism, a global socioeconomic doctrine with intellectual roots in Chicago. Emanuel was a key architect of the trade agreement, which ultimately cost tens of thousands of U.S. jobs and brought social and economic devastation to Mexico.

To the extent that Emanuel genuinely wants to make the world a better place for working people, he thinks market forces and business models are the way to do it, and he clearly (and perhaps rightly) thinks that he understands these institutions far better than any teacher or crossing guard or nurse. From that viewpoint, the messy attributes of democracy—sit-ins, protests, rallies, people demanding meetings and information and input—simply slow down and encumber the streamlined, bottom-line-driven process Emanuel knows is best. But many regular Chicagoans see injustice, callousness and even cruelty in this trickle-down, authoritarian approach to city governance. They see the mayor bringing thousands of new corporate jobs subsidized with taxpayer dollars while laying off middle-class public sector workers like librarians, call-center staffers, crossing guards, and mental health clinic therapists. They see him closing neighborhood schools, throwing parents' and students' lives into turmoil. They see him (like Daley) passing ordinances at will through a rubber-stamp City Council, leaving citizens with few meaningful avenues to express their opposition to policies changing the face of their city.

If there's one thing Chicagoans have demonstrated ever since the city rose out of a swamp of stinking onions, it is that they will not quietly acquiesce when they sense injustice. This rich tradition stretches from the Haymarket Affair of 1886 to the garment workers strikes of the early 1900s; from the 1968 Democratic National Convention protests to the first massive immigration march of 2006. Like the proud Chicagoans who came before them, the Chicago Teachers Union, the Mental Health Movement, and other contemporary groups are committed to questioning and shaping the meanings of democracy, leadership, power and justice.

Rahm Emanuel's tenure as mayor of Chicago has provided a stage for these populist and progressive institutions to grapple with other powerful forces in a drama about the continual evolution of a great American city.

HANDS OFF OUR SCHOOLS

How would Emanuel's tenure be judged through the lens of history? Would he be seen as popular and effective? Or autocratic and brutal? Or both?

That question was not a rhetorical one for the scores of parents and students who attended the more than a hundred meetings in the winter and spring of 2013 about plans to close up to 100 or more public schools. In countless interviews with reporters, comments at public meetings, and chats with friends, the idea was often repeated: School closings were a clear sign that certain residents were no longer welcome in Chicago, that they weren't part of the future plan. Emanuel and his supporters continued repeating their talking points about creating schools where all students would have equal opportunity, about allowing low-income minority youth to fulfill their dreams. But increasingly many Chicagoans—particularly African-American ones—were not buying it.

At the school closing hearings, parents, teachers and students begged the mayor and education board—often tearfully—to save their schools. In promoting charter schools Emanuel and other backers frequently invoked the image of "parent choice." With scores of public schools on the chopping block, hundreds of parents made their choice quite clear: they and their kids wanted their schools to stay open.

By March schools officials had, they said, analyzed the input from the community hearings. On March 21, the big news came: the list of schools to be closed. There were 54: one small high school and 53 elementary schools. Additionally some schools would be combined with other schools, shoehorned into the same buildings. The closings were mostly in low-income African-American neighborhoods on the South and West Sides. It made national headlines as the largest-ever mass school closing plan.

The reaction was immediate.

Families saw the closing of their local school as the unmooring of one of their few anchors. Walking an extra mile— even an extra half mile—would mean significantly increased danger of violence. Parents and community activists demonstrated this point to reporters and some sympathetic aldermen by taking them on the new paths their kids would have to take, past loitering gang members, boarded up buildings, and busy intersections.

A week before the school board vote, students and activists staged a "die-in" on the South Side, near an elementary school slated for closure. The die-in was organized by Fearless Leading by Youth, the group of teenagers from the largely African-American, low-income neighborhoods on the South Side.

They lay down in the street in white T-shirts adorned with fake blood; five were arrested. Among them was Jesus "Chuy" Campuzano, an energetic young activist who was a central part of the Mental Health Movement. The protest got him "eleven hours in lockup" on charges of disorderly conduct, as he recounted a week later. "Some people didn't believe I was up to that arrest, but I did it and I'm willing to do it again."

The weekend before the board vote, Karen Lewis was reelected president of the Chicago Teachers Union with 80 percent support. Over the next three days, hundreds of parents, students, and teachers marched throughout the city visiting schools to be closed and protesting the plan. They rallied at City Hall, and 23 were arrested for blocking elevators. Students walked out of classes to join the demonstration—more than 100 by organizers' count.

Not surprisingly, Campuzano was there all three days. It was a grueling week, but at times like that he would think of Helen Morley. He remembered her struggling with various physical ailments but refusing to go home, even when other activists would try to persuade her to. "She was the one who taught me to stand up for what I believe in," said Campuzano. "She taught me not to let myself get bullied. The big bully in this town is the mayor. And if Helen were still here, he'd be having to deal with her every day."

The night before the vote, Campuzano sat in a brightly decorated Mexican taquería in Rogers Park, the North Side neighborhood where he'd been staying with friends since falling out with his parents. The air was humid and electric with the feel of a gathering storm. Campuzano chatted with the restaurant staff as he flipped through photos from the past week on his cellphone. There was one of him being pushed roughly into a squad car at the die-in, a grimace on his face. A shot of him with Maxine, a union janitor he met on the first of the three-day marches. Her goddaughter was killed in a shooting that night, he later learned. "On the third day she was there again," said Campuzano, his unwavering gaze and steady voice providing a sharp contrast to his animated chanting style. "She said she couldn't take it anymore, that she had to stand up to this person who was taking their jobs away. She was talking about Rahm."

Another of Campuzano's pictures showed Pilar, a teenage girl with burgundy streaks in her dark hair who was also arrested at the die-in. She would be elected prom queen a few nights after, he noted. Then there was Asean Johnson, a 9-year-old student at Garvey Elementary School, slated for closing. Asean's mother noticed Campuzano's style and told her son to emulate him. So Asean stuck near Campuzano during the march, shouting, "Education is a right, that's why we have to fight!" Videos were widely circulated online showing the diminutive boy speaking out passionately and confidently. People suggested he should run for mayor, or even president. "I'm like, 'What did we create here?' " said Campuzano later. "Another me!" "

When those children become adults, there will be a brighter future for the city," he concluded. "Thanks to the mayor, there will be a better Chicago."

PART IV

Chicago Government

Introduction

Local governments in the Chicago region are fragmented and frequently dysfunctional, having been created in earlier times. This plethora of antiquated local governments inhibits accountability, efficiency, effectiveness, and coordination. At the same time, in the city of Chicago, there is no participatory level of neighborhood government, where citizens can have an active voice in effecting local decisions that most affect their lives. Seven Chicago wards use a participatory budgeting process to allow citizens to vote on spending $1.3 million in the aldermanic menu of city services per ward.[1] A few more Chicago wards have held neighborhood hearings on local zoning issues. For the most part, however, governing is left entirely to government officials in both the city and the suburbs.

As those who have studied Chicago city government have learned, it is also inefficient because of the remains of machine politics patronage and the historical evolution of government services. Frequently in the past, the cost of city services in Chicago has been 100 percent more than in other comparable cities. Continual budget cuts and the privatization of some city services have made government somewhat more efficient over the years, but waste still remains. Some government services are also not equitably delivered. It is not uncommon for black and minority communities to receive fewer city services than white communities within the city and in the suburbs.

In 1989, the City Club of Chicago proposed ten reforms needed for the Chicago City Council. Chief among those reforms were 1) Public disclosure of information on legislation; 2) Improving the City Council committee system; 3) Better and more democratic City Council procedures; and 4) Greater citizen participation. Of the initial ten City Club proposals, only five have been partially adopted. Chicago's city council remains a rubber stamp, simply endorsing the proposals put forth by the mayor's administration, rather than serving as a democratic and deliberative legislature.

From 2011 to 2015, the Chicago City Council under Mayor Rahm Emanuel was more of a rubber stamp than under either Mayors Richard J. or Richard M. Daley. By 2016, however, the city council became somewhat more independent and less of an absolute rubber stamp. Only 28 aldermen (56 percent) voted with the mayor 100 percent of the time, and 13 aldermen (26 percent) provided a loose opposition to the mayor's administration. The reason for the change to a weaker rubber-stamp council was the mayor's loss of popularity, with only 25 percent of the voters approving of the job he has done, and two major challenges: the high crime and murder rates, especially in the African American communities; and a budget crisis greater than any faced since the Great Depression.

The city council normally approves the city's more-than seven-billion-dollar budget unanimously. But the city faced a large budget gap in 2016, a huge deficit in all its pension funds, and a decline in state funding during the state budget crisis. Property and other taxes were increased by $755 million and more than $1 billion was borrowed to pay the bills. Tax increases are never popular, and some aldermen opposed them. The final vote on the budget was divided, with 36 aldermen voting for the budget and 14 against. Mayor Emanuel continues to reign over a more or less compliant council, but there is increasing dissent.

Since the mayor and aldermanic elections of 2011, we have entered a new post-Daley era. Political reformers have been elected as president and commissioners of the Cook County Board, and a few more progressive reform–oriented candidates have been elected to the Chicago City Council. A Republican governor of Illinois was elected for the first time in decades. By necessity, Mayor Rahm Emanuel, County Board president Toni Preckwinkle, and Governor Bruce Rauner have been forced to cut expenditures to close permanent structural budget deficits. Yet, even with the political will to bring about fundamental reforms, it can be very hard to make major changes to a structure so mired in overlapping jurisdictions and competing interests.

Previous transition team reports of both Chicago city government and Cook County government have found a variety of problems that each new administration has attempted to fix. Frequently, there is a lack of management information needed for our governments to operate efficiently; there is an even greater lack of information for the public to hold our city and county governments accountable. This lack of information has persisted, despite Freedom of Information requests by civic groups and the increase in information available on official government websites. This lack of information decreases productivity and is compounded by outdated technology, methods, and practices, which have only gradually improved and changed since Richard J. Daley and George Dunne controlled our city and county governments.

While much more data is available on official city and county government websites, it is like a firehose of information. It has become increasingly difficult to decipher what information is important and needed by our governments to be productive. It is also increasingly difficult for civic watchdog agencies, community groups, and citizens to weed through all of this information in a meaningful way that improves accountability. For instance, while four hundred pages (with two hundred thousand line items) of the city budget are now online, neither the city nor the county provides audited performance data on the goods and services they deliver. Therefore, for most local government services, it is impossible to calculate a reliable cost per unit in order to set realistic goals of measurable increases in productivity. In general, no one knows for sure whether Chicago services are produced as efficiently as services in other cities.

City and county government departments have grown up organically over the last century. Each was originally created with a clear purpose and often with a small staff. Each used the technology available at the time of its creation to deliver city services. Over time, however, conditions changed. Departments have added more functions and personnel, but they continue to deliver services as they had in the past. There has been no genuine zero-sum budgeting process and no rethinking of the entire operation of government agencies and departments. Under both Chicago Mayor Emanuel and Cook County President Preckwinkle, this has begun to change. Mayor Emanuel, for example, has redesigned how city garbage is collected, moving from a ward-based system to a new grid system. President Preckwinkle was an early adopter of the federal Affordable Care Act, which has resulted in millions of new dollars available for patient care at the county hospital. In addition, the city inspector general has reviewed city agencies and programs like the garbage pickup system and recommended additional reforms. But new budget cuts and increased pension costs are going to require further increases in productivity—providing more government services at less cost. They are also likely to demand local tax increases, which both aldermen, county commissioners, and constituents are likely to protest.

Beyond the city of Chicago, there is a crazy quilt of 540 governments with taxing authority in Cook County and 1,200 in the metropolitan region. There is considerable waste, duplication, and inefficiency in this fractured, multilayered government system that has grown up haphazardly over the last one hundred fifty years. The multiplicity of local governments is due in large part to state constitutional limits on taxing and borrowing. New special units of government, with their own taxing authority, were formed when a larger unit could not finance and administer a particular government service due to constitutional limits. Special districts were also created when a natural service area did not correspond to existing political boundaries (mosquito abatement districts) or to achieve economies of scale (Metropolitan Water Reclamation District).

Perhaps the biggest problem in local government, however, is the political corruption brought by machine politics. Public corruption in Illinois has a long history, dating from the first scandal involving Chicago aldermen and Cook County commissioners in the 1860s, and to even earlier scandals involving Illinois governors. In the 1860s, Chicago aldermen and county commissioners participated in a crooked contract to paint city hall. Today, crooked contracts still cost the taxpayers millions of dollars a year and crooked politicians still go to jail.

More than two thousand individuals have been convicted of myriad forms of public corruption since 1970. Thirty-three Chicago aldermen (current and former) have been convicted of public corruption since 1970. Based upon testimony before the Illinois Reform Commission, the cost of corruption, or "corruption tax," for the Chicago and Illinois tax-payer is at least $500 million a year.

Chicago remains the most corrupt metropolitan region in the nation, and Illinois the third most corrupt state.[2] And 2015 was a banner year for corruption in Illinois.[3] Our city and state are losing the battle against this evil. Corruption convictions in 2015 and 2016 continued for Illinois congressmen, Chicago police officers, Cook County officials, suburban officials, state legislators, and doctors involved in Medicare and Medicaid fraud. Political campaign contributions that often lead to fraud and corruption continue to grow as US Supreme Court decisions have removed restrictions on giving and resulted in the proliferation of Super PACs. Illinois, unsurprisingly, topped the list of most populated states in Super PAC spending of $11.1 million in just the first months of 2016.[4] California and New York, which are larger in population, spent only $10.5 and $3.6 million, respectively. States like Texas spent only $1.2 million.

Only comprehensive reforms can lessen the level of corruption in Chicago and Illinois, currently the capitals of corruption in the United States. Given the high cost of corruption, we cannot hope to adopt a prudent city, county, or state budget without such reforms. Without reform, we will continue to pay too much for government services, we will keep honest businesses from locating here, and we will slow economic recovery. While citizens will continue to distrust government at all levels and consider tax increases unfair, curbing public corruption is the first step in reestablishing trust and pride in our government.

NOTES

1. See http://www.pbchicago.org for details.
2. Gradel, Thomas J., and Dick Simpson. *Corrupt Illinois: Patronage, Cronyism, and Criminality.* Urbana: University of Illinois Press, 2015.

3. Simpson, Dick, et al. "2015 a Banner Year in Illinois Corruption: Anti-Corruption Report Number 9," Chicago: University of Illinois Department of Political Science, March 2016.

4. "Illinois Tops List of Most Populated States in Super PAC Spending," Illinois Sunshine Website published by the Illinois Campaign for Political Reform, May 26, 2016. Detailed information available at www.illinoissunshine.org

A Tradition of Corruption

By Elizabeth Brackett

Chicago and Illinois politics have been fraught with corruption for decades. This tradition of corruption has led, in many cases, to arrests and the prosecution of those involved. This should have served as a lesson and warning to Rod Blagojevich, yet surprisingly it did not.

The following chapters from journalist Elizabeth Bracket's book Pay to Play: How Rod Blagojevich Turned Political Corruption into a National Sideshow *provides a portrait of former Illinois Governor Rod Blagojevich and the tradition of corruption in Illinois.*

" IF ILLINOIS isn't the most corrupt state in the United States, it's certainly one hell of a competitor." The FBI's Robert Grant hurled those words into the atmosphere at the press conference following the arrest of Governor Blagojevich. While it may have made some Illinois politicos wince, the FBI chief didn't receive much argument from them. Illinoisans have a long love/hate relationship with their state's reputation for producing scoundrels and scallywags. The colorful characters who dot the state's political landscape are part and parcel of the state's raucous, brawling identity, particularly in the city of Chicago.

The antics of Mike "Hinky Dink" Kenna and "Bathhouse John" Coughlin, two bosses who ruled Chicago's First Ward from the late nineteenth century until World War II, are legendary. The ward, which later became much of what is now known as "The Loop" in downtown Chicago was one of the most infamous havens for vice in the entire United States, home to magnificent gambling palaces, ornate houses of prostitution, and saloons, bars, and dives of immense variety. "Hinky Dink" was the brains behind the operation while the gregarious "Bathhouse John" was the front man. As Democrats, the two men controlled the party and its coffers, and both served as alderman of the First Ward. They immediately sold protection to the ward's pimps, prostitutes, and gamblers, which included lawyers who would be on the spot if arrests came. In exchange Kenna and Coughlin received a cut of the proceeds from the illegal activities. ...

Corruption got an early start too in the state capital in Springfield. Governor Joel Aldrich Matteson (1853-1857) tried to cash in $200,000 in government script, explaining that he had "found" it in a shoebox. A judge bought the governor's explanation that he had no idea how the script had made its way into the shoebox. The judge agreed not to accept an indictment if the governor turned the money over to the state.

Another Illinois governor escaped indictment in the 1920s despite substantial evidence that he had embezzled more than $1 million in state funds while in office. Governor Lennington Small went on to serve seven more years in office.

And though he was never governor, Illinois Secretary of State Paul Powell appears to have gotten away with fleecing the taxpayers out of more money than anyone before him. Powell, who was elected to the office in 1964 and again in 1968, had a simple definition of political success: "There's only one thing worse than a defeated politician, and that's a broke one." Powell was never defeated and, as it turned out at his death, he was not broke either. The highest office Powell ever held was secretary of state, and the highest salary he ever received was $30,000 a year. Yet after a lifetime of public service, when Paul Powell died in 1970 at the age of sixty-eight he left an estate that exceeded $3 million. Police officers gathering up his belongings from the Springfield hotel suite where he had been living did not believe anything suspicious had occurred until they came across $800,000, *in cash,* stuffed in shoeboxes, briefcases, and strongboxes in the closet. Upon investigation they realized that when Illinois residents came to the secretary of state's office to renew their driver's license and were told to write out their checks simply to "Paul Powell," at least part of the money really did go to Paul Powell. Taxpayers were both aghast and amused by the idea of Powell stuffing hundreds of thousands of dollars into shoeboxes, all the while continuing his modest way of life.

Powell was emblematic of the Illinois politicians who built their political organizations—and apparently their personal fortunes—on patronage. In his role as secretary of state, 'Powell had more than two thousand jobs to handout. He understood and wielded the power those jobs gave him. Whenever the subject of state jobs came up, he was known to say, "I can smell the meat a-cookin.'"

Those who were awarded jobs were expected to give back, perhaps by working for Powell's election and reelections, or contributing to his campaigns, or both. This was the "pay-to-play" politics of its day, which at the time no one saw as corrupt. It was simply the "way things worked" in Illinois.

Political corruption in the state had its roots in the momentous population movements of the nineteenth century. As Irish, Germans, Poles, and others came to Illinois, jobs were hard to come by. The new immigrants faced intense discrimination and grew to realize they would have to organize themselves politically in order to gain power. As their political organizations gained strength and began taking control of precincts, then wards, and finally city and state governments, immigrant politicians built these organizations by handing out jobs. Once a new immigrant had a job, walking a precinct for a candidate or a political party seemed like a small price to pay for holding on to that job. It wasn't long before working a precinct became a requirement for getting a job, enabling these political organizations to gain more and more control over who would work in state and local government.

Richard J. Daley, the legendary boss of Chicago, took over the Cook County Democratic party when he became mayor in 1955 and proceeded to build the nation's strongest political machine. Daley's predecessor, Martin J. Kennelly, had been seen as an ineffectual reformer. So it was, on the election night when Richard J. Daley took the throne, that Alderman Paddy Bauler danced a jig and belted out his now-famous words, "Chicago ain't ready for reform!" Over the next twenty-one years, Daley's machine delivered again and again in providing city services and in getting out votes for the Democratic party. Handing out city jobs in exchange for precinct work or political contributions was never seen as corruption. Rather, it was seen as a means of providing "good government and good politics," as the mayor liked to say.

***

Most Chicagoans believed he was a personally honest man. But plenty of those around him got caught with their hands in the city's coffers. Thomas Keane, Daley's longtime floor leader in the City Council, was convicted and served prison time for federal wire fraud and for making millions of dollars on secret land deals. The day after Keane's conviction, his law partner, Alderman Paul Wigoda, was convicted for income tax evasion on a $50,000 bribe he'd taken from a real estate developer for pushing a zoning change through the City Council. And the day after that Daley's former press secretary, Earl Bush, went down on eleven counts of federal mail fraud. It marked the beginning of the end of America's last great political machine.

***

With so many Chicago politicians before him taken down by federal prosecutors, Rod Blagojevich had to know the rules had changed. But somehow he seemed to think those changes did not apply to *him*. Federal prosecutors and the FBI were amazed—and angered—by Blagojevich's brazenness in the wake of the convictions of politicians who preceded him. On the day of the governor's arrest, the FBI's Robert Grant told reporters, "Many, including myself, thought that the recent convictions of a former governor [George Ryan] would usher in a new era of honesty and reform in Illinois politics. Clearly the charges announced today reveal that the Office of Governor has become nothing more than a vehicle for self-enrichment, unrestricted by party affiliation, and taking Illinois politics to a new low."

The low road of Illinois politics had been well-traveled by previous governors. Three of the seven who served before Blagojevich were convicted and served serious jail time.

Democratic governor Otto Kerner, a tall, handsome man, had a perfect profile for politics: a graduate of Brown University, law degree from Northwestern, married to a former Chicago mayor's daughter, Bronze Star for service in World War II. Elected in 1960 and 1964, Governor Kerner served without a hint of scandal. Appointed to the U.S. Court of Appeals in 1968, he resigned in disgrace in 1974 after he was convicted on seventeen counts of bribery and related charges. The manager of two Illinois racetracks had given then Governor Kerner $356,000 worth of stock in her horse-racing operation. In exchange the governor had arranged for her track to have the best racing dates of the season. Kerner was sentenced to three years in prison but was diagnosed with terminal cancer and released after serving eight months. Such were the circumstances of dealings with Illinois public officials that Marge Lindheimer Everett, the tracks manager, actually believed the bribe was a legitimate, federally deductible expense for doing business with the state.

Horse racing has long been a magnet for corruption in Illinois. One of the charges against Blagojevich in the federal criminal complaint accuses him of demanding a campaign contribution before signing a bill that would direct a percentage of casino revenues to the horse-racing industry.

After Otto Kerner, the next governor to wind up behind bars was Dan Walker, a Democrat who ran as a reformer against Daley's Democratic machine. Without the benefit of the Democratic organization to turn out the vote for him, Dan Walker set out to *walk* across Illinois, a distance of 1,197 miles, wearing his signature red bandana, work shirt, and jeans in order to relate to everyday voters.

His stunt caught the imagination of the media—and Illinois voters—and Dan Walker won a single term as governor, from 1973 to 1977. But it wasn't easy. Walker had hoped for cooperation from the Illinois legislature, but in his autobiography, *The Maverick and the Machine,* he describes the confrontational relationship that developed. "Right of the box, my own party leaders deserted me and refused to confirm my Cabinet appointees. In effect, they spit in my face, and the Republicans kicked me in the ass. But what are you going to do? Lay down, or fight them? So I fought them." When the Democrats won majorities in both houses of the legislature during the last two years of Walker's administration, he was able to bring some reform to the state with new ethics legislation and tighter laws regarding political patronage. …

Like former Governor Kerner, Dan Walker's legal troubles began after he left office when he was convicted for obtaining fraudulent loans for his business and personal use from a savings and loan bank he owned. At his sentencing, U.S. District Judge Ann Williams told him, "It's clear to this court that a pattern was established and that you, Mr. Walker, thought this bank was your own personal piggy bank to bail you out whenever you got into trouble." He was sentenced to seven years and served eighteen months at a Duluth, Minnesota, federal prison.

In 2001, when Patrick Fitzgerald arrived in Chicago, political corruption trials reached a new level. Fitzgerald went after city, county, and state politicians with an aggressiveness never before seen from the U.S. attorney's office. One of the sacred cows he took on was the political patronage system in the city of Chicago. Richard M. Daley had been mayor for twelve years and held firm control of the city's political operations when Fitzgerald took over as U.S. attorney. The city had flourished in many ways under Daley's leadership, and he credited the professional managers and staff he had placed in key departments for the city's success. Revamping the city's schools under the leadership of his appointee Paul Vallas was the mayor's toughest challenge, and he touted the important progress Vallas made. Neighborhoods were revitalized across the city, helped by good economic times and a well—run city Department of Planning—led at one point by Valerie Jarrett, currently one of President Barack Obama's chief advisers. Where his father had been the "Boss," Daley frequently referred to himself as the city's "CEO." He did not take the job as chairman of the Cook County Democratic party, as his father had, and he often said that the Democratic machine and the old patronage system were long gone. Nonetheless, through his corporation counsel young Daley challenged the Shakman Decrees, alleging that they "interfered with the smooth operation of city government and were no longer needed."

It was an imaginative effort, but the argument came to a screeching halt on July 18, 2005, when Patrick Fitzgerald brought federal charges against leading city officials in Daley's administration for "violating the Shakman Decrees' against the political hiring and firing of city employees." in a news conference announcing the charges, Fitzgerald reiterated that "Every resident of Chicago has the right to compete fairly for a job if he or she is qualified, without regard to political affiliation or whether they do campaign work. Every applicant who sits for an interview is entitled to an honest evaluation. And the residents of Chicago are entitled to the best-qualified laborers, plumbers, foremen, and inspectors. And when a federal court order requires that people be hired or promoted without regard to political affiliation, the court order must be followed. Yet, for a decade, certifications by city officials that the law has been complied with have often been fraudulent. Qualified persons sat for interviews for jobs that had already been doled out as a reward for political work. The defendants are charged with a pervasive fraud scheme that included fixing applicant interviews and ratings, guaranteeing that preferred job candidates would be chosen over other equally or better-suited individuals, and then falsifying personnel documents to conceal their wrongdoing." He added, "The diversion of public resources to benefit political organizations, by using fraudulently obtained jobs and promotions as currency to compensate political workers, cheats the city and its employees, and improperly advantages those political organizations with influential government sponsors."

***

Rod Blagojevich slid easily into [Father-in-Law, Dick] Mell's organization. City payroll records show he was being paid by as many four different City Council committees in one year. But Blagojevich told the *Chicago Tribune* he never worked in City Hall; rather, he said, he worked in Mell's ward service office where he organized community events and held free legal clinics. The U.S. attorney's office launched an investigation into ghost payrolling at that time, concentrating on whether some of those listed on city payrolls, like Blagojevich, were being paid for doing no work. A handful of Mell's office workers were questioned, but the investigation never resulted in indictments. Blagojevich was snagged by the city's ethics ordinance, however, when he represented legal clients from his private law practice in personal injury and workmen's compensation cases. The ethics ordinance bars city employees from representing personal clients in cases against the city. The ethics complaint against Blagojevich went to the City Council Rules Committee, chaired by—who else?—Alderman Dick Mell. The charges were dropped.

Rod and Patti Blagojevich had been married for two years when the phone rang one Sunday evening. Dick Mell, on the other end of the line, needed a candidate to run for state representative—and he needed one *now*. "Are you interested?" he asked Rod. It was the beginning of Rod Blagojevich's political career.

***

Windy City Corruption Blows Across the State

By Melissa Mouritsen, David Sterrett, Dick Simpson,
and Thomas J. Gradel[1]

For a long time—going back to at least the Al Capone era—Chicago and Illinois have been known for high levels of public corruption. Recent statistical analysis now proves the city, suburbs, and the state are among the most corrupt in the nation.

With 1869 elected officials, appointees, government employees and a few private individuals convicted in Illinois since 1976, the state of Illinois now ranks third in the nation for absolute public corruption convictions.[2] Illinois is only surpassed by California with 2357 convictions and New York with 2552—both states with much larger populations.

A breakout of public corruption conviction statistics shows that the Northern District of Illinois, containing the Chicago metropolitan region, leads all other districts with 1,561 convictions. This means that the Northern District leads the nation's cities in corruption just like the Capone era when the mob financed, elected and controlled Mayor Big Bill Thompson.

The two worst crime zones in Illinois in terms of federal corruption convictions are the Governor's mansion in Springfield and the City Council Chambers in Chicago. No other state can match our dubious distinction.

Adapted from "Chicago and Illinois, Leading the Pack in Corruption: Anti-Corruption Report Number 5" and "Green Grass and Graft: Corruption in the Suburbs: Anti-Corruption Report Number 6." University of Illinois at Chicago, Department of Political Science. December 8, 2014.

A STATE OF CORRUPTION

Since 1970, four of the last seven Illinois governors have been convicted of corruption. More than half of the state's governors have been convicted in the past forty-two years. Otto Kerner, who served from 1961 until his resignation in 1968 to accept a federal judgeship, was convicted in 1973 of mail fraud, bribery, perjury, and income tax evasion while governor. Dan Walker, who served from 1973–1977, was convicted in 1987 of obtaining fraudulent loans for the business he operated after he left office.

George Ryan, who served from 1999–2003, was found guilty in 2006 of racketeering, conspiracy and other charges going back to his days as Secretary of State. Many of these charges were part of a huge scandal, later called "Licenses for Bribes" which resulted in the conviction of more than 40 state workers and private citizens. Secretary of State employees allowed unqualified truck drivers to receive licenses in exchange for bribes, part of which would ultimately end up in Ryan's campaign fund. The scandal came to light when a recipient of one of these licenses crashed into a van and killed six children.

Perhaps the most famous of all modern Illinois corrupt officials is former governor Rod Blagojevich, who served from 2003 until his impeachment in 2009. Blagojevich was ultimately convicted of trying to sell the U.S. Senate seat vacated by Barack Obama. Other charges included his attempting to shake down Children's Memorial Hospital for a campaign contribution in return for state funding and his trying to extort a racetrack owner. Blagojevich gave state commission appointments to cronies who rigged overpriced crooked contracts in exchange for campaign contributions and later potential gifts and appointments to the private sector.

CAPITAL CITY OF CORRUPTION

Not to be outdone, the City of Chicago has seen its share of convicted officials. The first conviction of Chicago aldermen and Cook County Commissioners for accepting bribes to rig a crooked contract occurred in1869. Since 1973, 31 more aldermen have been convicted of corruption. Approximately 200 aldermen have served since then, which is a conviction rate of about one-sixth of the council members. In 1973 and 1974, four aldermen were convicted of bribery, income tax evasion and mail fraud in a scandal involving zoning changes. In the 1980s, three aldermen pleaded guilty or were found guilty in Operation Incubator, an FBI investigation into Chicago corruption. The convictions included bribery, racketeering, extortion, mail fraud and tax evasion. Less than 10 years later, seven more aldermen were convicted as part of Operation Silver Shovel, an FBI investigation into corruption in Chicago in the 1990s. Between 1996 and 1999 these seven were convicted of bribery, money laundering, fraud and tax evasion.

But not all of the convictions were part of larger FBI stings. In 1974, Thomas Keane, former 31st ward alderman and Mayor Richard J. Daley's floor leader, was convicted of conspiracy and 17 counts of mail fraud in connection with questionable real estate deals. In 2008 Ed Vrdolyak, former 10th ward alderman, was also convicted of fraud in a real estate sale involving the Chicago Medical School.

Corruption sometimes occurs multiple times in the same ward. Joseph Potempa and his successor Frank Kuta, aldermen of the 23rd ward, were both convicted in the same zoning scheme in 1973. After Thomas Keane, the 31st ward saw two more of its alderman convicted. In 1987, Chester Kuta pleaded guilty to fraud, income tax evasion, and violation of civil rights stemming from a payoff scheme. In 1997, 31st ward Alderman Joseph Martinez was convicted as part of Silver Shovel. The 13th, 20th, and 28th wards have seen multiple convictions as well. One has to wonder if certain wards especially breed corruption.

Corruption can even run in the family. In 1983, William Carothers, Alderman of the 28th ward, was found guilty of conspiracy and extortion. In 2010, his son Isaac Carothers, 29th ward alderman, pled guilty to accepting campaign contributions from an FBI agent posing as a developer seeking zoning changes. This father-son aldermanic team was convicted for almost the same crimes twenty years apart. The bond of marriage can also serve to bond a couple in corruption. Former 7th Ward Alderman Sandy Jackson pled guilty to tax fraud charges stemming from the misuse of campaign funds that belonged to her husband, United States Congressman Jesse Jackson Jr., who also pled guilty to several charges including misuse of funds.[3]

SUBURBANIZATION OF CORRUPTION

The City of Chicago attracts local, national, and even international attention for its long and salient culture of corruption. But the media and the general public tend to overlook the abundant political corruption that also exists in many of the region's suburbs. The predominant stereotype of the suburbs is that they have clean, efficient governments. Yet patronage, nepotism, cronyism, abuse of power and criminal activity flourish, sometimes for decades, in numerous city halls, police stations and special purpose government agencies in suburbs surrounding Chicago and in the collar counties. Public corruption has afflicted the north, south, and west suburbs. It impacts upper income and lower income villages, towns and cities.

More than 130 individuals have been convicted of corruption related schemes in the suburbs since the 1970s, including more than 100 public officials in the last two decades. Far from being an escape from the corrupt practices of the big, bad city, many of the suburbs seem determined to imitate them.

There are six categories of corruption-related convictions in suburban Chicago: Public officials with ties to organized crime, nepotism, police officers aiding or extorting criminals, kickbacks and bribes to officials and administrators, bribes from large development projects and stealing of funds by leaders of school districts and special purpose districts.

Organized Crime. West suburban Cicero illustrates the problems that arise when organized crime corrupts city officials. Organized crime took root in Cicero in the 1920s when Al Capone decided to settle there. During the following decades, attempts to eradicate corruption proved unsuccessful as organized crime maintained a strong presence in Cicero with mob bosses such as Frank "The Enforcer" Nitti and Tony "Big Tuna" Accardo overseeing liquor, gambling and strip joints in the city.[4]

Cicero's most recent problems with mobbed-up public officials again gained public attention in 1990 when 20 people were indicted for participating in a gambling and extortion scheme. At the time, authorities called it one of the largest-ever crackdowns on Chicago-area organized crime.[5] Organized crime's influence in Cicero continued under the leadership of Betty Loren Maltese who became town president in 1993. In 2002, she was convicted of racketing, wire fraud and mail fraud for her role in a mob scheme that stole more than $12 million from the city's insurance fund.[6] An organized crime boss and five others would also be convicted in this scheme. This came 11 years after her husband, former Cicero Town Assessor Frank Maltese, had pleaded guilty himself to fraud related to gambling.[7]

Corruption associated with organized crime has also surfaced in suburbs such as Rosemont, Northlake, Chicago Heights, Franklin Park and Stone Park.[8]

Nepotism. Nepotism has long been a significant issue in many Chicago suburbs and the village of Rosemont demonstrates how public officials can use their power to enrich friends and family. Donald Stephens served as mayor of Rosemont from 1956 to 2003 and he helped transform Rosemont from a small subdivision into a booming suburb. However, many of the beneficiaries of village contracts under Stephens' administration had business or family connections to the mayor.

In the late 1980s four firms owned by Stephens' relatives received millions of dollars in city business contracts without a competitive bidding process.[9] Likewise, three firms owned by Stephens' business associates received more than $18 million worth of contracts to expand the Rosemont Exposition Center in the 1980s.[10] Firms owned by his wife and son would also receive million dollar contracts.

Nepotism remained as prevalent under Rosemont Mayor Bradley Stephens as it was before his father died in 2007. In 2010, ten members of the Stephens family received a combined $950,000 from the village.[11]

Nepotism undermines the principles of hiring the best-qualified candidates and giving contracts to companies that will provide the best government services at the lowest cost. It undermines employee morale as workers learn that promotions and assignments are not based on merit and qualifications. It hinders accountability within city governments because it is difficult for a supervisor to discipline a family member of a top official. Ultimately, nepotism reduces efficiencies, raises the cost of government, leads to higher taxes and lowers the quality of government services.

Police Corruption. Corruption has surfaced too often within police and law enforcement agencies throughout the Chicago suburbs. Since the 1970s, more than 30 suburban law enforcement officers have been convicted of crimes related to corruption. Many of the convictions involve officers aiding or extorting criminals.

In Chicago Heights, multiple officers have been convicted of helping or extorting drug dealers.[12]

Officers have also been convicted of bribery or extortion in suburbs such as Melrose Park, Harvey and Lyons. Dispensing police powers has also been a source of corruption. In 1997 the Village of Dolton began a deputy marshal program to back up the police department. The mayor of Dolton handed out 18 badges to private citizens who were also authorized to carry guns, though none of these individuals have ever been called to service.[13] Three of those given badges were later convicted on drug charges, and at least one said he purchased the badge for $30,000—40,000.[14] In 2003, Harvey Mayor Eric Kellogg gave out a number of such badges, resulting in several arrests and convictions when a number of deputy marshals abused their police powers.[15]

Bribery and Kickbacks. Many elected officials and top government bureaucrats in suburban Chicago have been convicted of using their authority to solicit bribes from business and individuals. A corruption scandal in the middle-class suburb of Niles illustrates how elected officials can use their positions to enrich themselves. Nicolas Blasé served as a mayor of Niles for 47 years until he resigned in 2008 under the pressure of federal corruption charges. That year Blasé pleaded guilty for his role in a kickback scheme that involved him steering local businesses to a friend's insurance company.[16] Prosecutors said Blasé pocketed more than $420,000 over three decades in return for pressuring businesses to use Ralph Weiner and Associates as their insurance broker.[17] And according to a recent investigation, Blasé also handed out about a half of a million dollars' worth of perks for six retiring or retired village employees. These perks came in the form of retirement bonuses, village cars and cash payments authorized by Blasé, and apparently not approved by the Village Board at an official meeting, which may be a violation of Illinois Open Meetings Act.[18]

Top officials in suburbs such as Chicago Heights, Calumet City, Oak Forest and Fox Lake also have been convicted of taking kickbacks. Elected officials also have been convicted for accepting money in return for helping businesses receive approval for development projects in suburbs such as Lyons, Berwyn and Hoffman Estates.[19]

If bribes aren't forthcoming, some officials take advantage of whatever is available. In 1987, Arlington Heights Treasurer Lee Poder was arrested for using $20 million in fire department pension funds to buy and sell securities, keeping profits for himself but passing along the losses to the village.[20]

Big Developments. The lure of big developments in suburbs has also been a source not only of potential corruption but massive conflicts of interest, and not just in Rosemont. A recent *Chicago Tribune* exposé of Bridgeview cites the suburb's total debt at $230 million—a $196.4 million increase from the year 2000—making it by far the largest debt burden of any suburb.[21] A town of only 16,446 residents, this amounts to almost $14,000 for every man, woman and child residing in Bridgeview. This has caused Standard & Poor's to down grade its credit rating to near-junk status.[22]

This money was used mainly to build Toyota Park, home to the Chicago Fire, a professional men's soccer team, and a concert venue. But it was the mayor's friends and associates who were getting contracts to build and maintain the park. Among those receiving contracts were the town's financial advisor, Austin Meade; the mayor's brother, owner of P.B. Food Products; and Mayor Stephen Landek's former company, Eco-Chem. The mayor had ownership transferred to his girlfriend or his nephew while the stadium was being built. Also favored with a contract was CDK Accounting, which rents office space from a building the mayor owns.[23] Since the project was proposed, Mayor Landek received $170,000 in political contributions from Toyota Park contractors and vendors.[24]

Mayor Landek has other conflicts of interest in Bridgeview. He was recently appointed to replace retiring State Senator Louis Viverito, and has since been reelected in 2012. He chairs the Lyon's township political fund, after resigning about a year ago as Lyon's Township Supervisor, and he was previously the highway supervisor.[25] Mayor Landek holds or has recently held multiple government jobs, which have allowed him to influence decisions and to provide many benefits for family, friends, and contributors.

SUBURBAN SCHOOLS AND SPECIAL PURPOSE DISTRICTS

Corruption has affected a number of suburban school districts and special purpose districts. Two major corruption scandals rocked the Dixmoor Park District before it disbanded in 1998. Bobby Jackson, a former Dixmoor Park District trustee, pleaded guilty in 1998 to stealing $100,000 from the agency.[26] The money collected from property taxes was supposed to be used to pay off construction bonds for a recreation center that was never built. Instead, Jackson spent the stolen money on a political campaign and shared it with political allies.[27] Prosecutors said Jackson and two former Dixmoor Park District trustees—Bonita Wright and Parnell Jackson—stole $500,000 of taxpayer funds.[28] All three were convicted. The district never operated recreation programs and only oversaw one tot lot. However, state officials estimate the park district had amassed more than $1.6 million in bond issues, loans and tax levies.[29]

Corruption also tainted the Dixmoor Park District Police Department.[30] Officials working for special purpose districts have also been accused or convicted of corruption related charges in suburbs such as Batavia, Posen and Maywood.

CONCLUSION

For decades Chicago has been known for its corruption. Unfortunately, this is not just a problem in the city but the suburbs and the state as well. Corruption has many forms from simple till-skimming to bribery and kickback schemes, from nepotism to sweetheart contracts. The history runs deep and it shows no signs of stopping.

NOTES

1. We are indebted to Emily Marr, Mike Ramirez, Nick Yodelis, Doug Cantor and Esly Sarmiento for their help conducting the research contained in this article. *Chicago and Illinois, Leading the Pack in Corruption: Anti-Corruption Report Number 5* and *Green Grass and Graft: Corruption in the Suburbs: Anti-Corruption Report Number 6* are available at http://www.uic.edu/depts/pols/ChicagoPolitics/anticorruption.htm

2. 2011 figures according to the Department of Justice Public Integrity Section. Available at http://www.justice.gov/criminal/pin/

3. Skiba, Katherine and Jeff Coen and Jeff Ventiecher. "Jacksons' Guilt a Tale of Excess." *Chicago Tribune*, February 21, 2013.

4. Rodriguez, Alex and Andrew Zajac. "Feds Trace Origins of Cicero Plot." *Chicago Tribune*. June 17, 2001.

5. O'Connor, Matt and Maurice Possley. "For Mob, It's Not Like Bad Old Days." *Chicago Tribune*, August 25, 2002.

6. Fountain, John. "Town President Is Convicted In Scheme to Steal $12 Million." *The New York Times*. August 24, 2002.

7. Braden, Wiliam. "Frank Maltese, 63, Former Town Assessor For Cicero." *Chicago Sun-Times*, October 21, 1993.

8. Sterrett, David, Melissa Mouritsen, Thomas J. Gradel, Dick Simpson, Emily Marr, Mike Ramirez, Nick Yodelis, Doug Cantor and Esly Sarmiento. *Green Grass and Graft: Anti-Corruption Report Number 6*. Published June 25, 2012. Available online at http://www.uic.edu/depts/pols/ChicagoPolitics/SuburbanCorruption.pdf.

9. Gibson, Ray. "Striking It Rich in Rosemont." *Chicago Tribune*. May 27, 1990.

10. Ibid.

11. Griffin, Jake. "Family Connections In Rosemont Net $2 Million In Pay." *Daily Herald*. August 31, 2011.

12. Sterrett, David, Melissa Mouritsen, Thomas J. Gradel, Dick Simpson, Emily Marr, Mike Ramirez, Nick Yodelis, Doug Cantor and Esly Sarmiento. *Green Grass and Graft: Anti-Corruption Report Number 6*. Published June 25, 2012. Available online at http://www.uic.edu/depts/pols/ChicagoPolitics/SuburbanCorruption.pdf.

13. Main, Frank. "Dolton Badges Tarnished?" *Chicago Sun Times*, April 26, 2002.

14. Main, Frank. "Drug dealer testifies Shaw sold him badge—Dolton mayor says testimony in cops' trial 'totally untrue.'" *Chicago Sun-Times,* April 25, 2002.

15. Main, Frank. "Harvey's armed marshals accused of breaking law—Lack of training puts them in violation, state official says." *Chicago Sun-Times*. January 15, 2011.

16. Ahmed, Azam and Kristen Kridel. "Ex-Niles Mayor Pleads Guilty in Kickback Scheme." *Chicago Tribune*. November 02, 2008.

17. Ibid.

18. Robb, Tom. "Perks Aplenty: Niles Records Detail Hand Outs of Cash Bonuses, Vehicles to Ex-Village Employees. *Des Plaines Journal & Topics*. June 15, 2012.

19. Sterrett, David, Melissa Mouritsen, Thomas J. Gradel, Dick Simpson, Emily Marr, Mike Ramirez, Nick Yodelis, Doug Cantor and Esly Sarmiento. *Green Grass and Graft: Anti-Corruption Report Number 6*. Published June 25, 2012. Available online at http://www.uic.edu/depts/pols/ChicagoPolitics/SuburbanCorruption.pdf.

20. Gary Wisby."FBI seeking Arlington Heights treasurer in investment ploy," *Chicago Sun-Times,* May 8, 1987; Art Petaque. "$5 million rip off? Arlington Hts. still toting up ex-aide's take," *Chicago Sun-Times,* June 7, 1987.

21. Mahr, Joe and Joseph Ryan. "Soccer Ball and Chain." *Chicago Tribune*, June 10, 2012. Page 18.

22. Ibid.

23. Mahr, Joe and Joseph Ryan. "Some firms faced little competition on contracts." *Chicago Tribune.* June 10, 2012. Page 19.

24. Mahr, Joe and Joseph Ryan. "Soccer Ball and Chain." *Chicago Tribune*, June 10, 2012. Page 18.

25. Koebel Foster, Wynn. "Landek to resign Lyons Township post." *The Doings.* May 12, 2011. Page 18.

26. Wilson, Terry. "Ex-Dixmoor Parks Chief Admits Role in Graft." *Chicago Tribune.* June 04, 1998.

27. Ibid.

28. Ibid.

29. Colarossi, Anthony. "Settlement Offered in Failed Dixmoor Park District Case." *Chicago Tribune.* September 1, 1999.

30. O'Connor, Matt. "2 Plead Guilty in Selling of Park Police Badges." *Chicago Tribune.* July 19, 2001.

Curing Corruption in Illinois

By Thomas J. Gradel and Dick Simpson

Adapted from the book Corrupt Illinois, *this article reminds us that ending machine politics and corruption requires hard work, day after day, year and year. It is not over with one speech, one election, one report, or one new law. The authors propose an eight-step strategy to end corruption*

In Illinois, the most common method employed to end corruption has been to convict individuals practicing it. It has been the practice of the U.S. Attorney, and the occasional State's Attorney (usually from the opposite political party from those in power) who prosecute corruption, to focus on convicting guilty individuals. One prevailing theory has been that corruption is a matter of the "rotten apple in the barrel." Getting rid of a few bad guys and gals will clean up government. Second, prosecutors have believed that if they convict some individuals and have them serve significant prison sentences, other government employees and business people will decide corruption is too dangerous. With 1,913 federal convictions in Illinois from 1976-2012, those theories seem inadequate. Prosecuting corruption is a necessary, but not sufficient to cure corruption.

Nonetheless, some corruption scandals have brought legislative changes, both locally and nationally. Media coverage and public outcry has forced changes. In 1912, William Lorimer, was ousted from the U.S. Senate after it was revealed that bribes had been paid to Illinois state legislators to secure the seat. This scandal helped to pass an amendment to the U.S. Constitution requiring the direct election of Senators. Unfortunately, this did not prevent the planned sale of the Illinois U.S. Senate seat by Governor Blagojevich a century later.

Scandals in federal-government hiring, especially under presidents like Andrew Jackson, led to the Civil Service Reform Act of 1883 and the Hatch Act of 1939. They helped end patronage in the federal government and prevented federal employees from engaging in partisan activities. However, civil service has been slower to take root in Illinois.

In general, major legislation curbing corruption came much later to Illinois than to the rest of the country. The first Chicago Ethics Ordinance wasn't passed until 1987, during the final days of the Harold Washington Administration and a hundred years after the Civil Service Reform Act. And that ordinance has had to be amended a number of times to close loopholes revealed by various ethics scandals and corruption convictions. … After Mayor Rahm Emanuel was elected in 2011, he appointed an Ethics Reform Task Force headed by distinguished Chicagoans including former State Senator and Comptroller, Dawn Clark Netsch. The mayor's task force fell short of getting aldermen and their staff members covered under the Chicago Inspector General. And, despite the ethic ordinance and its many amendments, Chicago corruption persists.

Serious campaign-finance reform legislation wasn't passed at the state level until after Governor Blagojevich's indictment, impeachment and eventual conviction. Until then Illinois was the "wild west" of campaign finance regulations, with almost no limits on who could contribute and how much they could give. After Governor Pat Quinn replaced Blagojevich in 2009, he created the Illinois Ethics Commission, which proposed fundamental reforms to state laws, but only a few of those were adopted.

In general, legislative reforms in Illinois have tried to narrow the opportunities for graft and corruption by governmental officials and to increase the penalties for offenses. As Cynthia Canary and Kent Redfield have written, "[L]aws do matter and new laws can make a difference. Laws define what is legal and illegal. They set the tone for what society considers acceptable behavior and allow us to draw a line in the sand." Canary and Redfield maintain that additional key "changes in the laws that govern Illinois politics would significantly reduce both actual corruption and the appearance of corruption."[1] The problem is to generate sufficient public support and the necessary legislative votes to pass new restrictions and to provide new resources, such as public funding of elections.

On a different front, reformers have been more successful in promoting transparency laws and practices. Today more information about campaign contributions, government contracts, and government actions by both the legislative and executive branches is available than ever before in Illinois' history. While this has limited the types of corruption pursued and the techniques employed, the rate of convictions and the media reports of corruption have not decreased.

A COMPREHENSIVE ANTI-CORRUPTION STRATEGY

To end the never ending parade of corruption in Illinois, we need to do more than convict the bad guys and gals who get caught. We need to forge a comprehensive anti-corruption strategy to be implemented over a long period of time. This is necessary to create a new political culture in which public corruption is no longer tolerated.

We propose an eight-step program, going from the easiest to the most difficult steps to end corruption:

1. Demanding more transparency and accountability;
2. Hiring more inspectors general, including in the suburbs;
3. Providing civic engagement programs in our schools;
4. Encouraging more citizen participation in government and politics by steps like moving primary elections to warmer months, online voter registration, and making it easier for bills in the state legislature to get to the floor to be voted upon;
5. Adopting public financing for political campaigns;
6. Electing better public officials who will promote reforms;
7. Changing how we remap legislative districts; and
8. Ending political party machines, thus changing Illinois' culture of corruption.

Ultimately, changing the culture of corruption in Illinois requires that public officials no longer expect to be bribed and citizens no longer expect to bribe them to get legitimate government services, a government job, or a government contract.

To achieve this requires that we voters elect Illinois officials pledged to bring about reforms and carry out their promises once in office. They will have to fire subordinates who engage in corrupt or unethical practices. They will have to eliminate the remnants of patronage hiring, ghost payrolling, favoritism in the delivery of government services, and in granting government contracts.

Many of the long-term changes must happen through education. The improvements proposed in the Burnham plan for Chicago did not happen with the publication of the report or his speaking tours around Chicago in 1909. Charles Wacker produced *Wacker's Manual of the Plan of Chicago* for local schoolchildren. It was taught in the Chicago public school for decades. The end result was to produce civic leaders to promote the projects of the Burnham plan and the legion of educated voters to vote in referendum to fund the individual projects like the bridge over the river at Michigan Avenue and the merging of the three separate park districts into one unified system. We need to teach civic education, engagement, and ethics for the next decade or two as well as the cost of corruption, and its cures. Only then will we have produced the leaders and the citizens needed to finish the battle.

When Dick Simpson was in the Chicago City Council back in the 1970s, Alderman "Fast Eddie" Vrdolyak said in a speech on the floor of the council, "Anyone who would fight the machine had better bring lunch." What Vrdolyak meant is that ending machine politics and corruption requires hard work, day after day, year and year. It is not over with one speech, one election, one report, or one new law. Usually, it's not wise to heed advice from Fast Eddie, especially now after his felony conviction but what he said that day rings true.

NOTES

1. Cynthia Canary and Kent Redfield, "Lessons Learned: What the successes and failures of recent reform efforts tell us about the prospects for political reform in Illinois," Paper presented at *What's in the Water in Illinois? Ethics and Reform Symposium on Illinois Government.* Chicago, September 27-28, 2012, p 9.

City Council Still Mostly A Rubber Stamp

By Dick Simpson, Melissa Mouritsen, and Beyza Büyuker

The retirement of Mayor Richard M. Daley in 2011, along with many of the aldermen who had served under him, had the potential to change the face of politics in Chicago. Instead, Mayor Rahm Emanuel in his first term of office presided over a council that is more of a rubber stamp than it was under even boss mayor Richard J. Daley.

In his first term in office, Mayor Rahm Emanuel had more control over the council than his predecessor, Richard M. Daley had in his last term in office or even his father, Boss Richard J. Daley, had. Despite a louder and more organized opposition, and a recent slip in support, the average level of support by all aldermen on divided roll call votes was 90%. Mayor Emanuel does indeed preside over a "rubber stamp council." [1]

To assess support of the aldermen for Mayor Emanuel, a University of Illinois at Chicago study examined the voting records of all 50 alderman. The votes were then compared Mayor Emanuel's floor leaders, Alderman Pat O'Connor (40th) and Alderman Edward Burke (14th). The floor leaders' voting patterns were used to represent the official position of the mayor. [2]

Since May of 2011, when Mayor Emanuel took office, eight of the 50 aldermen voted to support his position 100% of the time and 29 aldermen voted with him from 90% to 99% of the time. Thus, over two thirds of the Chicago City Council always, or almost always, voted for the Mayor's agenda.

Adapted from: Büyuker, Beyza, Melissa Mouritsen and Dick Simpson. "Rahm Emanuel's Rubber Stamp City Council: Chicago City Council Report #7." University of Illinois at Chicago, Department of Political Science. December 9, 2014.

Figure 1: Aldermanic Agreement with Mayor Emanuel

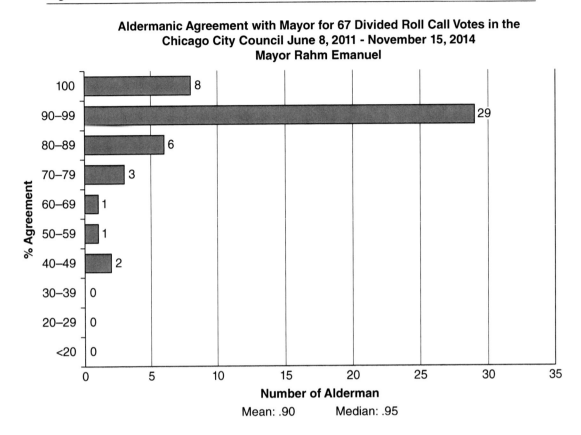

Aldermanic Agreement with Mayor for 67 Divided Roll Call Votes in the Chicago City Council June 8, 2011 - November 15, 2014
Mayor Rahm Emanuel

Mean: .90   Median: .95

Despite overall support of mayoral initiatives in the council, there are two self-proclaimed reform blocs. The Progressive Reform bloc is made up of the following Aldermen: John Arena (45th), Robert Fioretti (2nd), Scott Waguespack (32nd), Nicholas Sposato (36th), Leslie Hairston (5th), Ricky Munoz (22nd), Roderick Sawyer (6th), and Toni Foulkes (15th). This bloc votes on average only 67% of the time with the mayor, with Alderman Arena voting only 43% of the time, Alderman Fioretti, 45%, Alderman Waguespack, 54% and Alderman Sposato, 66%.

The second bloc, the Paul Douglas Alliance, is made up of the following Aldermen: Brendan Reilly (42nd), Michelle Smith (43rd), Pat Dowell (3rd), William Burns (4th), Ameya Pawar (47th), James Cappleman (46th), James Osterman (48th), Joe Moreno (1st), Rey Colon (35th), and Joe Moore (49th). This bloc votes with the mayor much more often: 91% of the time. Thus, they vote more or less consistently like the aldermen who do not label themselves as reformers and support the mayor. This block is mostly made up of aldermen representing lakefront "liberal" wards who want to be seen as representing their communities effectively, rather than being subservient to the mayor. Ameya Pawar, 47th Ward Alderman, votes most consistently with the Paul Douglas Alliance. As he has explained, "I do think that what is wrong with the way we do things is the narrative that we've created over many years, and if you simply vote 'no' you're a reformer, if you vote 'yes' you're a rubber stamp."[3] Aldermen in the Paul Douglas Alliance argue that they are able to influence legislation in negotiations with the mayor's office behind closed doors, and then are able to support his legislation in the final vote.

There were some controversial issues that split the city council during Emanuel's first term in office. In all, there were 67 divided roll call votes, over a third of which (24) only had one dissenting vote. Only 12 of the divided roll call votes had more than 5 dissenting votes, and only 7 had 10 or more. These seven issues were: fitting safety zones around schools with cameras to ticket speeders (33-14); amending the parking meter agreement (39-11); allowing public access to building energy consumption (32-17); redistributing surplus Tax Increment Finance (TIF) district funds (11-37); blocking a referendum that would allow for the election of the Chicago School Board (32-15); prohibiting large retail chains from using plastic shopping bags (36-10); and allowing ride-sharing services (like Uber and Lyft) to operate in Chicago (34-10). Although there were some contentious issues, most council votes were not. Some aldermen argue that they have supported the mayor so whole-heartedly because he, and his administration, have been willing to compromise with them on issues like cuts in library hours and protest rules at the NATO Summit.

It is important for citizens to understand that Chicago still has a strong rubber stamp council, unable to check and balance a strong chief executive like both Mayors Daley and now Mayor Emanuel. In a representative democracy a strong and deliberative legislative branch is critical to serve as a check and balance to keep the chief executive from making disastrous mistakes; and to introduce proposed laws and policies that better represent their constitutents.

NOTES

1. Buyuker, Beyza, Melissa Mouritsen and Dick Simpson. "Rahm Emanuel's Rubber Stamp City Council: Chicago City Council Report #7." *University of Illinois at Chicago Department of Political Science.* December 9, 2014.

2. On a few issues Alderman O'Connor and Alderman Burke voted differently. In these cases, the votes of the aldermen were compared directly to the Mayor's opinion as represented by his public opinion on these issues.

3. Dardick, Hal and John Byrne. "Emanuel's $7.3 Billion Budget Sails." *Chicago Tribune,* November 20, 2014.

TIF Districts

A Beginner's Guide to Chicago's 'Shadow Budget'

By Alex Nitkin

In the time it takes a Brown Line train to circle the Loop, dozens of secret deals can be made in Chicago. Some walk a blurry legal line, many are done with the common good in mind, and all of them benefit somebody. In the past few years, Tax Increment Financing (TIF) has come to epitomize this universal, yet very Chicago practice.

The weight of TIFs' complexity starts with the very term the acronym stands for. "Tax Increment Financing" sounds like the title of a chapter you'd be tempted to skip in an economics textbook, or the focus of an especially sleepy Ben Stein lecture [from the movie, *Ferris Bueller's Day Off*]. But the term stands for a process so hotly controversial—in part for its impact on schools—it [became]…a topic for debate in the 2015 Chicago mayoral election.

TIF is a process by which funding is diverted away from public education and into a network of government-controlled bank accounts, which now hold a combined $1.7 billion while school budgets continue to dwindle. It's a system that raises public money in some parts of the city to fund private mega-projects in others. It's an issue at the intersection of income inequality, education reform and government transparency. And it's a phenomenon seen in Cook County on a scale incomparable to anywhere else in the United States.

WHAT'S A TIF?

Understanding TIFs begins with property taxes. For each occupied building in Chicago, that property's owner has to pay taxes to the local government. More than half of those taxes go directly to the Chicago Board of Education (BOE), while the rest are divided between Cook County and the city of Chicago for public works projects, city college endowments and public park management.

But the Chicago City Council can vote to create areas within the city, called TIF districts, where some of that money is set aside for new construction projects outside those basic categories. TIF districts are meant to help revitalize neglected or depopulated neighborhoods by funding projects aimed to bring new economic development into the area. By design, this would attract jobs and raise property values in the long run.

As of this writing [in 2014], 153 TIF districts exist in Chicago. Some span entire neighborhoods, while others comprise just a few city blocks. In total, they cover about 32 percent of the city's geographic area.

HOW DO TIFS WORK?

As property values rise over time, property taxes rise with them. But inside a Chicago TIF district, property tax revenues are frozen in place for a period of 23 years. So year after year the same amount of money is going toward the city and BOE, while the money from each new tax increase goes into TIF accounts.

This rising value is the "I" in "TIF": each incremental tax jump means more TIF dollars generated. And TIF money, unlike public property tax money, is more-or-less spent at the discretion of the mayor and City Council.

In order for a TIF district to be created, though, state law requires that the area be "blighted"—that is, its properties must be largely old, vacant or in poor condition. This is essential to TIF's ultimate goal of bringing economic success to struggling neighborhoods. But a large question hanging over the practice is whether or not this part of the law is actually followed, as some TIFs have popped up in seemingly well-to-do areas.

WHAT'S THE BENEFIT OF TIFS?

TIFs give the city the ability to raise revenue for major projects without the political burden of raising taxes. Earthshaking developments like building a Whole Foods in Englewood, for example, simply could not happen without TIFs.

The system can also create money for massive public works initiatives, like the total reconstruction and renovation of the Howard CTA station in 2006.

By the most basic rules of urban economics, projects like these make surrounding properties more valuable and boost economic growth.

This is exactly how the upper levels of city government defend the system: in his most recent annual budget report, Emanuel has said TIFs are "promoting business, industrial and residential development in areas of the city that struggled to attract or retain housing, jobs or commercial activity."

HOW IS A TIF DISTRICT CREATED?

TIF districts are born in the city's Department of Planning and Development (DPD), whose commissioner is appointed by the mayor and operates under his direction. If the city's leaders decide to create TIF in a certain area, they'll hire a private consulting firm to prepare a "redevelopment plan," which includes an "eligibility study" that purports to 'prove' that the neighborhood is blighted.

The plan must include a detailed outline of the construction projects the TIF will make possible. However, in many cases these outlines can be as vague as "residential and commercial development."

DPD will then hold a public hearing to present the plan and hear public comment. But more often than not, if the plan has already reached this stage, it's not stopping for anything. Last Tuesday, for example, the DPD voted unanimously to create a new TIF district in Washington Park despite objections from community residents at the board's public hearing. Opponents cited a passage in the plan's fine print allowing for "displacement of residents," saying projects funded by the TIF may not always be in the community's interest.

Once the group approves the plan, it's sent straight to the City Council for what is usually a swift rubber stamp. The area's property taxes are then frozen, a TIF fund is created and from that moment private developers can make pitches to the DPD to bankroll its projects.

HOW LONG HAVE TIFS BEEN OPERATING IN CHICAGO?

The first TIF district in Chicago dates back to 1986, when then-Mayor Harold Washington introduced the system as part of an effort to bring life to the defunct Block 37. The so-called "cursed" city block in the middle of the Loop had long resisted developers' efforts to attract businesses and, even with the TIF, stayed vacant until 2005.

The use of TIFs skyrocketed under the leadership of Mayor Richard M. Daley, and by 2010 they brought in more than half a billion dollars in combined revenue each year. If considered as a collective taxing body, TIFs would represent the third-largest district in the county, behind only the Board of Education and the City of Chicago itself. In their 28-year lifespan, TIFs have generated about $5.5 billion in total.

WHY ARE TIFS SO CONTROVERSIAL?

When it comes to the areas designated for TIFs, the city has maintained a pretty loose definition of the word "blighted." Even though it's intended as a catalyst of positive change in squalid neighborhoods, most TIF revenue over the years has actually gone toward well-financed projects in relatively wealthy areas. The Near South TIF district, by far the most lucrative in the city (it generated more than $60 million in 2013) runs along Michigan Avenue between Jackson and Cermak—hardly a site of extreme poverty. And before expiring in 2008, the legendary Central Loop TIF pulled in almost a billion dollars on its own, which it shoveled into massive projects like the construction of Millennium Park in the early 2000s.

Although most TIF money goes toward public projects, a substantial chunk of it goes toward private companies as an incentive to open or expand their Chicago offices. All in all, TIFs have doled out $15 million to the Chicago Mercantile Exchange, $3.2 million to the Coca Cola Company, and in one high-profile move by the mayor, $5 million to Vienna Beef. Even Willis Tower (formerly the Sears Tower), the city's colossal beacon of wealth and power, has gotten nearly $4 million in TIF funding. Public school advocates are quick to point out that TIF, which siphons directly from CPS's largest source of revenue, is a common source of funding for charters... In 2013, TIFs generated about $412 million, which is about 20 percent of CPS's total yearly budget. That begs the question: If it weren't for TIFs, would the district still face the kind of budget shortfalls that force it to close dozens of schools at a time?

Not all TIF funding stays in the district where it was raised. In a process called "porting," the DPD can freely transfer money from one district's TIF account into another. Because of porting, about $145 million—that's 35 percent of total TIF revenue—was transferred from one district's account into another in 2013. The 24th and Michigan TIF, for example, which comprises about 10 square blocks in the Near South Side, received almost $44 million in 2013 from other TIF accounts around the city. So even though TIF is intended to raise money for individual districts, it isn't uncommon for property taxpayers in Kenwood on the South Side to be paying for constructions projects in Edgewater on the North Side.

It isn't by accident that TIFs have come to be known as the city's "shadow budget." Since the system reroutes public money from its regular channels into one-off projects controlled by the DPD, it's difficult to know exactly how much money is being spent where. And aside from obligatory public meetings where two-minute slots are allotted for citizen comment, residents of TIF districts aren't part of the decision-making process for development projects. Critics often use terms like "slush fund" and "portal hole" to refer to the massive sum of property tax money that's more or less available at the pleasure of the mayor.

SO, TIFS HAVE BEEN AROUND FOR YEARS. HAVE WE FOUND OUT ANYTHING NEW ABOUT THEM?

Since TIFs are so heavily shrouded in the tangle of municipal bureaucracy, it can be hard to keep up with them year after year. But due in part to research efforts like the TIF Illumination Project, run by Chicago's Civic Lab [see www.civiclab.us/tif_illumination_project], we're finding out more every day.

The Civic Lab's…2013 TIF analysis…reviewing 151 of the city's annual TIF reports… reached a few staggering new revelations:

…About $1.7 billion is sitting idle in TIF funds. This means that either this money is all reserved for imminent projects, or that it's sitting in wait to be used as the city sees fit.

In 2013, more than 90 percent of total property taxes were diverted to TIF accounts in 21 TIF districts. In three districts, 100 percent of property tax money went to TIF.

Even though TIF money is supposed to be used exclusively for construction projects, the DPD extracted about $7.6 million from 91 TIF districts to pay for city staff and administration costs. The TIF Illumination Project report called this process "skimming from the skim."

PART V

Global Chicago

Introduction

Chicago, once known for its gangsters and meatpacking industry, has evolved into a global city. Located at the crossroads of the United States, Chicago is economically, politically, and culturally significant across the globe. Michael Moskow, vice chairman of the Chicago Council on Global Affairs and a former president of the Federal Reserve Bank of Chicago, recently declared that, "it's not just Chicago versus other cities in the Midwest these days—it's Chicago versus cities all over the world."[1] In a 2007 speech at the University of Illinois–Chicago, Mayor Richard M. Daley said, "If you don't become a global city, you live in the past." When announcing his first candidacy for mayor, Rahm Emanuel said: "The choices we make in the next few years will define Chicago for future generations … they will determine whether we remain a world-class city—or fall back."[2] As a global city, Chicago is a tourist and convention destination, where the promotion of consumerism and culture play important roles. Chicago has nearly 40 million annual visitors, who make stops at sites like Navy Pier, Millennium Park, and various museums.[3] Hundreds of thousands attend Chicago sporting events and concerts at Wrigley Field, Cellular Field, Soldier Field, and the United Center. People from the metropolitan region, the nation, and the world come to Chicago for knowledge, entertainment, shopping, and vacations. To reach our status as a global city, Chicago has become an influential hub of business, culture, sports, and international policy debate. We have drawn people from around the world—both to visit and to settle here.

In 2015, Chicago was ranked as the seventh most global city in the world. Describing the city's ranking, A.T. Kearney, a global management consulting firm, stated, "a consistent top performer, Chicago especially stands out for its human capital, aided by excellent universities and a sharp uptick in the number of international schools."[4] Although Chicago has achieved the *status* of a "global city," it is struggling to *become* a global city that is both livable and humane. One in which wealth and prosperity are shared.

Chicago's postindustrial economic transformation began in the 1970s. Our switch to the global economy is as momentous as the Industrial Revolution in the nineteenth century. It is marked by Chicago:

1. Becoming the immigration capital of the Midwest.
2. Continuing to have the most manufacturing jobs in the country.
3. Quietly gaining the most high-tech jobs in the country.

By the mid-2000s, the *Economist* declared that, "Chicago has come through deindustrialization looking shiny and confident."[5] However, as Aaron Renn has pointed out, "parts of Chicago suffer from a legacy of deindustrialization: blighted neighborhoods, few jobs, a lack of investment, and persistent poverty."[6]

According to Saskia Sassen in her book *The Global City*, the definition of a global city is as a "site of production of specialized services needed by the complex organizations for running a spatially dispersed network of factories, offices, and service outlets and as the production of financial innovations and the making of markets which are central to the internationalization and expansion of the financial industry."[7] As Sassen stresses, global cities provide services for firms and industry rather than individuals. Yet, these top-level service firms and the people they employ create a demand for meagerly paid lower-level service workers, like those in the retail and hospitality industries, and personal services like nannies, house cleaners, and dog walkers.

The downside of the globalization of Chicago has been not only a "widening color gap," but a shrinking middle class and a widening wealth gap between the rich and the poor in the region. The forces of globalization have produced fewer jobs that pay middle-class wages, but more jobs that pay higher- and lower-class wages. This increasing inequality has been called an hourglass economy. As globalization has transformed our city, the middle class has nearly disappeared, having been squeezed out by ever expanding rich and poor populations. Chicago now ranks eighth nationally among US cities in inequality. The wealthiest 5 percent of residents have a household income of $201,460 or more, while the poorest 20 percent have a household income of $16,078 or less.[8]

As detailed in Figure 1, most of the city was middle class in 1970. Figure 2, while graphically demonstrating the city's shrinking middle class, also shows the growth of rich and poor populations across the city.

Figure 1. 1970 median family income as a percentage of the median family income for the Chicago metropolitan region, by census track.

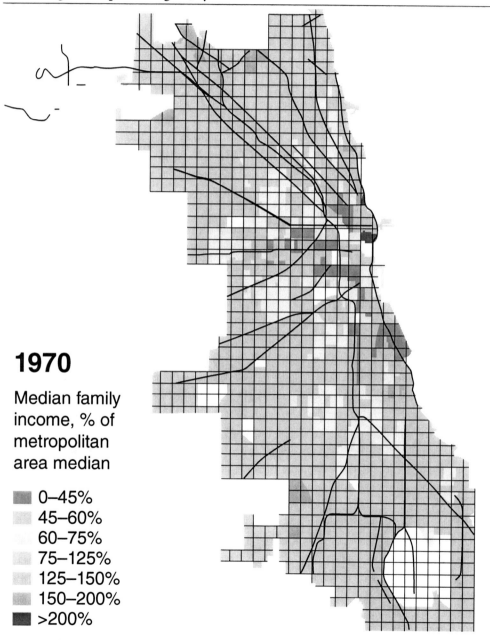

1970

Median family
income, % of
metropolitan
area median

- 0–45%
- 45–60%
- 60–75%
- 75–125%
- 125–150%
- 150–200%
- >200%

Source: Daniel Kay Hertz[9]

Figure 2. 2012 median family income as a percentage of the median family income for the Chicago metropolitan region, by census track.

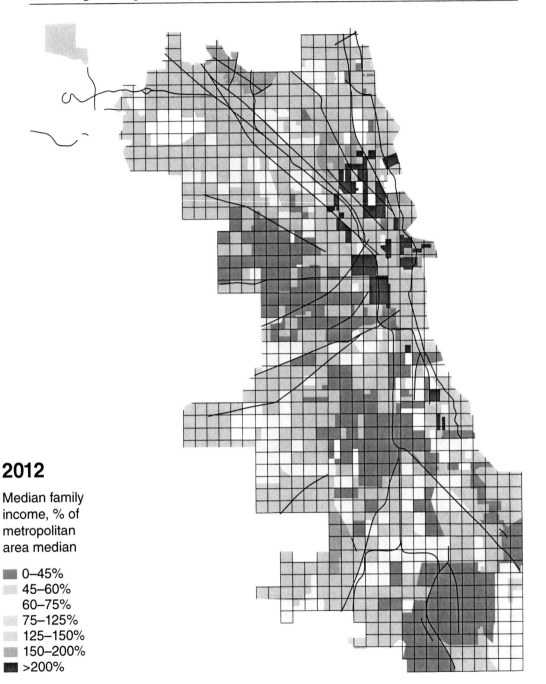

2012

Median family
income, % of
metropolitan
area median

- 0–45%
- 45–60%
- 60–75%
- 75–125%
- 125–150%
- 150–200%
- >200%

Source: Daniel Kay Hertz[10]

While Chicago leaders have been focused on the glamour that comes with being a global city, little attention has been given to the middle and working classes living in neighborhoods outside of the city core. The American Historical Association has noted "large swaths of the city outside the central area appear more 'rust belt' than 'cutting edge.'"[11] The articles in this section explore whether or not Chicago can make it in the long run as a global city, how that transformation is occurring, and how the forces of globalization are changing the "Hog Butcher for the World."

NOTES

1. Rodriguez, Alex. 2014. "How does Chicago stack up?" *Chicago Tribune*, January 26.
2. Emanuel, Rahm. 2010. Speech announcing his candidacy for Mayor of Chicago. Coonley Elementary School, Chicago, IL November 13.
3. "Facts and Statistics." City of Chicago. www.cityofchicago.org/city/en/about/facts.html
4. "Global Cities Index and Emerging Cities Outlook." 2014. A.T. Kearney. www.atkearney.com/research-studies/global-cities-index#sthash.vglmPRjX.dpuf
5. "A success story." 2006. *Economist*, March 16.
6. Renn, Aaron M. 2012. "The Second-Rate City?" *City Journal*, spring.
7. Sassen, Saskia. 1991. *The Global City: New York, London, Tokyo*. Princeton, NJ: Princeton University Press, p.5.
8. Berube, Alan. 2014. "All Cities Are Not Created Unequal." *Brookings Metropolitan Opportunity Series*, February 20. www.brookings.edu/research/papers/2014/02/cities-unequal-berube
9. Hertz, Daniel Kay. 2014. "Watch Chicago's Middle Class Vanish Before Your Very Eyes." *City Notes*, March 31. http://danielkayhertz.com/2014/03/31/middle-class
10. Ibid.
11. Hunt, D. Bradford. 2011. "Welcome to Chicago, Global City. American Historical Association, October. www.historians.org/publications-and-directories/perspectives-on-history/october-2011/welcome-to-chicago-global-city

A Global City

By Adele Simmons

Chicago's rich immigrant tradition since its inception has made it an international city long before "global city" became a buzzword. Through business, medicine and science, art, and music and dance, Chicago exhibits its global heritage.

In Chicago, my hometown, the local florist's lilies may come from Holland, the grocer's grapes from Chile, the computer assembler's chips from Taiwan, the bicyclist's brakes from Japan. While those goods are flying in, Chicago academics are flying out—to advise the governments of Chile, Indonesia, and Nigeria, to name a few. Scientists from all over the world gather to conduct experiments at our laboratories—particularly Argonne National and Fermi Laboratory—and human rights activists from every continent doff their hats to their comrades here, without whom the new International Criminal Court might not exist. Chicagoans import and export goods, ideas, and people, hourly. To us, this is no big deal.

The fact that Chicago has become one of the world's great global cities has yet to impress most Chicagoans, in part because the global fabric is so thickly woven here. In a city with 130 non-English newspapers, where an emergency call to 911 can be responded to in 150 languages, a foreign tongue turns few heads. Similarly, no face seems out of place—each one seems legitimate for a Chicagoan. (We concede native status without much regard for nativity. If you're here, not living in a hotel, and not wearing any Green Bay Packers paraphernalia, we assume you're one of us.) Immigrants make up 22 percent of the city's population and they send an estimated $1.8 billion annually to the families they've left behind. Entire villages depend on that Chicago money. To us, this is old news. People have always come. Money has always gone back.

Adele Simmons, "Introduction," *Global Chicago*, ed. Charles Madigan, pp. 7-14. Copyright © 2004 by the University of Illinois Press. Reprinted with permission.

A Chicagoan who favors a local Korean dry cleaner, the Thai restaurant down at the corner, and an Eastern European tradesman recommended by a neighbor is unlikely to pay much notice to the Loop offices of foreign multinationals like Societe Generale, Sumitomo Bank, and ABN Amro. Similarly, the consular offices of seventy nations, clustered mostly around the Loop, make few Chicagoans ponder the city's place in the world. We expect those diplomats to be here. And city residents traveling abroad don't think twice anymore when they see a logo of some hometown corporation—McDonald's, Motorola, Boeing, and the Bulls, to name a few. We expect them to be there too.

The curiosity of the native Chicagoan might have been aroused recently when two candidates for the office of governor of the Mexican state of Michoacan campaigned for votes here. Then again, Chicagoans are accustomed to candidates trolling far and wide for votes, sometimes even into the afterlife, and thus the Mexican campaign may have appeared more like Cook County politics than anything particularly foreign. Similarly, the globalization of crime seems not so new here. Yes, we have ethnically varied criminal networks, but we've had those before. We have immigrants exploited in the workplace, but that too is not new. The exploiters may have changed and the number of exploited may have increased, but the act is an old one.

We're a tough crowd. We don't impress ourselves. We've become an economic and cultural powerhouse, a commercial and artistic center of growing international importance. Mayor Richard M. Daley created World Business Chicago to promote the city to business investors from all over the world and to ensure that foreign trade delegations connect with the right partners in Chicago. Foreign delegations routinely stop by city hall for a chat, where they may board elevators with German architects filing their drawings, Irish contractors applying for building permits, or Italian restaurateurs petitioning for liquor licenses. Globalization touches all of our lives daily, sometimes hourly. Most of us take no notice at all...

GLOBAL BEFORE "GLOBALIZATION"

Chicago's interaction with the world began long before "globalization" became a buzzword, embraced by some and reviled by others. From its inception in the 1770s as a fur-trading post founded by Jean-Baptiste Point du Sable, an immigrant from Sainte-Domingue (Haiti), Chicago has been a place where cultures, languages, and traditions have mixed.

Here, Native Americans intermingled with settlers from France, Great Britain, and Germany. Rather than being hurt by being situated in what was then the western part of the American territories, the outpost profited from its location at the mouth of a river flowing into the largest body of water in the region. It was this fortuitous location that helped transform a fur-trading outpost into a national hub for transportation. Transportation brought immigrants, and those immigrants brought skills, and those skills have built a metropolitan area that is home to more than eight million residents.

The 1893 World's Columbian Exposition in Chicago set in motion the city's transformation into the gleaming, bustling metropolis it is today. The exposition's Chicago organizers staged the grandest and most memorable world's fair ever held. They broke new ground in showcasing each country—the exhibits were designed by the members of each exhibiting country and not by Americans. As a result, each exhibit represented its country's particular sensibility and how its people saw themselves—rather than how Americans saw them. Chicagoans were thus infected with new ideas and perspectives. The Ho Ho Den building in the Japanese Village, for example, profoundly influenced Frank Lloyd Wright, and he incorporated elements of the building's design in his renowned Prairie style of architecture. Nearly three decades later, the Japanese hired Wright to design the Imperial Hotel in Tokyo, completed in 1922—a neatly closed loop of Chicagoans influenced by the world and the world influenced by Chicagoans.

That pattern repeated itself in industry, science, religion, and the arts in the decades that followed. Fifty years after the exposition, within a mile of the site where Wright had been inspired, a team of physicists led by the Italian refugee physicist Enrico Fermi created the world's first self-sustaining nuclear reaction. The experiment, staged under the football stadium at the University of Chicago, redefined energy development, altered the terms of international conflict, and changed the course of diplomacy around the world.

A hundred years after the exposition, the World's Parliament of Religions, one of the enduring legacies of the Chicago fair, marked its centennial by forging a consensual document entitled "Towards a Global Ethic." Commonly referred to as "The Chicago Declaration," the document is a pledge to work for a just social and economic order, for mutual understanding among peoples and nations, and for a recognition of the interdependence of all living things.

GLOBAL CHICAGO AT WORK

A glimpse into the life of Chicago and its citizens during one spring month in 2002 shows the international dimension of everyday activities of individuals from all walks of life.

On a typical day in May, Robert Langlois, director of international relations at Motorola, walks into his office in Schaumburg at seven in the morning. "I get in early so that I have a few hours of overlap with my colleagues working in Europe, Africa, and the Middle East," he says.

On this particular morning, Langlois checks his e-mail and responds to a message from a colleague at the company's production facility in Israel. He calls the Moscow office to talk about the sale of Motorola pagers. He then calls Cairo and talks with the country manager for Egypt. At 10:30 A.M., he leaves his office for downtown Chicago, where he attends a luncheon for the vice president of Botswana. After lunch, he calls on the South African consulate to discuss that government's order of Motorola walkie-talkies. He ends the day by giving a talk on the international business climate to a group of young professionals.

In the Loop offices of Perkins and Will, one of Chicago's most respected architectural, interior design, and planning firms, William Doerge and Ralph Johnson have spent a good portion of the same day negotiating the timeline for construction of a university in Luanda, Angola. Eighteen of their colleagues in the Chicago office work on the project, while five others are in Mumbai, India, where they are retrofitting an existing concrete structure to accommodate a hospital. A dozen other international projects are in various stages of planning and completion. The firm, which is accustomed to exporting expertise, has no hesitation to import it as well. Consultants from Britain advised Perkins and Will on the design of two green "sustainable" projects—a middle school in Bloomington, Indiana, and a courthouse in Los Angeles.

While Perkins and Will is planning for the Angolan university, Flying Food Group is dispatching meals all over the globe. FFG was founded in Chicago by Sue Ling Gin in 1983, and it now caters meals for twenty-eight international airlines that fly out of Chicago's airports. During the month of May, the O'Hare kitchen alone made 183,598 meals. Says Gin, "Flying Food Group is a global company not only in its sales, but in its people. The 1,800 people who work for us come from all over the world, so we are truly global from production to sales to end users."

Minority-owned Blackwell Consulting Services, Inc., has a similarly international work-force. Blackwell employs natives of Cuba, Russian, India, Ireland, and Venezuela to advise clients on management and information technology, and this May they are laboring on a project for a local client, Waste Management. "Our clients call us the League of Nations," says Bob Blackwell, founder and CEO of the Chicago-based firm. "Our employees come from around the world and each person brings something different to the team. We do better work because of our diversity."

MEDICINE AND SCIENCE

In early May, Dr. Robert Murphy, who works in the infectious diseases lab at Northwestern University, is preparing to leave for the 2002 HIV/AIDS conference in Barcelona. One of the world's leading HIV/AIDS treatment researchers, Murphy is the only non-French citizen to serve on France's Conseil d'Administration, Objectif Recherche Vaccin SIDA, a committee for the discovery of a therapeutic AIDS vaccine. Working with Dr. Toyin Falusi, a Nigerian who directs HIV/AIDS clinical research at Cook County Hospital, Murphy recently established the Nigerian Adult Clinical Trials Group (NACTG) in Ibadan, a city sixty miles north of Lagos, Nigeria. The goal of the Nigerian project is to set up an AIDS treatment infrastructure to be run by Nigerians for Nigerians. To that end, AIDS specialists from Chicago will spend two weeks in Nigeria and their Nigerian colleagues will spend three weeks at three Chicago hospitals. Murphy will head to Masai country in Kenya where he is helping a local doctor upgrade a general clinic so it can treat HIV/AIDS patients.

While that AIDS treatment infrastructure is being planned on the city's north and west sides, Dr. Olufanmilayo Olapade, another native of Nigeria, is working on the South Side. Olapade directs clinical and laboratory research program in cancer genetics at the University of Chicago's School of Medicine. She is investigating why black women develop breast cancer at younger ages and why they suffer higher mortality rates from cancer than other population groups. Her research in Chicago and Nigeria will eventually examine the genetic material of 100,000 women who developed breast cancer before the age of forty-five.

At the Field Museum in May 2002, Debbie Moskovitz, director of the museum's Environment and Conservation Program, is talking on the phone with Alaka Wali, curator of the museum's Center for Cultural Understanding and Change. Wali is in Peru meeting with residents of Tocache, a town in the Huallaga Valley, and with staff from local nongovernmental organizations (NGOs). To ensure the protection of the Parque Corillera Azul, created through the collaboration of the museum, the government of Peru, and Peruvian conservationists, Wali and her team want to help Tocache residents find ways of sustaining their livelihoods while minimizing ecological damage to the buffer zone that surrounds the park. Wali tells Moskovitz that she began to make real progress in Tocache after the mayor realized that his cousin was a volunteer for the Field Museum.

ART

At the Cultural Center of Chicago, Mike Lash, the director for the City of Chicago's Office of Public Art, is on the phone with Sylvie Fleury, an artist in Geneva, Switzerland. Fleury is a Swiss national who has agreed to do a project sponsored by the city, Tiffany's and Sears, where she will explore consumerism in a series of photographs and paintings.

For Millennium Park, Chicago's ambitious scheme to turn its lakefront park into a major cultural attraction, Lash's department has recently approved two other major pieces from European artists. A metal sculpture by Anish Kapoor, a London-based artist, will measure forty-seven feet by thirty-three feet by sixty-six feet and will be the largest noncommemorative piece of art in the world, weighing more than a hundred tons. The new park will also feature a fountain designed by the Spanish artist Jaume Plensa with LCD screens that will project images of Chicagoans.

The city's willingness to embrace the unorthodox in art is not new. "In the nineteenth century and the beginning of the twentieth century, Chicago art patrons had an appreciation for European artists, such as the impressionists," says the cultural historian Tim Samuelson. "Chicago art patrons were not constrained by the East Coast and European orthodoxy, and so they collected impressionist paintings before the rest of the East Coast and European art collectors came to value it. This was a reflection of the pioneering, open-minded attitude that characterized Chicagoans from the start. It was because of this openness that there are so many famous impressionist paintings at the Art Institute."

This pioneering spirit and the willingness to embrace new ideas is alive and well, as evidenced by Art Chicago, one of America's largest international contemporary art expositions. Two hundred six galleries from twenty countries exhibited work at the five-day festival in May 2002, the tenth anniversary of the event.

May is also a busy month for Carlos Tortolero, the founder and executive director of the Mexican Fine Arts Center Museum in Pilsen, a neighborhood in Chicago where many Mexican immigrants have settled. He spends a week in Mexico finalizing which pieces would appear in an upcoming exhibition of artwork from the Museo de Arte Carillo Gil, meeting with officials from the Instituto Nacional de Antropologia y Historia (INA) regarding an exhibition of clothing from the pre-Columbian period to the present, and planning for an exhibition of art from the Gelman Collection planned for January thrugh April.

"Much of my work is creating bridges between Mexico and the U.S.," he says. "While I was in Mexico City, I also met with the director of INA and discussed a possible collaboration over an amnesty program which would allow historical artifacts trafficked into the U.S. to be returned anonymously, displayed in the museum, and then repatriated to Mexico."

MUSIC AND DANCE

The Chicago Symphony Orchestra (CSO) has its home in Symphony Center, located across Michigan Avenue from the Art Institute. Considered an orchestra with few peers, the CSO is an unofficial ambassador of Chicago to the world, while also bringing the world to Chicago. Daniel Barenboim, the CSO's artistic director, hails from Argentina, was educated in Europe, and has lived in Israel.

In May 2002, Barenboim is preparing for the Fourth Annual West-Eastern Divan Workshop, a program he created to bring together seventy gifted young musicians from Isarel and Arab countries for three weeks of intensive musical training. The program is unique in its format and makeup. The participants would otherwise never interact. Held on the campus of Northwestern University in 2001, the workshop will be in Seville, Spain in 2002.

Chicago's vibrant jazz scene also draws world-class performers to the city. The Empty Bottle's Annual International Festival, held every April, brings internationally known musicians to play alongside local jazz artists. The festival is directed by John Corbett, a Chicago producer, writer, and musician, who has created numerous collaborations between European and Chicago-based musicians. While the CSO's Barenboim prepares for his Divan, Corbett is in Europe organizing the program for the 2002 Berlin Jazz Festival, for which he is artistic director. He is a good example of the large number of musicians who call Chicago home while collaborating with artists all over the world.

Dance in Chicago is also a global importer and exporter of ideas and personnel. In May, while dancers from Burkina Faso are performing at Columbia College in Chicago, the Hubbard Street Dance Company is touring the United Kingdom. Twenty-five percent of Hubbard's world-renowned company members are from outside the United States.

WHY THE FUSS?

At this point, the true Chicagoan might say, "Yeah, so what's the big deal?" Paul O'Connor, executive director of World Business Chicago, puts it like this:

> "We invented the skyscraper, split the atom, made our river flow backwards, created a lakefront from scratch, figured out the transistor, drew all the railroads to us, pioneered and continuously dominated commercial air travel, broadcast the world's first all-color TV station, built the number-one manufacturing city of America, invented risk management markets, won more Nobel Prizes than any city on earth, communicate more data on a daily basis than any other city on earth, threw away more basic industries than most other cities ever had, you know, like, hog-butcher, stacker of wheat, steel capital of America. Should we tell anyone?"

Well, the answer is yes, we should. Being known as a global city is an economic and cultural asset. It helps attract corporations of Boeing's magnitude. It reminds us and our friends around the world that we are no longer a city defined by a manufacturing and industrial base, that we have a history of transformation, that we welcome new ideas, new markets, and new kinds of business opportunities. Being a beautiful city with twenty-nine miles of lakefront is not enough to guarantee our future. We must continue reinventing ourselves and keeping pace with global opportunities.

Can Chicago Make It as a Global City?

By Janet L. Abu-Lughod

Chicago is a global city and has been since the 19th century, but its transition has not been even. Can it make it as a vital, growing, commanding center in the new configuration of the global economic system? In this paper, based on a presentation made in November, 1999, Abu-Lughod argues that Chicago's future is shaped by local, regional, national, global forces. It must overcome its racial discrimination and the city/suburban split if it is to make it as a global city in the 21st Century.

I s Chicago an international city? Of course it is. It has been ever since the second half of the nineteenth century: (1) when it was British bond investments that funded the rail lines to open the prairies and the west to the New York port; (2) when midwest corn and wheat began to supply Europe's bakeries; and (3) when new techniques of curing and refrigeration permitted the delivery of Chicago's meat to distant and even foreign markets.

And talk about a cosmopolitan population! Recall that at the turn of the century, four-fifths of Chicago's residents had either been born abroad or were the children of those who had. Attracting international capital, offering banking and financial services to tributary cities and towns, producing goods for export, and drawing diverse immigrant labor are all characteristics of a dominant global center.

Is Chicago now a global city? Of course it is. It has all the contemporary earmarks: high tech, producers' services, the MERC, and the busiest airport in the country, even though its attractiveness to migrants now trails Los Angeles and New York.

Nonetheless, Chicago is a city that for half a century first denied and then succumbed to "rustbelt anxiety," at best whistling in the dark. And especially after the census ignominiously demoted it to "third city," it has been the object, inter alia, of a glossy (even hysterical) Chamber of Commerce report in 1992, boasting that, like any third world country or depressed American city, it was prepared for a race to the bottom: Comparing the city to its "rivals" (especially New York and Los Angeles), the Chamber propaganda stresses that Chicago has lower wages, congestion, lower rents for office space, lower utility rates, corporate and individual, and a more "cooperative" administration.

While the slick brochure does not spell out the implications of these advantages, it is evident that lower wages and lower taxes can only mean more poor people and fewer funds to assist them. More recently, a similar anxiety shows through the Commercial Club's Plan to "fix" the metropolis by the year 2020, a report stronger on analysis than prescription.

There are good reasons for anxiety. But if the causes of a problem are not realistically diagnosed, proposed solutions may prove ineffectual. In present discussions of Chicago's future, it has become fashionable both to blame the global system for generating problems at the local level (a la Bill Wilson), but, paradoxically, also to lust after even globalization as the panacea (a la Chamber of Commerce). However, simply invoking the buzzword "global" neither advances the analysis of decline nor offers an easy way out.

I want to take a dispassionate look at the realities of Chicago's uneven development and possible stagnation, and to suggest some radical solutions that may be only tangentially related to "making it as a global city," although they are essential to making it "a city that works" …

But first, what do we mean by these new terms: globalization and global cities? I take a somewhat deviant position. From an historical point of view, the present phase of globalization is just a continuation, albeit at a faster pace and via new technologies, of what has been going on for much of human history. In its most literal sense, globalization simply refers to an ongoing process whereby larger and larger portions of the world have become increasingly linked to one another via material exchanges of resources, commodities and currencies, as well as through a widening of the geographic range over which populations move, whether temporarily or permanently. Inevitably, this process not only entails more "integration" on the economic and political levels, but also permits more contact on the symbolic and cultural levels, either directly or indirectly …

A global city is therefore simply an urbanized node through which disproportionate fractions of national and international interactions flow. Such flows are also neither symmetrical nor equally rewarding. Indeed, the enormous scale at which globalization now operates often camouflages clear lines between causes and effects, as capital and labor move with increasing freedom not only across national borders but beyond metropolitan boundaries as well.

Being designated as a "global city," then, gives no assurance of special rewards. Degrees of economic, political and cultural dominance help to distinguish more powerful from less powerful global cities. But even within the class of dominant global cities, the effects of globalization vary, not only between global city regions but also within them. Paradoxically, because globalization often flows through the increasingly disembodied cyberspace of information and high finance, its advantages do not necessarily fall directly on the physical ground that lies beneath their electronically flashing nodes and circuits.

There is, then, no contradiction between the proliferation of transactions in cyberspace, such as those that flow through the computers of the MERC, and the evisceration of localized functions. This disengagement means that even a healthy growth in command functions cannot protect those parts of the system (whether highly localized, at the national level, or at the global level) that are "out of the loop." Such marginalized zones can now be found in Bangladesh and many parts of the African continent, in Manchester and Sheffield, England, in downtown Detroit, in South Central Los Angeles and in the south and west side areas of Chicago! …

My book, *New York, Chicago, Los Angeles: America's Global Cities*, compares America's three largest global cities: New York, Los Angeles and, with reservations, Chicago. The book emphasizes differences, tracing over time the ways specific technologies, economic functions, geographic sites, demographic compositions, and cultural responses have shaped these three particular urban regions. It argues, moreover, that even the same forces emanating from the global system at any given time always interact with active agents on the ground who operate within distinctive political cultures that have been honed over long periods of time.

So it is easy to answer one question implied in part of the title of my talk. Of course, Chicago is a global city. It always has been. But the answer to the second part of the title: "Can Chicago make it as a vital, growing, commanding center in the new configuration of the global system?" is not so evident.

And here I am going to take an unpopular position. I think Chicago will continue to lose ground unless it diagnoses its strengths and weaknesses more realistically, and works not with some mythological "force" such as globalization, on which it can blame all its problems and through which it can dream of salvation, but on the energetic grittiness of its special history and people. I begin with the premise that Chicago's future is shaped by local, regional, national, global forces, and failure to attend to all four simultaneously cannot yield adequate policies.

There is an old prayer that I quote inaccurately. "God give me the strength to accept what can't be changed, the energy to alter what can be changed, and the wisdom to know the difference." That is how I propose to organize my talk.

WHAT CAN'T BE CHANGED: CHICAGO'S LOCATION IN GEOGRAPHIC SPACE

Chicago is where it is, in the heartland of the subcontinent, a region whose population growth rate now falls below average. Even though O'Hare's boast that it is "the busiest air terminal in the country" is not to be dismissed, it must be acknowledged that the vast midwestern and plains hinterlands of Chicago have not been growing as before, and indeed, the population in many of its parts has actually been in decline.

To some extent, the demographic "failure to thrive" of the midwest, Chicago's service area catchment zone, has had serious repercussions on the city's economic health, repercussions that compound those caused by the shrinkage of heavy industry. Thus, not all of Chicago's problems stem from specifically local causes, such as post-Fordism or even Chicago's contentious race relations, although the effects have been experienced most severely by poor people of color.

In the four decades between 1950 and 1990, the population of the larger Chicago region grew by only 40 percent (well under its rate of natural increase). The city itself lost one-fourth of its population and the number of suburban Cook County's residents virtually stagnated. True, the population in the other five collar counties almost tripled, but this was insufficient compensation. The New York CMSA—and especially the Los Angeles CMSA whose population almost doubled in the 30 years between 1960 and 1990—have been growing faster; much faster because their hinterlands have been.

Reflecting the Januslike position of the contemporary US as both an Atlantic and Pacific power, and eventually, the greater integration of North America with the Caribbean and the Latin American continent, the three seacoasts of the US have become increasingly important magnets for internal migrants. In recent decades the population of the United States has been decanting toward the coasts, not only in the older directions of east and west but now, southward as well. ...

The "hollowing out" of the continent has been achieved not only through low rates of natural increase and heightened internal emigration from the Great Plains but, increasingly, through the recently enlarged streams of immigrants from abroad whose "ports of entry" remain the coastal cities. Chicago is no longer the magnet for immigrants that it once was. By 1990, despite the great burst of immigration to the US since 1965, only 11 percent of the residents of the Chicago CMSA had been born abroad, compared to two and three times that percentage in New York and Los Angeles. The recent demographic recovery of the New York urbanized region and, even more so, the growth of the Los Angeles megalopolitan region are clearly attributable to the heightened immigration from abroad that resulted not from changes in local policies but national ones.

How do these larger demographic trends affect Chicago? For one, Chicago's "central place" function as chief market for the midwest is undermined. Furthermore, because Chicago is far from the coasts; it benefits less from the new larger scale of global exchanges that move via sea or air. Chicago's rank among American ports is low: 59th in 1990. The ports of New York take in 15 times more raw tons of freight than Chicago and export 7 times as much weight; Los Angeles's ports export 11 times as much tonnage as Chicago. Even in air freight, Chicago handles only a small fraction of international commerce.

Thus, because of its location, Chicago can be neither the prime gateway to Asia that now makes the ports of Los Angeles engines for that city/region's growth, nor the gateway to Europe and Eastern Europe that underlies New York's dominance in international trade and traffic. Flows through cyberspace can supplement, but will never supplant, the movements of people and material. (In any case, cyberspace marketing is now done in back offices in small cities of the plains and Rockies.)

The Chicago region has also fallen behind the other two in attracting foreign capital and employment in foreign-owned firms. The value of direct foreign investment in Illinois is less than half that invested in either New York/New Jersey or California, and foreign firms are generating many fewer jobs here than elsewhere.

While size isn't everything, it is something, especially in national politics. The Chicago region's relative demographic losses have weakened its voice in Washington, an increasingly important force underlying the economies of states located in what Ann Markusen has called the "defense perimeter." She has shown how little money the Department of Defense actually spends on research and development, innovative weaponry, or even production in the Illinois/Chicago region. Whereas in 1951 Illinois was still near the middle rank of the 18 states she studied as measured by "Per Capita Prime [Defense] Contracts Relative to U.S. Average," by 1984 Illinois had dropped to the very lowest rank in defense contracts, below the remaining midwest states on their list, such as Wisconsin, Michigan, Ohio, and Indiana.

In contrast, California continues to grow in strength and New York, New Jersey, Connecticut, and Massachusetts still retain their attractiveness to defense investments. Chicago has not ... Plant closings and reductions in the industrial labor force had already appeared in the Chicago region as early as the late 1940s, and these reductions persisted throughout the prosperous 1950s and mid-1960s, a period when the US still monopolized the world's production. Such losses not only preceded the recent phase of globalization and the "shift" to the services but have continued into the 1990s in parts of the region! ...

Even though some of this deficit has been compensated by a growth in services, not much of that growth has been in the much-touted (i.e., high paying) services that are hall-marks of the "new globalization: FIRE (finance, insurance and real estate) and producers' services, for example. Between 1974 and 1985, the number of FIRE jobs in the Chicago region increased by only 7 percent, whereas they grew by 21 percent in New York and 63 percent in Los Angeles.

True, there was one exception. Chicago was able to "capture" some share in "the new economy" after the 1973 recession by innovating in the upper circuit of arbitrage and fi-nancials via the remarkable transformation in the Chicago Mercantile Exchange. By a bold stroke of anticipating a global market for financial futures and currency options, the then-foundering Chicago Mercantile Exchange was the first to grasp this opportunity which, by 1995, came to account for some 90 percent of its contracts. However, because the market is international and unregulated, the MERC is already seeing some of its base erode through competition from private deals and unregulated non-US exchanges. But even if the MERC had retained its monopoly, one must acknowledge that very few persons are employed in this and the other new sectors of the global economy, and what is worse, their multiplier effects are very narrow. Few of the profits of these "global" operations filter down to the local population. Furthermore, in comparison to New York (which moved almost directly from pre-Fordism to post-Fordism), and Los Angeles (which has grown more Fordist and industrial with time), the increases in producer services and high tech R&D in Chicago have lagged considerably behind those two competitors. In short, globalization is saving Chicago.

WHAT CAN BE DONE?

Some other midwest cities have faced similar losses and yet appear to be thriving. Why? Industrial production continues and expands. Connections to the global system and the knowledge industry increase. What handicaps does Chicago face that these do not?

And here I am going to be very blunt. In prosperous times, Chicago could afford to be profligate with its space and people. It could afford to leave its contradictions unresolved and its confrontations raw. J. W. Sheahan, writing in 1875, suggested that Chicago, instead of trying to resolve its divisions like the cities of the East Coast and Europe, had made its conflicts the basis of its identity. "Divisions that might paralyze other places provided the very condition for Chicago's existence."

I contend that these divisions no longer work, if they ever did. They now sap the city's vitality. Today, new ways must be found to fully utilize its space and people, ways that will not only adjust to the city's diminished role in the global system but also build upon its formidable local strengths. Perhaps, if this opportunity is seized, a new healthy basis for the region's economy and social life can be forged.

But to do that, Chicago's historical racism must be acknowledged as a "luxury" this city region can no longer afford!

Two "facts" must be faced honestly. Enormous sections of the city now lie "fallow," denuded of their industries and businesses. What a waste of sunk investments and potential resources! It is not that all growth has ceased, but that it has been taking place exclusively in the Loop, in Edge City or the outlying portions of the collar counties, especially along the almost exclusively white growth corridors to the northwest and, leaping over inlying urban quarters, in suburban sections of the southwest's growth corridor.

Second, Chicago's metropolitan region remains one of the most, if not the most, segregated places in the country. Not only does the region demonstrate the greatest inequality between its wealthy (white) and poor (minority) areas and suburbs, but the gap has been widening precipitously. Hyper segregation in housing, as Doug Massey has clearly shown for Chicago, underlies the increased poverty and isolation of minorities not only from jobs but from hope. ...

The combination of these forces means that not only land but whole fractions of Chicago's regional labor force also lie fallow. The underutilization of their labor power drags Chicago's growth down and saps its vitality as production center, market place and provider of desperately needed local infrastructure and services.

To claim that such inequalities are new and an inevitable product of globalization is false and self-serving, because it denies the local and long-term causes of this situation. And, in my mind, it is the failure of proposals for rescuing Chicago such as those advocated by the Chamber of Commerce report or even the Commercial Club's 2020 Plan to acknowledge the historic evolution of this situation and to advocate real, but hard and long-term correctives, that I want to address in the time left to me. Neither of these two reports, nor, for that matter, most other business analyses of Chicago's economic future, take seriously or even cite the penetrating analysis of racism by critics such as Greg Squires, or scholars associated with the Chicago Urban League and Metro Chicago analyses that demonstrate the systematic disinvestment in the people and places that now lie fallow in the region.

I am not claiming that all of the resulting inequalities in the Chicago region are due to racism, just as I have argued that not all of them are due to "globalization." Many are attributable to more national causes: increasingly unprogressive income tax rates, the obscenely high and hidden compensations paid to CEOs who "downsize," the atrophy of union strength and its substitution by flexible production without fringe benefits, the reforms to welfare without the accompanying substitute services to mothers, and the politically gated suburban communities that beggar their neighbors. All of these "choices" affect the growing gap in income and wealth distribution not only in Chicago but in New York and Los Angeles, as well as other places.

But Chicago's situation is extreme because of the very long time during which the conditions of the minority poor have not only been neglected but perversely exacerbated. Chicago's race problems cannot be simply explained on the grounds of numbers. Taken as a whole, the region has no higher a percentage of minority residents than the New York region: black non-hispanic residents constitute slightly under a fifth in both CMSAs and black hispanics are more numerous in New York than in Chicago, and combined minorities are even higher in Los Angeles.

However, neither New York nor Los Angeles has the same degree of cleavage as Chicago between the central city and its politically powerful "white" collar counties. And it is cleavage, which was the result of racism that stands in the way of a solution. ... As early as the 1919 riot, when African Americans constituted only a tiny percentage of the total population, racism had become the organizing principle of Chicago life, whereas in the political cultures of New York and Los Angeles, it was only one theme among many others.

Given this long history, I think white Chicago owes reparations and an investment in healing that can belatedly compensate for the pain, suffering, and demoralization it has created. And I also believe that if Chicago is to make it as a global city, it must make this investment its highest priority.

WHAT POLICIES ARE NEEDED?

My reading of the 2020 Plan is that its programmatic suggestions are both too and little too late. Let me first address the latter because I want to end with the former. Too Late: There is absolutely nothing wrong with Adele Simmon's section that strongly advocates investing heavily in educating the young, paying special attention to underserved minority children. But this approach, even in the unlikely event that it were to receive overwhelming support and generous funding and that it achieved spectacular success, would not, in itself, either bind the city and collar counties into an integrated economic unit nor bind its populations into a common community. It is a necessary but not a sufficient cure. That is because education is very long term! And in the meantime, shorter-term payoffs are essential. If conditions of material deprivation, isolation, and hopelessness are allowed to persist through the present generation while we wait for the kids to grow up, even the best and brightest of the next generation may not be able to resist demoralization. Motivation requires real evidence of opportunity not in promises but on the ground. Unless massive reinvestment in the present is undertaken simultaneously, better math courses and computer literacy will not save us.

TOO LITTLE AND IN THE WRONG PLACES

Conservative reformers are fond of dismissing solutions that merely "throw money" at problems (although they tend to overlook the fact that the systematic withdrawal of funds is the most basic cause of problems) I agree, especially when only modest amounts are appropriated in relation to needs and when such investments are accompanied by unrealistic expectations of stunning and rapid results. They are bound to disappoint. Nickel and dime investments may yield an occasional bonanza in the stock market lottery, but they will make little dent on the task that really needs to be done, which is nothing short of rebuilding the fallow land and integrating its displaced labor. The long-accumulating deficiencies in large minority areas of Chicago cannot be repaired in a few years nor can we expect modest "incentives" to make philanthropists out of investors.

No. Given at least half a century during which jobs, hopes, and values have been drained from the African American and Latino hyperghettos of the south and west sides, only massive investments right now and continuing for many years can begin to repair the damage.

I am not here to tell Chicago how to do this, although redistributing the wealth of the entire region to replace the jobs that have been drained from the south and west sides of the city seems to me to be an indispensable starting point. That means breaking down the imaginary line between Cook County and the collar counties physically, politically, legally, and financially. Unless this can be achieved, the resources will be insufficient and the potential gains from both local and global sources of strength will continue to elude us.

Chicago's early history tells us that its ability to harness the labor and the "will" of its people was the basis for its past prosperity. It is time to do that again. The "living with contradictions" that Sheehan thought was Chicago's unique way of dealing with its social cleavages is no longer working. The contradictions must be acknowledged and resolved. The entire region can only harness its untapped power in a climate of hope. And hope requires not only preferential education but also the breaking down of the powerful spatial barriers that racism has consciously built into the region and that continue to deny opportunities to most of its minorities. Here we are, in the Harold Washington Public Library, a stunning building surmounted by what I take to be copper phoenixes that ever present image of hope in Chicago. More than ever before, this city needs hope and the realistic will to overcome its inequalities. That will require honest acknowledgement that a city cannot prosper with so large a fraction of its terrain and people underutilized and unintegrated into the spatial and economic fabric.

Most causes of growth and decline do not originate from global forces and most solutions to decline require careful attention to more localized causes. It will not be easy, but its payoffs will not only change Chicago into a region that "makes it" but one that "makes it globally."

Economic Restructuring

Chicago's Precarious Balance

By David Moberg

Although Chicago has a diverse economy, it remains trapped in a precarious balance. In this article, David Moberg argues that for Chicago to succeed in a global world it must address economic inequality among individuals and communities. This can only be accomplished through regional cooperation and planning.

After spurring cities across the country into a bidding war for its favors, Boeing Corporation announced, in March 2001, that it was moving its corporate headquarters from its long-time Seattle home to downtown Chicago. Although $56 million in public subsidies brought only 450 jobs, Chicago political and business leaders celebrated the capture of the nation's leading exporter and iconic global corporation as proof of the city's intrinsic attractions as a world corporate center. [1]

On the other hand, relatively little fanfare erupted when Brach's Confections Inc. announced two months earlier its plans to shut down the world's largest candy manufacturing plant at the end of 2003. It was easy to see the loss of roughly 1,000 jobs on Chicago's still-poor West Side as an episode in the oft-told "Rust Belt" story of a fading industrial past giving way to a postindustrial service and knowledge economy. The company's transfer of production to Mexico followed more than half a million other manufacturing jobs that, over the decades since World War II, had largely moved out of the central city to the suburbs, to the South, and to foreign countries. [2]

But what looks like a paradigmatic tale of the emergence of a new Chicago economy is not so clear and simple. After all; both Boeing and Brach's are manufacturing companies.

David Moberg, "Excerpts from Economic Restructuring Chicago's Precarious Balance," *The New Chicago: A Social and Cultural Analysis,* pp. 32-34, 37-43. Copyright © 2006 by Temple University Press. Reprinted with permission.

Globally, manufacturing obviously has not died. Neither has it all migrated. At the time Brach's was closing, metropolitan Chicago had the largest number of manufacturing jobs of any U.S. metropolis. Despite other shutdowns, it was still the candy capital of the country, and even without its once-famous stockyards by far the national leader in food processing.

Brach's was a local icon, cited by *Industry Week*[3] as one example why Chicago was the premier location for manufacturing in the United States. But, starting in 1986, Brach's was subjected to a wave of corporate buy-outs and spin-offs that imposed shifting and disastrous marketing strategies. Despite many years of both pressure and assistance (including $10 million from the city), community groups and the workers' union could not persuade the changing cast of owners and managers that they could succeed by improving technology and training workers rather than pursuing cheaper workers (and sugar) across the border.[4]

Attracting Boeing was a public relations coup, but it also raised troubling questions. If the subsidy wasn't critical, as a key Boeing executive said, what did the outsized enticement say about Chicago's confidence in its own merits? Might the $56 million have been better spent on improving schools, fixing infrastructure, training workers, or enriching cultural life? Ultimately, Boeing generated far fewer ancillary economic benefits than projected in the rosy, never-released analysis justifying the public subsidies. Another Chicago corporate giant, Arthur Andersen, had prepared the analysis not long before that one-time symbol of Chicago's strength in business services folded in the aftermath of the Enron debacle.[5]

The city's roster of corporate headquarters remained mixed, despite optimistic projections that Boeing heralded the beginning of a new era. Starting in 1998, Chicago had lost a string of headquarters, such as Amoco, Ameritech, and Inland Steel, mostly to corporate takeovers.[6] In January 2004, J. P. Morgan Chase & Co. bought Bank One, depriving Chicago of the headquarters for its largest bank. Also, corporate headquarters were nearly as likely to be in the suburbs as in the central city.[7]

Nevertheless, both suburbs and city could take comfort in the dramatic growth of business services, such as architecture, personnel, and consulting firms, which provided specialized assistance to the corporate managers of far-flung empires.[8] In one of the nation's fastest-growing employment sectors, with moderately above average salaries, metropolitan Chicago was either first or second nationally in the number of business service workers, depending on who's counting (World Business Chicago or the Harvard Cluster Mapping Project), and many of those jobs were in the city.

Also, despite its lingering Rust-Belt image, metropolitan Chicago had the largest concentration of high-tech workers of any urban region in the country (and tied with Washington, D.C. for the greatest number of information technology jobs). The city ranked considerably lower in the proportion of all workers in high-tech and in the ratio of high-tech manufacturing to services (whereas cities like San Jose and Seattle ranked at the top), and it lagged on measures of innovation and rate of growth.[9] But Chicago's history as an electronics and telecommunications center left a legacy of companies, research institutions, and skilled workers that could be a foundation for growth.

The wired world, analysts like Saskia Sassen have argued, does not eliminate the need for personal contacts among the decision-makers, professional advisors, and technical elite of the business world. Consequently, certain key cities—especially in their traditional cores— were likely to be centers of corporate control for the global economy.[10] Yet, just as cities like Chicago were gearing up to compete for global-city status, growing indications hinted that many highly skilled, business professional jobs—computer programmers, software engineers, architects, securities analysts, and others—could be outsourced to India, China, and other lower-wage locations, as were the manufacturing jobs before them.[11]

CHICAGO: REGIONAL CAPITAL WITH A GLOBAL REACH

So what, if anything, do Boeing and Brach's reveal about the new Chicago economy? First, Chicago is increasingly globalized, shaped for both good and ill by the force of global markets in goods, services, capital, and labor and by the strategies of global corporations. Workers at factories like Brach's got the short end. Many new business professionals are winners—at least for the moment. However, ultimately, globalization and related factors, such as a declining union movement, contributed to growing economic inequality and insecurity.

Chicago will have to adapt to the constraints and opportunities posed by globalization, but it is not a "global city" that can be reasonably confident of a controlling position like that enjoyed by New York, London, and Tokyo. Despite the growing presence of foreign multinationals, significant trade, and a renewed and varied influx of immigrants, metropolitan Chicago remained, in the early twenty-first century, a strong regional capital with a global reach. Its best opportunity to extend its global importance may depend as much on the health of the wider Great Lakes region as on the steps both the city and metropolitan Chicago take locally to shape their economic future.

It is not simply greater global interconnectedness that is shaping Chicago and other cities or that defines most contemporary conceptions of a "global city."[12] Rather, contemporary globalization embodies a distinctive set of rules for an economic game that are heavily influenced by global corporations. With different rules, such as stronger worker rights around the world, an end to U.S. farm subsidies, the cancellation of most less-developed country debt, or a "Tobin tax"[13] on currency, and financial transactions, Chicago would still be a globalized city, but one with different opportunities.

More broadly, the Boeing and Brach's cases both underscore how market relationships have intensified and penetrated more deeply into social and economic life, a political and economic process driven partly by globalization. For example, deregulated financial markets spurred the market in corporate control, which subjects to the solvent of financial calculations ties that might have bound parts of corporations together or business facilities to a particular location. Cheap transportation and communications provide technical means for a geographic dispersal of factories and offices, but a distinct business strategy, often shaped by short-term profit horizons, is the driving force behind the often frenzied relocation of operations. Just as Brach's can be easily detached from Chicago, other corporate centers of control, like Boeing's head office, increasingly separate themselves from the gritty reality of the enterprises they manage and the cities or nations where they have headquarters. While the corporate centers retain control over dispersed and contingent empires,[14] managers devote much effort to managing risk—such as through the Chicago futures markets—and, above all, to shifting risk to employees, contractors, governments, and the general public.

There are implications for cities like Chicago in these intensified trends. One economic rationale for cities is that they provide agglomeration advantages, such as large labor pools, nearby suppliers, easy transportation, ready customers, and a climate of both cooperation and competition that generates useful information. A variety of networks of businesses develop, including both industrial districts made up of small firms, such as the old printers' row or garment districts in Chicago's Loop outskirts, and those networks fanned around a government institution or a dominant corporation, the most common pattern in Chicago as it industrialized. These relationships often made businesses more efficient, but in the process they created a kind of "stickiness" or reason to stay in place.[15] Even ownership made a difference. A privately held business run by owners who live in the same area, or a worker-owned business, is likely to be less mobile than publicly held nationals, which were disproportionately quick to relocate out of both the city and the country.[16]

In the newly globalized world of intensified market relations, capital becomes ever "slippery."[17] The capitalist ideal of liquidity is exemplified in the global financial markets, but both people and places can suffer from an excess liquidity of investment and employment. Stickiness can yield economic benefits, for example, through stimulating businesses to increase productivity by building on human skills, cooperative community relationships, or technical innovation to cut costs rather than fleeing to lower-wage locations.

* * *

CHALLENGES TO CHICAGO'S FUTURE AS A "GLOBAL CITY"

Saskia Sassen, the influential urban sociologist, argues that global cities have a new role as producers of services, such as the work of lawyers and financial specialists, for the demanding task of managing global corporate empires. These services thrive on face-to-face interaction among business and professional people in city centers, which is more effective than communication at a distance by telephone or the Internet.[18]

At first blush, this certainly seems to be happening in Chicago, with its expansion of business services, construction of new Loop office buildings, recycling of older office buildings into downtown condominiums, and the creation of new and more affluent residential neighborhoods near the Loop.

By most accounts, Chicago clearly ranks among the second tier of global cities, in the company of cities such as Hong Kong and Frankfurt. Some economic strategists envision a "global Chicago," with a central city featuring more of both multinational corporate headquarters and related financial, professional, and service firms. But even the relatively flush decade of the 1990s contained some worrisome signals.

First, while Chicago pursues corporate headquarters and their elite business service partners for the city center, corporate headquarters have been shifting to suburbs and "edge cities." Consequently, Sassen argues that "'the center' now has many centers, as the business activities associated with downtown spread into the suburbs."[19] But if "instant cyber-touch" permits this redefinition of the center for corporate headquarters, businesses serving global corporations may also not be a reliable engine for central city employment growth.

Second, a detailed analysis of Chicago's economy during the 1990s raises questions about the quality and quantity of future growth. For example, personnel supply services constitute by far the largest business service category and the category with the largest increase during the 1990s. But this industry includes not only executive recruiters and global giants, such as Manpower, but also proliferating day-labor agencies, like Laborama or Ready Men, which are concentrated in Latino neighborhoods. While about a fifth of temporary workers are professionals, most temp jobs are low-wage, degraded versions of former full-time office and laborer jobs.[20]

Some higher-end corporate service jobs, such as engineering and architectural services, research and testing services, and advertising, grew slowly or even declined during the 1990s. A dramatic decline even occurred in sectors that serve global corporations, such as legal services (down by 25 percent, for a loss of more than. 8,000 jobs) and depository institutions (a 17 percent loss, typically in banks). However, employment doubled at non-depository financial institutions, which include currency exchanges and payday loan offices—unlikely servants to global business.

During the 1990s, security and commodity brokers increased by nearly half, a byproduct of the stock bubble, but the subsequent bust almost certainly reduced those numbers, at least temporarily. Job prospects are at risk as the city's futures, options, and stock exchanges face both rising global competition and a shift from the open outcry system—and its face-to-face interactions—to electronic trading. Overall, employment in the broad category of finance, insurance, and real estate, as a share of total employment, declined after the stock bust—at a rate slightly faster than the national average—in both the city and the metropolitan area.[21]

Third, corporations will likely subcontract more managerial activities, thus generating demand for public relations, data management, and other business services. But, as economist David Gordon argued, for decades, corporations in the United States have had a much higher ratio of managerial to non-managerial workers and greater workplace conflict than that of competitors from countries like Germany, Japan, and Sweden.[22] Those more cooperative economies performed better in terms of investment, productivity growth, inflation, and unemployment. If U.S. corporations maintain high managerial burdens, then workers are more likely to lose jobs or income in a competitive global economy. But if corporations turn more cooperative and efficient, then the need may be reduced for some business services on which Chicago depends.

Fourth, many of the jobs that strategists hope will grow rapidly in the new global Chicago are now being performed at a fraction of the cost by well-educated workers in India, China, Russia, and other newly industrializing or transition countries. Management consultants— a business service growth industry in Chicago—now tell businesses that they must relocate both blue and white-collar work to China and elsewhere if they want to succeed.[23]

CHALLENGES TO THE "HIGH ROAD" ADAPTATION TO GLOBALIZATION

The new challenge of globalization strikes at the heart of even the more progressive strategies of adaptation to global competitive pressures and capital mobility, such as educating workers to perform higher-skilled, better-paying jobs even as lower-wage workers in developing countries do tasks like sewing clothes or assembling automobiles. But millions of educated workers in both the rich and poor countries are up the same skill ladder, applying downward income pressure even on those jobs that may remain in the United States.

Inspired by the success of Silicon Valley, Chicago strategists have also longingly looked for salvation from manufacturing losses through the development of high-tech industries, as biotechnology, business software, nanotechnology, or advanced manufacturing and materials. But metropolitan Chicago's large pool of science and technology workers is distributed throughout a wide range of both "new" industries, from pharmaceutical companies (such as Abbott Laboratories and Baxter Pharmaceuticals) to electronics firms (such as Motorola or Tellabs), and "old" industries, from steel mills to machine tool and fastener makers. Indeed, Chicago ranks quite low in high-tech specialization and just below the national average in the number of patents per employee.[24]

Metropolitan Chicago has also not been especially hospitable to new technology businesses. Very little venture capital is available. The region's universities and research centers have, until recently, done little to link research to local business development.[25] Also, the required critical mass of workers has rarely existed in any particular emerging high-tech industry to create an environment of intellectual exchange, cooperation, public institutional support, and competition that can stimulate the growth of new companies in a geographic region. The symbol of the region's high-tech slipups is Marc Andreessen, who developed the computer code for an Internet browser as a student at the University of Illinois but had to go to California to find venture capital to launch his business, Netscape. Also, the local giant, Motorola, has faltered, losing an early lead in the cell phone business. In 2003, it closed its five-year-old, $100 million factory in the collar county town of Harvard, where 5,000 workers once were making and distributing cell phones. Now that building may become an indoor water park, an unwelcome symbol for the region's high-tech hopes.[26]

Many urban economic development analysts argue that innovation is nurtured by the clustering of businesses in a particular industry, whether around a dominant firm or as a district of small businesses. Chicago has a large number of highly concentrated clusters of related businesses, making goods for trade rather than for local consumption, in which the metropolitan area's share of national employment is greater than its share of the national work force. But Chicago is not known for one or two hallmark industries, such as computers and aerospace in Seattle, finance in New York, or entertainment in Las Vegas. Local leaders are proud that Chicago is, according to one study, the most diverse urban economy in the nation. While diversity helped Chicago rebound from the 1980s manufacturing collapse, it is no guarantor of future success. The varied cities following Chicago in the diversity ranking are questionable models: Little Rock, Baltimore, Salt Lake City, and Buffalo.[27]

Indeed, in most of Chicago's strongest industrial clusters, the metropolitan area was losing share throughout the 1990s, not an indication of growing strength. According to the Cluster Mapping Project of Harvard University's Institute for Strategy and Competitiveness,[28] Chicago gained national share among its most concentrated clusters only in the processed food industry and the education and knowledge cluster. Chicago remained the leading metropolitan area for employment in metal manufacturing, food, plastics, communications equipment, production technology, lighting and electrical equipment, heavy machinery, and medical devices. It also had a very high relative concentration in other clusters: transportation and logistics (second among all metropolitan areas), publishing and printing (second), distribution services (third), chemical products (second), business services (second), and financial services (third). Yet, at the same time, it was losing national share in all those clusters, suggesting that they were not serving as the needed seedbeds of innovation and superior economic growth.

The focus on diversity leaves unanswered a big question: What will be the engines of both job and income growth for the Chicago region? The strongest sectors have been lagging behind national averages in employment growth. Many of the biggest corporate pillars— United Airlines, McDonald's, Allstate, Sears, Motorola, and even the new star, Boeing—are experiencing hard times for varied reasons. Outside takeovers continue to undermine the city's position as a corporate decision center. Chicago's big-business exhibition and convention business faces Sun belt competition (Orlando and Las Vegas), economic doldrums, and *post-9/11* travel jitters. Even a rapidly growing local film industry has been undercut by the industry's shift to foreign locales: Toronto often serves as the backdrop for television shows or movies supposedly set in Chicago, according to a *New York Times* report.[29]

At the start of the new century, neither high-tech nor financial industries are poised to be the new drivers of a growing economy. Despite efforts to retain manufacturing and upgrade workforce skills and technology, manufacturing is unlikely to yield job growth. Business services, perhaps even education, have promise but also vulnerabilities. In all those sectors, a base exists that could be developed, but it seems likely that, in 2020, Chicago's leaders will still be touting diversity rather than a new job-generating champion.

INEQUALITY: THE ECONOMIC AND SOCIAL THREAT

The economic challenge for the city is not simply to create jobs, but to generate adequate income from good jobs. In the competition to attract businesses, pressure always exists to sell a city as offering cheap labor, but the prospect of earning low incomes does not attract talented people. If workers earn more, they can invest in their homes, buy goods and services for local consumption, and strengthen their communities, making the city even more attractive. An economically thriving population can afford to pay for the schools and infrastructure that make the city more livable and businesses more productive. But raising average incomes is not enough. The metropolitan area will be more likely to thrive if there is greater economic equality among individuals and among communities. Urban regions with higher economic inequality typically grow more slowly, hurting both central-city and suburban residents.[30]

Inequality has grown both among different geographical communities within the metropolitan region and among households. From 1989 to 1999, an increase occurred in the percentage of families in the metropolitan area in the lowest quintile of national income and in the highest quintile, but a decrease occurred in the broad middle-income quintiles.[31] By 2000, household income was more unequal in metropolitan Chicago than in the nation as a whole. Among the central cities of the 40 largest metropolitan areas, the city of Chicago ranked fifteenth in income inequality in 1999.[32]

But metropolitan Chicago scored even worse in the contrast between poverty levels in the city and its suburbs. With its central-city poverty rate 3.5 times the poverty rate in the suburbs, metropolitan Chicago was the eighth most unequal urban region in terms of poverty level.[33] The suburbs are richer than the city largely because many suburbanites work at well-paid jobs in the city, even though suburban corporate headquarters also increasingly provide high-paid jobs.[34] Suburban workers prosper disproportionately from the higher wages in the city, but they pay local taxes to support communities that escape much of the costs of social inequality.

Sassen argues that increasing inequality is "built into the new growth sectors" of global cities.[35] That is partly because of the intrinsic effects of competition in the global labor market, but it also reflects the lack of unionization in many growth sectors. Although Chicago has long been a union stronghold, unions represented only 19 percent of metropolitan area workers in 2002, more than the 13 percent nationally, but a decline from the 22 percent of workers in unions during the mid 1980s. Yet, unions representing janitors and hotel workers have recently won significant gains for these workers, suggesting that current levels of inequality are not intrinsic to the new economy.

Just as inequality exists among workers and families, the disparities among geographic communities, including individual suburbs and city neighborhoods, are deepened by the exodus of manufacturing from the central city and by suburban sprawl. Because of persistent discrimination and the historically high degree of racial segregation in Chicago, the mismatch between the skills of black inner-city residents and service and manufacturing jobs in the suburbs is particularly severe.[36] Sprawl also has created huge public and private external costs—such as traffic congestion and environmental destruction—and shifted public spending away from modernizing inner suburb and city infrastructure. On balance, the social costs of sprawl have roughly equaled the private benefits. Sprawl thus transfers income from low—and middle-income workers to upper-income business owners, especially if one takes into account the state's highly regressive taxes.[37] Suburban growth thus made it harder, even if the good will existed, to reduce racially based economic inequalities and to resolve the racial contradiction in post-war Chicago urban development.

Although businesses that sell goods and services outside the region typically have a disproportionate effect on the region by stimulating the growth of related jobs, roughly two-thirds of all jobs provide goods and services for local consumption.[38] These local businesses, from grocery and hardware stores to restaurants and theaters, affect both the economic vitality and livability of the diverse micro-economies within the broader urban region, from depressed and depopulated communities like Lawndale on the city's West Side to wealthy Kenilworth in the north suburbs.

Although the influx of new immigrants to Chicago has strengthened many neighborhood economies, the central city overall is undersupplied with retail stores. Many businesses fled—just as banks deprived the same neighborhoods of credit—because they did not want to serve black neighborhoods. By the late 1990s, the federal government estimated that Chicago had a "retail gap" of $9.9 billion, second only to New York. But, because land is scarce and the "big box" store has emerged as the retail model, initiatives by retailers to replicate their suburban-style stores often conflict with the need to preserve manufacturing jobs. After concluding that the city gained more economically from manufacturing than from retail or residential development, Mayor Harold Washington protected several key manufacturing districts from real estate speculation.[39] Also, anti-union discount retailers, such as Wal-Mart, put downward pressure on wages and benefits and are likely to lead to a net loss of jobs.[40] In 2004, community and labor critics of Wal-Mart proposed that future "big box" retailers meet certain minimum standards on wages, hiring, and other policies.

CREATING AN ECONOMICALLY COHERENT REGION

Beyond such problems as the mismatch between job location and willing workers or the inequities of tax revenue among different jurisdictions, this dispersal of jobs through a large number of competing municipalities unravels the metropolitan area's economic coherence. As major firms or factories moved out, small businesses whose fates had once been linked to them failed, followed, or adapted to a more national market. A few local businesses still benefit from their proximity to one of the remaining giants, and some local suppliers to big corporations such as McDonald's have expanded their national or global operations.[41] Ford is also creating a new supplier park close to it's South-Side assembly plant.

Businesses now rely on ties within the Midwest or Great Lakes region much in the way that they once looked to links within the city or metropolitan region. During the 1990s, the average firm in the Chicago region relied much more on external customers and suppliers than in previous decades. But, despite the growing importance of international trade, especially with Canada and Mexico, Illinois companies' trade with other states is roughly four to five times larger than trade with other countries.[42]

Chicago could thus gain greatly from a strategy to develop the region: strengthening the manufacturing base, providing business services, and developing new high-tech firms that complement the region's needs. This refocusing of the region's economic ambitions does imply two strategic changes.

First, the political will would be necessary for the entire region to stop its low-road tragedy of attempting to compete in the world—and often among the states and cities of the region—by offering cheap labor, lower taxes, and direct public subsidies. Instead, a commitment to a high-road regional strategy is necessary, one that emphasizes research, education, skilled workers, high wages, innovation, and productivity.[43] Trying to pursue both is impossible. The low road continually undermines the potential for the high road.

For the region to be more economically integrated, it needs a dramatic increase in infrastructure spending designed to increase regional efficiency, such as upgrading existing streets, expanding public transportation, and making Chicago the hub of a high-speed rail network. Despite substantial infrastructure investment in Chicago during the 1990s, key areas were neglected (such as upgrading the city's intermodal freight capacity), and public investment was often misguided (especially tax increment financing for Loop businesses).[44]

Before Chicago can hope to implement a vision of an integrated Midwestern region, it must first confront the political and economic conflicts within the metropolis itself. Part of the business elite, as well as many neighborhood groups and labor unions, now recognize the need for a regional approach that includes control of sprawl, balanced growth, improved energy and transportation efficiency, a strengthened manufacturing sector, and enhanced education and training.

Ultimately, regionalism will only work effectively if strategies are also implemented to share tax revenues throughout the region, starting with state efforts to equalize funding for public schools, but including more regional tax sharing as well. Growing disparity among local governments' capacity to raise revenues feeds on itself in a spiral of growing inequality. From 1980 to 1993, 26 suburbs (mainly black and poor to start with) lost tax base by as much as 36 percent, but the tax base increased by more than 48 percent in 77 suburbs (mainly white and affluent).[45]

Regionalism—whether it spans metropolitan Chicago or the Midwest—will be most successful if leaders can unite a divided metropolis around a vision of self-consciously creating good jobs and communities for all, rather than relying on the trickle-down effects from an increasingly unequal region. Chicago was initially "the city of the [nineteenth] century"[46] partly because it embodied a vision of both the city and its industries opening up the Great West. It was driven with class conflict, but it had a vitality that was captured in the classic odes to Chicago by Carl Sandburg, who was a keen socialist critic of the city. Chicago in this era was rough-edged, but it was also coherent.

THE FUTURE OF CHICAGO IN A GLOBAL ECONOMY

In the decades after World War II, Chicago lost much of that vitality, as people and jobs, especially in manufacturing industries, moved to suburbs not integrated within one metropolitan area, and as racial discrimination divided the central city and fed the suburban exodus. As businesses moved out or simply folded, the metropolitan region became less politically and economically coherent as well. Inequalities grew, among individuals and communities, and these inequalities undercut the economy of the entire region.

The form that globalization took exacerbated the tensions within the urban region, putting severe pressure on traded-goods manufacturers, but opening new opportunities for corporations to move production to meet short-term performance goals. Globalization reinforced the trend toward the dominance of financial interests and the transformation of corporate power into remote strategic centers distanced from routines of production, whether of candies or airplanes, and from the communities in which they operated.

These tendencies towards a less coherent and less egalitarian metropolis deepened even during the 1990s, but after a horrendous previous decade of manufacturing job losses and economic hardship, there was a tenuous recovery of both economic and population growth. Surviving manufacturers had reorganized and reinvested to survive, new business service firms were expanding in the central city, and a renaissance occurred around the Loop and even in some outlying neighborhoods. New efforts were made to exploit Chicago's historic advantages and economic legacy, to enrich the amenities of community and cultural life, and to give new focus to the neglected needs of deprived communities and of the region.

A growing awareness has arisen of Chicago's economic role in the wider world. With the forces of globalization nibbling away at highly skilled white-collar jobs, as well as both skilled and unskilled blue-collar jobs, it is becoming difficult to make increasingly slippery jobs stick in the city or metropolitan area. Local government can foster supportive cultures among businesses in common industries and professions, guarantee adequate infrastructure, and improve education and both basic and advanced job skills, but it needs more progressively generated revenue from regional, state, and federal governments. Local government can also encourage management cooperation with workers and an organized voice for workers themselves, but Chicago's economy could benefit as well from closer cooperation with universities and research centers and from a greater variety of investment and credit, including both more venture capital and more neighborhood capital (such as lending by community-oriented development banks).

If Chicago is to become a global city, it is likely to do so by first becoming an integrated metropolis that serves as the capital of a more integrated Midwestern region. Globalization is full of contradictions for Chicago, destroying and creating opportunities, generating inequalities, and encouraging a less parochial outlook while ungluing local ties that bind. Chicago's hold on the business service firms that cater to the needs of global corporations, as well as the headquarters of many of those corporations, will depend on the health of the Midwest region and the quality of life in the metropolitan area. In the end, local government can have little effect, even with its most generous subsidies and tax breaks, on the shifting winds of globalization and markets for corporate control. It may achieve most on the skills of its citizens and of the quality of life in the region.[47]

Far from being a Rust Belt relic, high-tech incubator, or global city, the new Chicago economy is precariously balanced, retaining a diminished but transformed legacy of industrial greatness and expanding its potential as a center of high-skilled services. Chicago is the globally important capital of a region larger than nearly all other national economies, yet it lacks metropolitan political and economic coherence. It also lacks the commitment to renewal that would create a more integrated, egalitarian region. Those shortcomings are as much a threat to the region's economic future as are the shifting winds of national politics or economic globalization.

NOTES

1. Ginsburg, Robert, Xiaochang Jin, and Sheila McCann. E.J. Brach: *A Misadventure in Candyland*. Chicago: Midwest Center for Labor Research, 1994.

2. Verespej, Michael A. "The Atlas of U.S. Manufacturing." *Industry Week*. April 5, 1999.

3. Ginsburg, Robert, Xiaochang Jin, and Sheila McCann. E.J. Brach: *A Misadventure in Candyland*. Chicago: Midwest Center for Labor Research, 1994; Langly, Alison. "Swiss Maker of Chocolate Will Acquire Brach's Candy." *New York Times*. September 2, 2003.

4. McCourt, Jeff and Greg LeRoy with Phillip Mattera. "A Better Deal for Illinois: Improving Economic Development Policy." Washington: Good Jobs First, 2003.

5. Looking only at the biggest companies, Chicago's share of corporate headquarters dropped by 40 percent over two decades. But, by other measures, the metropolitan region was second to New York and growing (counting corporations with 2,500 or more employees) or in fourth place and declining (counting corporations with more than SOD employees) (Klier and Testa 2001; Strahler 2003).

6. "Special Report: Top 100 Companies." *Chicago Tribune*. May 18, 2003; Economic Focus. World Business Chicago: November, 2002.

7. An increase of 42.7 percent occurred in professional and business services employment (NAICS code 54) in metropolitan Chicago from 1990 to 2000, according to U.S. Census Bureau figures compiled by Glen D. Marker, Director of Research, World Business Chicago.

8. Markusen, Ann, Karen Chapple, Greg Schrock, Daisky Yamamoto, and Pingkang Yu. "High-Tech and I-Tech: How Metros Rank and Specialize." Minneapolis, MN: The Hubert Humphrey Institute of Public Affairs, 2001.

9. Sassen, Saskia. "A Global City." In *Global Chicago*, C. Madigan , ed. Urbana: University of Illinois Press, 2004.

10. Engardio, Peter, Aaron Bernstein, and Manjeet Kripilani. "Is Your Job Next?" *Business Week*. February 3, 2003.

11. Sassen, Saskia. "A Global City." In *Global Chicago*, C. Madigan , ed. Urbana: University of Illinois Press, 2004.

12. Named after economist James Tobin, who first proposed it, a very small tax on international financial transactions could dampen speculation and some of its destabilizing effects (ul Haq, Kaul, and Grunberg 1996).

13. Harrison, Bennet. *Lean & Mean: Why Large Corporations Will Continue to Dominate the Global Economy*. New York, NY: The Guilford Press, 1994.

14. Markusen, Ann. "Sticky Places in Slippery Space: A Typology of Industrial Districts." *Economic Geography* 72:294–314. 1996.

15. Squires, Gregory, Larry Bennett, Kathleen McCourt and Philip Nyden. *Chicago: Race, Class and the Response to Urban Decline*. Philadelphia: Temple University Press, 1987.

16. Markusen, Ann. "Sticky Places in Slippery Space: A Typology of Industrial Districts." *Economic Geography* 72:294–314. 1996.

17. Sassen, Saskia. "A Global City." In *Global Chicago*, C. Madigan , ed. Urbana: University of Illinois Press, 2004.

18. Ibid.

19. Peck, Jaime and Nik Theodore. "Contingent Chicago: Restructuring the Spaces of Temporary Labor." *International Journal of Urban and Regional Research*, 25 (3):471–96. 2001.

20. Economic Report of the President. Washington, D.C.: U.S. Government Printing Office, 2004; SOCDS: State of the Cities Data System. Http://socds.huduser.org.

21. Gordon, David. *Fat and Mean: The Corporate Squeeze of Working Americans and the Myth of Managerial "Downsizing."* New York, NY: The Free Press, 1996.

22. Engardio, Peter, Aaron Bernstein, and Manjeet Kripilani. "Is Your Job Next?" *Business Week*. February 3, 2003; Goodman, Peter. "White Collar Work a Booming U.S. Export." *Washington Post*. April 2, 2003; Roberts, Dan and Edward Luce. "As Service Industries Go Global More White Collar Jobs Follow." *Financial Times*. August 19, 2003; Uchitelle, Louis. "A Statistic That's Missing: Jobs That Moved Overseas." *New York Times*. October 5, 2003.

23. Markusen, Ann, Karen Chapple, Greg Schrock, Daisky Yamamoto, and Pingkang Yu. "High-Tech and I-Tech: How Metros Rank and Specialize." Minneapolis, MN: The Hubert Humphrey Institute of Public Affairs, 2001; Porter, Michael E. n.d. Cluster Mapping Project. Harvard Business School, Institute for Strategy and Competitiveness. Http://data.isc.hbs.edu/isc.

24. Johnson, Elmer W. *Chicago Metropolis 2020: The Chicago Plan for the Twenty-first Century*. Chicago: University of Chicago Press, 2001.

25. Tita, Bob. "A White Elephant Tramples Harvard." *Crain's Chicago Business*. May 5, 2003; Tita, Bob. "Trying to Make a Splash with Harvard Water Park." *Crain's Chicago Business*. July 21, 2003.

26. Moody's Investor Services. "CMBS: A New Economic Diversity Model for a New Economy." June 9, 2003.

27. Porter, Michael E. n.d. Cluster Mapping Project. Harvard Business School, Institute for Strategy and Competitiveness. Http://data.isc.hbs.edu/isc.

28. Bernstein, David. "Films Flee the Loop, but Chicago Fights Back." *New York Times*. April 9, 2003.

29. Dreier, Peter, John Mollenkopf, and Todd Swanstrom. *Place Matters: Metropolitics for the Twenty-first Century*. Lawrence, Kansas: University of Kansas Press, 2001; Moberg, David. "Separate and Unequal." *The Neighborhood Works*. August/September 2001.

30. SOCDS: State of the Cities Data System. Http://socds.huduser.org.

31. Rodgers, Angie and Ed Lazere. "Income Inequality in the District of Columbia is Wider than in Any Major U.S. City." Washington, D.C.: D.C. Fiscal Policy Institute, 2004. www.cbpp.org.

32. Ibid.

33. Dreier, Peter, John Mollenkopf, and Todd Swanstrom. *Place Matters: Metropolitics for the Twenty-first Century*. Lawrence, Kansas: University of Kansas Press, 2001.

34. Sassen, Saskia. "A Global City." In *Global Chicago*, C. Madigan , ed. Urbana: University of Illinois Press, 2004.

35. Wilson, William Julius. *The Truly Disadvantaged: The Inner-City, The Underclass and Public Policy*. Chicago: University of Chicago Press, 1987.

36. Persky, Joseph J. and Wim Weivel. "Introduction." In *Suburban Sprawl*, W. Wievel and J.J. Persky eds. Armonk, NY: M.E. Sharp; Chicago Case Study Working Group of the Great Cities Institute. Metropolitan Decentralization in Chicago. Chicago. Great Cities Institute, University of Illinois at Chicago. 2001; Gardner, Matthew, Robert G. Lynch, Richard Sims, Ben Schweigert, and Amy Meek. "Balancing Act: Tax Reform Options for Illinois." Washington: Institute on Taxation and Economic Policy, February 2002.

37. Porter, Michael E. n.d. Cluster Mapping Project. Harvard Business School, Institute for Strategy and Competitiveness. Http://data.isc.hbs.edu/isc.

38. Clavel, Pierre and Wim Wiewel, eds. *Harold Washington and the Neighborhoods: Progressive City Government in Chicago 1983–1987*. New Brunswick, NJ: Rutgers University Press, 1991.

39. Mehta, Chirag, Ron Baiman and Joe Persky. "The Economic Impact of Wal-Mart: An Assessment of the Wal-Mart Store Proposed for Chicago's West Side." Chicago: University of Illinois at Chicago, Center for Urban Economic Development, March 2004.

40. Gupta, Sapna. "The Global Corporation: McDonald's, A Case Study." In *Global Chicago*, C. Madigan, ed. Urbana: University of Illinois Press, 2004.

41. Hewings, Geoffrey J.C. n.d. "Infrastructure and Economic Development: Perspectives for the Chicago and Midwest Economies." 2004. www.chicagofed.org/newsandevents/conferences/midwest_infrastructure/documents/hewings_infrastructure.ppt.

42. Swinney, Dan. "Building the Bridge to the High Road." Chicago: Center for Labor and Community Research. 1998.

43. PRAGmatics (Chicago). "Looking Into Tax Increment Financing." Summer 2002.

44. Chicago Case Study Working Group of the Great Cities Institute. Metropolitan Decentralization in Chicago. Chicago: Great Cities Institute, University of Illinois at Chicago. 2001.

45. Miller, Donald L. *City of the Century: The Epic of Chicago and the Making of America*. New York: Simon and Shuster, 1997.

46. Markusen, Ann. "Sticky Places in Slippery Space: A Typology of Industrial Districts." *Economic Geography* 72:294–314. 1996.

The Second-Rate City?

By Aaron Renn

In response to the manufacturing and industrial decline in the North in the 1970s and 1980s, Chicago set out to rebuild itself as a global city. Yet in the process poor political leadership and lack of foresight in public policy decisions may have doomed it from the start. Key changes are needed for Chicago to truly be the global powerhouse it wants to be.

I n the 1990s, Chicago enthusiastically joined the urban renaissance that swept through many of America's major cities. Emerging from the squalor and decay of the seventies and eighties, Chicago grew for the first time since 1950—by more than 100,000 people over the decade. The unemployment rate in the nation's third-biggest city was lower than in its two larger rivals, and per-capita income growth was higher. Chicago's metropolitan area racked up 560,000 new jobs, more than either New York's or Los Angeles's in raw numbers and over twice as many on a percentage basis. A rising Chicago spent lavishly to improve itself, investing in a new elevated line to Midway Airport, a major street-beautification program, and new cultural facilities costing hundreds of millions of dollars. The capstone was Millennium Park, a $450 million showplace featuring work by such celebrities as architect Frank Gehry and sculptor Anish Kapoor.

The idea was to portray Chicago as a "global city," and it was successful, to judge from the responses in the national media. As Millennium Park opened (a few years late) in the mid-2000s, *The Economist* celebrated Chicago as "a city buzzing with life, humming with prosperity, sparkling with new buildings, new sculptures, new parks, and generally exuding vitality." The *Washington Post* dubbed Chicago "the Milan of the Midwest." *Newsweek* added, "From a music scene powered by the underground footwork energy of juke to adventurous

Aaron Renn, "Second Rate City," *City Journal*, vol. 22, no. 2. Copyright © 2012 by Manhattan Institute for Policy Research, Inc. Reprinted with permission.

three-star restaurants, high-stepping fashion, and hot artists, Chicago is not only 'the city that works,' in Mayor Daley's slogan, but also an exciting, excited city in which all these glittery worlds shine."

But despite the chorus of praise, it's becoming evident that the city took a serious turn for the worse during the first decade of the new century. The gleaming towers, swank restaurants, and smart shops remain, but Chicago is experiencing a steep decline quite different from that of many other large cities. It is a deeply troubled place, one increasingly falling behind its large urban brethren and presenting a host of challenges for new mayor Rahm Emanuel.

Begin with Chicago's population decline during the 2000s, an exodus of more than 200,000 people that wiped out the previous decade's gains. Of the 15 largest cities in the United States in 2010, Chicago was the only one that lost population; indeed, it suffered the second-highest total loss of any city, sandwiched between first-place Detroit and third-place, hurricane-wrecked New Orleans. While New York's and L.A.'s populations clocked in at record highs in 2010, Chicago's dropped to a level not seen since 1910. Chicago is also being "Europeanized," with poorer minorities leaving the center of the city and forced to its inner suburbs: 175,000 of those 200,000 lost people were black.

The demographic disaster extends beyond city limits. Cook County as a whole lost population during the 2000s; among America's 15 largest counties, the only other one to lose population was Detroit's Wayne County. The larger Chicago metropolitan area grew just 4 percent—less than half the national average. What little growth Chicagoland had, then, was concentrated in its exurban fringes, belying the popular narrative of a return to the city. And even that meager growth resulted almost entirely from new births and immigrants, rather than domestic migration: over the decade, the Chicago metro area suffered a net loss of more than 550,000 people to other parts of the country.

Chicago's economy also performed poorly during the first decade of the century. That was a tough decade all over the United States, of course, but the Chicago region lost 7.1 percent of its jobs—the worst performance of any of the country's ten largest metro areas. Chicago's vaunted Loop, the second-largest central business district in the nation, did even worse, losing 18.6 percent of its private-sector jobs, according to the Chicago Loop Alliance. Per-capita GDP grew faster in New York and L.A. than in Chicago; today, Chicago's real per-capita GDP ranks eighth out of the country's ten largest metros.

Fiscal problems are commonplace these days among local governments, but Chicago's are particularly grim and far predate the Great Recession. Cook County treasurer Maria Pappas estimates that within the city of Chicago, there's a stunning $63,525 in total local government liabilities per household. Not all of this is city debt; the region's byzantine political structure includes many layers of government, including hundreds of local taxing districts. But pensions for city workers alone are $12 billion underfunded. If benefits aren't reduced, the city will have to increase its contributions to the pension fund by $710 million a year for the next 50 years, according to the Civic Federation. Chicago's annual budget, too, has been structurally out of balance, running an annual deficit of about $650 million in recent years.

As dire as Chicago's finances are, those of Illinois are in even worse shape. The primary cause, once again, is pensions, which are underfunded to the tune of $83 billion. Retirees' future health care is underfunded an additional $43 billion. There's a lot of regular debt, too—about $44 billion of it. And Illinois, like Chicago, has run large deficits for some time. Despite raising the individual income tax 66 percent and the corporate tax 46 percent in 2011, the state is projected to end the current fiscal year with an accumulated deficit of $5.2 billion. While California has made headlines by issuing IOUs to companies to which it owes money, Illinois has taken an easier route: it just stopped paying its bills, at one point last year racking up 208,000 of them, totaling $4.5 billion. Some businesses have gone unpaid for nine months or even longer. Unsurprisingly, Illinois has the worst credit rating of any state. Unable to pay its bills, it is de facto bankrupt.

What accounts for Chicago's miserable performance in the 2000s? The fiscal mess is the easiest part to account for: it is the result of poor leadership and powerful interest groups that benefit from the status quo. Public-union clout is literally written into the state constitution, which prohibits the diminution of state employees' retirement benefits. Tales of abuse abound, such as the recent story of two lobbyists for a local teachers' union who, though they had never held government jobs, obtained full government pensions by doing a single day of substitute teaching apiece.

If the state and city had honestly funded the obligations they were taking on, their generosity to their workers would be less of a problem. But they didn't. As *City Journal* senior editor Steven Malanga has written for RealClearMarkets, Illinois "essentially wanted to be a low-tax (or at least a moderate-tax) state with high services and rich employee pensions." That's an obviously unsustainable policy formula. The state has also employed a series of gimmicks to cover up persistent deficits—for example, using borrowed money to shore up its pension system and even to pay for current operations. At the city level, Mayor Richard M. Daley papered over deficits with such tricks as a now-infamous parking-meter lease. The city sold the right to parking revenues for 75 years to get $1.1 billion up front. Just two years into the deal, all but $180 million had been spent.

The debt and obligations begin to explain why jobs are leaving Chicago. It isn't a matter, as in many cities, of high taxes driving away businesses and residents. Though Chicago has the nation's highest sales tax, Illinois isn't a high-tax state; it scores 28th in the Tax Foundation's ranking of the best state tax climates. But the sheer scale of the state's debts means that last year's income-tax hikes are probably just a taste of what's to come. (Cutting costs is another option, but that may be tricky, since Illinois is surprisingly lean in some areas already; it has the lowest number of state government employees per capita of any state, for example.) The expectation of higher future taxes has cast a cloud over the state's business climate and contributed to the bleak economic numbers.

But that isn't the whole story. Many of Chicago's woes derive from the way it has thrown itself into being a "global city" and the uncomfortable fact that its enthusiasm may be delusional. Most true global cities are a dominant location of a major industry: finance in New York, entertainment in Los Angeles, government in Washington, and so on. That position lets them harvest outsize tax revenues that can be fed back into sustaining the region. Thus New York uses Wall Street money, perhaps to too great an extent, to pay its bills (see "Wall Street Isn't Enough," page 12).

Chicago, however, isn't the epicenter of any important macro-industry, so it lacks this wealth-generation engine. It has some specialties, such as financial derivatives and the design of super tall skyscrapers, but they're too small to drive the city. The lack of a calling-card industry that can generate huge returns is perhaps one reason Chicago's per-capita GDP is so low. It also means that there aren't many people who *have* to be in Chicago to do business. Plenty of financiers have to settle in New York, lots of software engineers must move to Silicon Valley, but few people will pay any price or bear any burden for the privilege of doing business in Chicago.

Chicago's history militates against its transforming itself into a global city on the scale of New York, London, or Hong Kong. Yes, its wealth was built by dominating America's agro-industrial complex—leading the way in such industries as railroads, meatpacking, lumber processing, and grain processing—but that is long gone, and the high-end services jobs that remain to support those sectors aren't a replacement. Chicago as a whole is less a global city than the unofficial capital of the Midwest, and its economy may still be more tied to that troubled region than it would like to admit. Like the Midwest generally, parts of Chicago suffer from a legacy of deindustrialization: blighted neighborhoods, few jobs, a lack of investment, and persistent poverty. Chicago is also the "business service center of the Midwest, serving regional markets and industries," Chicago Fed economist Bill Testa wrote in 2007; as a result, "Chicago companies' prospects for growth are somewhat limited."

It's easy to understand why being a global city is the focus of civic leadership. Who wouldn't want the cachet of being a "command node" of the global economy, as urbanists put it? It's difficult, too, to think of a different template for Chicago to follow; its structural costs are too high for it easily to emulate Texas cities and become a low-cost location. But just because the challenge is stiff doesn't mean that it shouldn't be tackled. Chicago isn't even trying; rather, it's doubling down on the global-city square. Senator Mark Kirk wants to make O'Hare the most "Asia-friendly" airport in America and lure flights to central China, for example. A prominent civic leader suggests that the city should avoid branding itself as part of the Midwest. One of Mayor Emanuel's signature moves to date has been luring the NATO summit to Chicago.

Another reason for Chicago's troubles is that its business climate is terrible, especially for small firms. When the state pushed through the recent tax increases, certain big businesses had the clout to negotiate better deals for themselves. For example, the financial exchanges threatened to leave town until the state legislature gave them a special tax break, with an extension of a tax break for Sears thrown in for good measure. And so the deck seems to be stacked against the little guys, who get stuck with the bill while the big boys are plied with favors and subsidies.

It also hurts small businesses that Chicago operates under a system called "aldermanic privilege." Matters handled administratively in many cities require a special ordinance in Chicago, and ordinances affecting a specific council district—called a "ward" in Chicago—can't be passed unless the city council member for that ward, its "alderman," signs off. One downside of the system is that, as the *Chicago Reader* reported, over 95 percent of city council legislation is consumed by "ward housekeeping" tasks. More important is that it hands the 50 aldermen nearly dictatorial control over what happens in their wards, from zoning changes to sidewalk café permits. This dumps political risk onto the shoulders of every would-be entrepreneur, who knows that he must stay on the alderman's good side to be in business. It's also a recipe for sleaze: 31 aldermen have been convicted of corruption since 1970.

Red tape is another problem for small businesses. Outrages are legion. Scooter's Frozen Custard was cited by the city for illegally providing outdoor chairs for customers—after being told by the local alderman that it didn't need a permit. Logan Square Kitchen, a licensed and inspected shared-kitchen operation for upscale food entrepreneurs, has had to clear numerous regulatory hurdles: each of the companies using its kitchen space had to get and pay for a separate license and reinspection, for example, and after the city retroactively classified the kitchen as a banquet hall, its application for various other licenses was rejected until it provided parking spaces. An entrepreneur who wanted to open a children's playroom to serve families visiting Northwestern Memorial Hospital was told that he needed to get a Public Place of Amusement license—which he couldn't get, it turned out, because the proposed playroom was too close to a hospital!

And these are exactly the kind of hip, high-end businesses that the city claims to want. Who else stands a chance if even they get caught in a regulatory quagmire? As Chicagoland Chamber of Commerce CEO Jerry Roper has noted, "unnecessary and burdensome regulation" puts Chicago "at a competitive disadvantage with other cities." Companies also fear Cook County's litigation environment, which the U.S. Chamber of Commerce has called the most unfair and unreasonable in the country. It's not hard to figure out why *Chief Executive* ranked Illinois 48th on its list of best states in which to do business.

Chicago's notorious corruption interferes with attempts to fix things. Since 1970, 340 officials in Chicago and Cook County have been convicted of corruption. So have three governors. The corruption has been bipartisan: both Governor George Ryan, a Republican, and Governor Rod Blagojevich, a Democrat, are currently in federal prison. A recent study named Chicago the most corrupt city in the United States.

But an even greater problem than outright corruption is Chicago's culture of clout, a system of personal loyalty and influence radiating from city hall. Influencing the mayor, and influencing the influencers on down the line, is how you get things done. There is only one power structure in the city—including not just politicians but the business and social elite and their hangers-on—and it brings to mind the court of Louis XIV: when conflicts do arise, they are palace intrigues. One's standing is generally not, as in most cities, the result of having an independent power base that others must respect; it is the result of personal favor from on high. One drawback with this system is that it practically demands what columnist Greg Hinz calls a "Big Daddy"–style leader to sustain itself.

Another is that fear of being kicked out of the circle looms large in the minds of important Chicagoans. Beginning in 2007, Mayor Daley launched an ultimately unsuccessful bid for the 2016 Olympics. Later, commentator Ramsin Canon observed that Daley "was able to get everybody that mattered—everybody—on board behind the push. … Nobody, from the largest, most conservative institutions to the most active progressive advocacy group, was willing to step out against him."

These organizations have good reason to fear reprisal for not toeing the line. When Daley signed his disastrous parking-meter deal, an advocacy group called the Active Transportation Alliance issued a critical report. After a furious reaction by the Daley administration, the organization issued a groveling retraction. "I would like to simply state that we should not have published this report," said executive director Rob Sadowsky. "I am embarrassed that it not only contains factual errors, but that it also paints an incorrect interpretation of the lease's overall goals." Sadowsky is no longer in Chicago.

It's easy to see how fiascoes like the parking-meter lease happen where civic culture is rotten and new ideas can't get a hearing. Chicago's location already isolates it somewhat from outside views. Combine that with the culture of clout, and you get a city that's too often an echo chamber of boosterism lacking a candid assessment of the challenges it faces.

Some of those challenges defy easy solutions: no government can conjure up a calling-card industry, and it isn't obvious how Chicago could turn around the Midwest. Mayor Emanuel is hobbled by some of the deals of the past—the parking-meter lease, for example, and various union contracts that don't expire until 2017 and that Daley signed to guarantee labor peace during the city's failed Olympic bid.

But there's a lot that Emanuel and Chicago can do, starting with facing the fiscal mess head-on. Emanuel has vowed to balance the budget without gimmicks. He cut spending in his 2012 budget by 5.4 percent. He wants to save money by letting private companies bid to provide city services. He's found some small savings by better coordination with Cook County. Major surgery remains to be done, however, including a tough renegotiation of union contracts, merging some functions with county government, and some significant restructuring of certain agencies, such as the fire department. By far the most important item for both the city and state is pension reform for existing workers—a politically and legally challenging project, to say the least. To date, only limited reforms have passed: the state changed its retirement age, but only for new hires.

Next is to improve the business climate by reforming governance and rules. This includes curtailing aldermanic privilege, shrinking the overly large city council, and radically pruning regulations. Emanuel has already gotten some votes of confidence from the city's business community, recently announcing business expansions with more than 8,000 jobs, though they're mostly from big corporate players.

Chicago also needs something even harder to achieve: wholesale cultural change. It needs to end its obsession with being solely a global city, look for ways to reinvigorate its role as capital of the Midwest, and provide opportunities for its neglected middle and working classes, not just the elites. This means more focus on the basics of good governance and less focus on glamour. Chicago must also forge a culture of greater civic participation and debate. You can't address your problems if everyone is terrified of stepping out of line and admitting that they exist. Here, at least, Emanuel can set the tone. In March, he publicly admitted that Chicago had suffered a "lost decade," a promisingly candid assessment, and he has tapped former D.C. transportation chief Gabe Klein to run Chicago's transportation department, rather than picking a Chicago insider. Continuing to welcome outsiders and dissident voices will help dilute the culture of clout.

Fixing Chicago will be a big, difficult project, but it's necessary. The city's sparkling core may continue to shine, and magazines may continue to applaud the global city on Lake Michigan—but without a major change in direction, Chicago can expect to see still more people and jobs fleeing for more hospitable locales.

A Tale of Two Cities

Public Education and Human Capital in Global Chicago

By Constance A. Mixon

In a global city divided by wealth, our educational institutions reflect an organized hierarchy that is segregated, like our neighborhoods, into haves and have-nots. Rather than offering hope and opportunity for those living at the margins in Chicago, our schools reinforce existing political, social, and economic stratifications. If Chicago is to remain competitive in a global, knowledge-based economy, we must recognize the critical role our educational institutions, at all levels, play in helping students, especially disadvantaged and under- represented students, reach their full potential. We must also recognize that our many of our schools will require additional public funding to achieve these goals.

Horace Mann said that education is the great equalizer. Yet, in Chicago and many other metropolitan regions, a high-quality education is increasingly available only to those who can afford to pay for private schools or move to better school districts, often in the suburbs. In a global city divided by wealth, our educational institutions reflect an organized hierarchy that is segregated, like our neighborhoods, into haves and have-nots. As is the case with most challenges facing Chicago in the twenty-first century, race and poverty are integrally connected to the challenges facing our schools.

Chicago Public Schools (CPS) enrolls approximately four hundred thousand students in 660 schools. It is the nation's third-largest school district. The vast majority of CPS students attend schools that are highly segregated by race and income. In 2012, the *New York Times* reported that Chicago public schools were the most segregated in the country.[1] In Chicago, "96 percent of black students attend majority non-white schools and 67 percent of white students attend majority white schools. In other words, white students tend to attend schools with other white students and black and Latino students attend schools with other

191

students of color."[2] While about 30 percent of the city's population is white, less than 10 percent of the CPS student population is white.[3]

CPS segregation extends beyond race, to income. Within CPS, over 86 percent of students are classified as economically disadvantaged.[4] Yet, the proportion of low-income families with children in Chicago is only 52 percent.[5] Racial and economic segregation within Chicago Public Schools is a persistent problem that concentrates poor minority students in low-performing neighborhood schools. Steve Bogira, a reporter for the *Chicago Reader*, has argued that racial and economic disparities persist at CPS "because so many middle-class parents are unwilling to send their kids to the city's public schools. Instead, they send them to private schools, or, when their children reach school age (or high school age), they move to the suburbs."[6]

SELECTIVE-ENROLLMENT CPS HIGH SCHOOLS

Globalization has transformed Chicago into two cities: one for wealthy residents and tourists, with a gleaming downtown; and another for the poor, with neglected and isolated neighborhoods. Our city schools mirror this global transformation. As Chicago is two cities, CPS is two school systems: one system with selective-enrollment schools that are among the best in the nation; and another system with neglected and isolated neighborhood schools that are among the worst.

Mayor Rahm Emanuel has said that the "biggest, anxious question that exists across the city of Chicago" is "Where am I going to send my child to high school?"[7] Like many other large US cities, Chicago has a hierarchical system of highly regarded selective-enrollment schools, embedded within the larger CPS system. One of the common complaints about CPS selective-enrollment schools is they "shortchange disadvantaged kids … Even simply requiring student candidates (and their parents) to be proactive, to take the time to fill out what are often laborious applications risks discriminating against the less fortunate."[8] Yet, every year, ambitious and proactive students from across the city find themselves in a fierce competition for admission to one of the elusive and exclusive CPS selective-enrollment high schools, like Northside, Walter Payton, Jones, Whitney-Young, and Lane. These schools admit top students from across the city based on test scores and grades. Arguably, it is "more difficult to get into one of the top CPS high schools than it is to get into Harvard or Yale."[9] For the 2015–2016 school year, 13,413 students applied for only 3,600 freshman slots at these selective-enrollment high schools.[10]

In Chicago, students who are accepted to selective-enrollment schools benefit from the best education available, while students trapped in impoverished and isolated neighborhood schools are too often left behind. These differences are readily apparent when one looks at college enrollment statistics. Seventy-one percent of all CPS selective-enrollment high school graduates enroll in four-year colleges, while only 29 percent of all CPS neighborhood high school graduates enroll in four-year colleges.[11] Elite selective-enrollment schools in Chicago rate among the best in Illinois—and in the nation. According to *U.S. News and World Report*, in 2015, half of the top ten schools in Illinois were CPS selective-enrollment high schools.[12] Each of the five selective-enrollment CPS high schools, identified as among the best in Illinois, is located on the city's North Side. Detailed in Chart 1, these five selective-enrollment high schools enroll significantly more white and Asian students and significantly fewer black, Hispanic, and low-income students than the CPS system as a whole.

Chart 1. Demographics of CPS Top Ranked Selective-Enrollment High Schools and CPS System, 2015

School	Asian	Black	Hispanic	White	Low Income
Northside	18%	9%	27%	38%	42%
Walter Payton	13%	15%	23%	44%	33%
Jones	11%	20%	31%	35%	46%
Whitney Young	15%	24%	28%	29%	43%
Lane	10%	9%	44%	33%	60%
CPS	4%	39%	46%	9%	86%

Source: Compiled by author with data from Chicago Public Schools.

Students enrolled at selective-enrollment CPS schools benefit from higher-quality educational opportunities and programs generally not found in most traditional neighborhood schools. At Northside College Preparatory High School, for example, the average ACT score is 29.1, and 90 percent of graduates go on to college.[13] The school also boasts extensive academic enrichment activities and programs including the Academic Olympics, Chess, Math, Speech, Technology and Debate Teams, a writer's workshop, and nearly every sport team imaginable. Students at Northside also have their pick of Chinese, French, Japanese, Latin, and Spanish language classes.[14]

In 2014, CPS rolled out a new five-tiered school performance rating system, designed to "help educators and parents better identify struggling and successful schools."[15] The highest-performing schools in the system now receive a Level 1+ rating, while the poorest performing schools receive a Level 3 rating. A Level 3 rating means "the school is in need of intensive intervention."[16] Excluding charter schools, nine CPS high schools were classified as Level 3 in the spring of 2016. All of these Level 3 CPS high schools are located on the South and West Sides of the city.

Robeson High School, located in Chicago's Englewood neighborhood, is one of the Level 3 CPS schools. Robeson has been on academic probation and in need of intensive support for 20 years.[17] At Robeson, only 3.8 percent of the students test at or above state standards (CPS average is 34 percent); the average ACT score is 13.9 (CPS average is 18.2); and only 47.3 percent of enrolled students go on to graduate (CPS average is 70 percent).[18] Demographically, 100 percent of Robeson students are classified as low-income, and

98 percent of the students are black.[19] Unlike CPS selective-enrollment high schools offering full portfolios of academic enrichment and support programs, the only extra programs at Robeson are summer school and supplemental tutoring.[20] Robeson students also don't have their pick of language classes. Spanish is the only language offered.[21]

CPS SCHOOL CLOSURES AND CHARTER SCHOOL EXPANSION

On the heels of a bitter, seven-day CPS teacher strike in 2012, Mayor Emanuel and the CPS Board closed nearly fifty CPS schools. It was the "largest single round of school closures in American history."[22] Thousands of students were displaced and forced to transfer to new schools, often at some distance from their home and across different gang territories. In a prepared statement, CPS said the closures "will consolidate underutilized schools and programs to provide students with the quality, 21st century education they need to succeed in the classroom."[23] Mayor Emanuel echoed the CPS statement, saying, "By consolidating these schools, CPS can focus on safely getting every child into a better performing school … Like school systems in New York and Philadelphia where schools are being closed, Chicago must make tough choices."[24]

Those tough choices have, according to many experts, resulted in further destabilization of communities already on the margins, experiencing disproportionate levels of foreclosures, unemployment, and violence. Brad Hunt, an urban historian, argues that the consequence of taking schools out of these communities is a "slow death."[25] The move to close CPS schools, which are located mainly on Chicago's South and West Sides, was contentious, spawning protests from students, parents, and the Chicago Teachers Union (CTU). Many, including CTU president Karen Lewis, called the closures racist. While only 39 percent of the students who attend CPS are black, 87 percent of the closed schools were majority black; 80 percent of students affected by the closures were black.[26] Commenting on the CPS closures, the Race Matters Institute argued,

> By closing these schools … problems in low-income areas are not resolved and the students in these schools have to learn to adjust to new schools in different areas of Chicago … Many African American elementary-aged students are generally already farther behind in school (particularly in reading success) than white students because of their low-income background and under-resourced schools. When CPS and the Board forces the closing of schools rather than fixing the existing schools, there is a serious possibility that the students' academic success is further threatened because of adjustment issues at their new schools. By simply eliminating schools, structural inequities are ignored and able to persist in Chicago.[27]

Often forgotten in the discourse about CPS school closings is how these closures were coupled with charter school expansion in Chicago. Just days after the 2012 teacher strike, the *Chicago Tribune* reported that Mayor Emanuel was "aiming to add 60 charter schools in the next five years with support from the Bill & Melinda Gates Foundation, which is trying to expand charters across the country."[28] In Chicago, "the number of charter schools ... soared under Mayors Richard M. Daley and Rahm Emanuel, with enrollment rising nearly sixfold from 2003 to 2013: 8,647 students to 48,707."[29] As of 2016, there were one hundred thirty charter schools in the CPS system.[30]

Charter schools are public schools, but they have fewer rules and regulations than traditional public schools. They operate under a contract, or charter. Although they must meet requirements set by the state, they have more flexibility—like offering a unique curriculum or limiting admission to certain students. They also are not required to hire union teachers. While charter schools are funded in much the same way as traditional public schools, they have significant funding advantages. Charters receive more funding from the federal government than local schools, which are heavily reliant on local property taxes. They also receive billions of dollars from corporate foundations like Gates's and Walmart's Walton Foundation. In 2014, the Gates Foundation directed over $2.5 million to charter schools in Chicago through Chicago Community Trust, the Illinois Network of Charter Schools, and the CPS Children's First Fund.[31]

Chicago is at the center of a national debate about privately run—but publicly funded—charter schools, and whether or not charter schools are a better formula for success than struggling inner-city schools. Despite the lack of credible evidence of charter school success, both Chicago Mayor Rahm Emanuel and Illinois Governor Bruce Rauner believe charter schools are a better formula. Speaking to a group in Springfield, Illinois, in 2015, Rauner said, "Every parent, every child, deserves a choice to pick a high-quality school ... As governor ... I want to expand your charter network and get high-quality charters in every community throughout the state of Illinois ... I will do everything I can to support increased school funding, equal funding for charter schools and make sure that charters are supported."[32]

Despite their popularity, the results on charter schools are mixed. A 2014 report from the Institute on Metropolitan Opportunity at the University of Minnesota Law School found that "Chicago's charter schools actually underperform their traditional counterparts in most measurable ways."[33] When asked about the report, Myron Orfield, who directs the institute, said, "The question is whether charters are the best path available to find ways to better serve low-income students and students of color, given that this approach has failed to improve overall student performance by most measures, and led to less racial and ethnic diversity in the city's schools."[34]

Charter schools are an integral part of a comprehensive and expanding urban policy agenda, which advances privatization, deregulation, and free markets. Writing in the *New York Times*, Pauline Lipman, a professor of educational policy studies at the University of Illinois at Chicago, claims that "Chicago was the birthplace of neoliberal education reform—high-stakes testing, closing neighborhood public schools and turning them over to private operators, expanding charter schools, running schools like businesses, test-based teacher evaluation, prescribed standards, and mayoral control of schools."[35] In many ways, education, long considered a public good, has been converted to a private good in Chicago, focused on choice. In fact, CPS spokesperson Bill McCaffrey even states that CPS is "a system of choice … parents consider many options when choosing the best school."[36]

CPS CORRUPTION AND FINANCIAL CRISIS

When Mayor Emanuel appointed Barbara Byrd-Bennett as CEO of Chicago Public Schools in 2012, he described her as "the best and brightest."[37] In October of 2015, a federal grand jury charged Byrd-Bennett with twenty-three counts of federal corruption for her role in steering over $23 million in no-bid contracts to her former employer (SUPES Academy) in exchange for bribes and kickbacks. Byrd-Bennett eventually pleaded guilty under an agreement providing for a sentence of only seven and a half years in prison, well below the eleven to fourteen years recommended under federal sentencing guidelines.[38] While the Byrd-Bennett case is the most notorious of corruption cases at CPS, corruption has been documented throughout the system. According to a 2015 report from the Office of the Inspector General, 1,300 complaints of theft, fraud, and corruption were filed in 2015. Of the 322 cases investigated, the inspector general "found, among other things, that some employees used the district's tax-exempt status to buy personal televisions and refrigerators, some parents lied to get their children accepted into schools with selective enrollment, and some employees stole money directly from the district."[39] Commenting on corruption within the CPS system, Zachary Fardon, the United States attorney for the northern district of Illinois, said, "Graft and corruption in our city's public school system tears at the fabric of a vital resource for the children of Chicago."[40]

After the resignation of Byrd-Bennett in 2015, Forrest Claypool, Mayor Emanuel's long-time ally and chief of staff, was appointed CEO of CPS, becoming the third CEO of CPS during Emanuel's tenure as mayor. Claypool now heads a district struggling to renegotiate teacher contracts and rapidly approaching fiscal insolvency, with its debt rated as "junk" by all three major rating agencies.[41] It is estimated CPS has more than $6 billion in long-term structural debt.[42] At the end of the 2015–2016 academic year, CPS officials projected that the system had about "$24 million in cash … less than two days worth of operating expenses."[43] This prompted Claypool to announce CPS would not open in the fall of 2016 without the state passing an education budget that includes $400 million more in state aid for CPS.

While many of the fiscal problems at CPS are due to mismanagement and corruption, disparities in the way the state of Illinois funds schools are also part of the problem. Like many other states, the Illinois K–12 education funding formula relies on property taxes. Thus, the amount spent per pupil in Illinois can vary greatly, depending on where the student lives and the wealth of his or her school district. At the top end in Illinois is Rondout School District, located on the suburban North Shore. Rondout spent $30,628 per pupil in 2015. At the bottom is Germantown School District, located just east of St. Louis. With the state supplementing local revenue, Germantown spent only $6,037 per pupil in 2015. The

Education Trust, a nonprofit education advocacy group, recently reported that "Illinois, with the largest funding gap in the nation, stands out for its unfairness. The highest poverty districts in the state get nearly 20 percent less per student than the lowest poverty districts."[44] Making a compelling case for more funding from Springfield for CPS, Forrest Claypool has mobilized parents, students, and some teachers around the district's "20 for 20" campaign. This campaign seeks to bring attention to the lack of funding for CPS by the state of Illinois, arguing that "Chicago's children are 20 percent of the state's enrollment, and their families and neighbors provide 20 percent of the income tax money that funds public education in our state." Yet, "Chicago's students receive only 15 percent of the state's spending on education."[45]

Given that the Illinois General Assembly and Governor Rauner are mired in a long-running budget standoff, securing additional state revenue for CPS seems unlikely. Looming threats of another CPS teacher strike add to the fiscal crisis at CPS. Recognizing that CPS is unlikely to receive any help from the state, the CTU has called for a "revenue recovery" initiative that includes additional local taxes on "financial transactions, higher fuel and hotel taxes, plus a tax on ride-share services."[46] Teachers have also argued that tax increment financing (TIF) surpluses (estimated at $100–350 million) should be used to offset CPS deficits. Union leaders and some aldermen from the council's progressive caucus believe TIF funding, which comes from local property taxes, siphons off funding that should go to CPS. In response to these proposals from CTU and aldermen, Mayor Rahm Emanuel has said, "You cannot either tax your way or TIF your way out of this problem."[47]

Declining state investment in K–12 education, pension liabilities, and increasing debt service rates have left the CPS system in a fiscal crisis. In the midst of these dire financial conditions, CPS is yet again struggling with contentious teacher contract negotiations. As the start of the 2016–2017 school year approaches, CPS will require a long-term solution to its ongoing fiscal problems. Such a solution will need to include new revenue (unpopular local property tax increases), increased state financial support, and unpleasant cuts in services and expenses.

HUMAN CAPITAL AND HIGHER EDUCATION IN CHICAGO

Urban theorist Richard Florida, renowned for his work describing knowledge workers (the creative class) who drive urban economies, finds that when it comes to human capital, Chicago is once again two cities. One Chicago is comprised of the "creative class" that "includes people who work in science and technology, business and management, arts, culture, media, and entertainment, law, and healthcare professions ... These are high-skilled, highly-educated, and high-paying positions where workers average $75,033 per year in wages and salaries."[48] The other Chicago is comprised of the "service class" who are "low-wage, low-skill workers who work in routine service jobs such as food service and preparation, retail sales, and clerical and administrative positions ... Service workers in the [Chicago metropolitan area] average $30,946 in wages and salaries."[49]

According to the Chicago Council on Global Affairs, "the most successful cities are those that are rich in people—in skilled, smart, educated, diverse, innovative, hardworking, productive people."[50] Harvard urban economist Edward Glaeser, thinking along these same lines, argues that "much of the success of Chicago as a global city depends on its attracting skilled people, keeping them and letting them innovate, letting them lead the city forward."[51] In a knowledge-based economy, education is the primary means by which global cities compete and succeed. Education expands and develops human capital while it drives the economic growth of a city.

The Alliance for Excellent Education estimates that "85 percent of current jobs and almost 90 percent of the fastest-growing and best-paying jobs require some postsecondary education."[52] The Alliance further contends that even manufacturing jobs in today's world require some postsecondary training and skills.[53] Given these estimates, concerns have surfaced about the ability of the United States and its cities to fully meet future labor demands. In a *New York Times* editorial arguing that the political and economic dominance of America is coming to an end, due in part to an "education gap," Thomas Friedman writes that "the dirty little secret that no C.E.O. wants to tell you" is that American businesses are "not just outsourcing to save on salary. They are doing it because they can often get better-skilled and more productive people than their American workers."[54]

Like all global cities, Chicago depends on its institutions of higher education to train and produce large segments of its workforce. This dependence, however, deepens existing conflicts at colleges and universities over the democratic purposes of education and global demands for increased job training. While it is often easy to point out disparities in our K–12 system, few pay much attention to the inequalities of higher education in Chicago. Higher education in Chicago, much like the city's K–12 system, is a pyramid organization of institutions reflecting larger societal stratifications. While the doors of higher education have opened to more segments of our urban population, access has not been equal, and the stratification between institutions of higher education amplifies disparities.

City Colleges of Chicago (CCC)

Higher education in Chicago is yet another tale of two cities. Within our metropolitan region, we have some of the most prestigious and competitive research universities in the world, alongside top-tier private colleges. Increasingly however, these institutions serve and cater to those who are able to pay $30,000–50,000 a year for tuition, fees, and room and board. Even with scholarships, loans, and financial aid, many of these colleges and universities are outside the reach of everyday Chicagoans. At the other end of the higher-education spectrum in Chicago, in what seems like an entirely different city, are our public community colleges. These colleges are often the first point of entry into higher education for minorities, women, first-generation, part-time, low-income, and working-class students.

The City Colleges of Chicago (CCC) enrolls nearly 115,000 students. Over 75 percent of CCC students are black or Hispanic.[55] More than 90 percent of new CCC students need remediation, and 36 percent of students fall below the federal poverty line.[56] In 2015, CCC reported that only 17 percent of its students graduate.[57] This rate of 17 percent is a significant increase from only 7 percent graduating in 2009.[58] This improvement has been questioned, most notably by *Crain's Chicago Business*, which reported CCC has used creative accounting, even awarding degrees to deceased former students, in "an all-out hunt to boost lagging graduation rates and polish a centerpiece of Mayor Rahm Emanuel's education agenda."[59]

Although always an important part of CCC's mission, workforce and vocational training have recently taken center stage. Much of the recent focus on human capital and preparing the workforce at CCC may be attributed to Mayor Emanuel, who often promotes CCC as a key component of his urban economic policy agenda. In December of 2011, Mayor Rahm Emanuel launched the "College to Careers" program at CCC. In a *Wall Street Journal* op-ed piece, he said that the program will be based on "partnerships between our community colleges and our top employers that will draw on their expertise to develop curricula and set industry standards for job training in high-growth sectors like health care, high-tech manufacturing, information technology and professional services."[60] Fittingly, the title of Emanuel's op-ed was "Chicago's Plan to Match Education With Jobs."

At CCC, market forces are not only driving the educational curriculum, but also designing it. The CCC webpage indicates that the system "is in the midst of a Reinvention ... to review and revise CCC programs and practices ... to ensure student success and become an economic engine for the City of Chicago."[61] The number one goal of this "Reinvention" project is "to increase the number of students earning college credentials of economic value."[62] Pushed by Mayor Rahm Emanuel, Cheryl Hyman, the chancellor of CCC, put a focus on the needs of business and industry in Chicago. "Campus by campus, she [created] specialized job-training programs," where businesses, rather than faculty, developed the curriculum.[63]

Former Mayor Richard M. Daley appointed Hyman chancellor of CCC in April of 2010. Writing in the *Chronicle of Higher Education*, Jennifer Gonzalez points out that Ms. Hyman, who lacks the doctoral degree typically required of someone in her position,

> has no prior experience in higher education, or in education at all. The Reinvention project, which she began almost immediately after being appointed, is modeled on a similar effort at ComEd ... where she had spent her career ... most recently as vice president for operations strategy and business intelligence. The structure of the Reinvention effort at City Colleges is almost identical to that of a project Ms. Hyman worked on at ComEd. (In fact, ComEd's logo for its rebates and savings programs is similar to the Reinvention logo. Both incorporate a green swirl) ... A few months after her April 2010 appointment, Ms Hyman asked six of the seven college presidents to reapply for their jobs. Only one did, and she replaced the five others with more vocational-focused candidates from outside the system.[64]

When asked about the vocational focus at CCC, Dr. Larry Goodman, president and CEO of Rush University Medical Center, said, "we've recognized that City Colleges has a different set of aspirations going forward. They're focusing their programs on where the jobs are expected to be and to provide the very best training for their students."[65]

As CCC's mission shifted from providing access and general baccalaureate education to vocational training during Hyman's tenure, there were increasing concerns that this shift limited the full potential of underrepresented, low-income, minority students. CCC faculty were the harshest critics, arguing the increased focus on vocational training was in conflict with "the seven-college system's historical mission, offering an affordable and accessible gateway to higher education for working people, minorities and immigrants."[66] In an interview with *Crain's Chicago Business*, Hector Reyes, a CCC chemistry professor said, "they're taking advantage of people's desperation for jobs ... there is no individual job that is worth consigning an entire community to an educational ghetto."[67] Students also expressed their concerns, especially those at campuses hardest hit by program consolidations under "Reinvention." When interviewed by Northwestern's Medill School of Journalism, Jonathan Talley, a student at Kennedy-King College in Chicago's Englewood neighborhood, said the increased focus on vocational training at CCC "marginalizes students on the south side to just be cooks. That's not what everybody wants to do. It almost feels like segregation in a way. You're saying we can only do these types of jobs and that's not true at all."[68]

In February of 2016, the faculty of CCC voted no confidence in the leadership of Chancellor Hyman, citing increased tuition rates, program consolidations, dismantling of academic affairs, and lack of shared governance. Tony Johnston serves as the president of the Cook County College Teachers Union, which represents nearly six hundred full-time faculty members at CCC. When asked about the vote of no confidence in Hyman, Johnston said, "She has a very private-sector, corporate mentality when it comes to public education ... we need administrators who know what it's like in the classrooms in colleges, and we do not have that in the administration at City Colleges."[69] In June 2016, after six tumultuous years at CCC, it was announced that Hyman would step down from her post as chancellor. As Mayor Emanuel and his appointed CCC Board now seek a new leader for the system of community colleges in Chicago, it is however unlikely the focus on vocational training will change.

If Chicago is to remain competitive in a global, knowledge-based economy, we must recognize the critical role our educational institutions, at all levels, plays in helping students—especially disadvantaged and underrepresented students—reach their full potential. CCC is in the unique position to offer opportunities to those who need further education, skills, and training. Yet, simply preparing students for jobs is not enough for full participation in today's global economy. In a rapidly changing global world, specialized job training will become obsolete, while the ability to think critically, communicate effectively, collaborate with others, and solve complex problems will always be in demand.

Despite the hopes of Horace Mann, education in Chicago has yet to achieve its equalizing potential. If a high-level quality education were available to all students across the city, many of our racial and economic disparities would be minimized, and our global economy would benefit. Unfortunately, rather than offering hope and opportunity for those living at the margins in Chicago, our K–12 schools and community colleges reinforce existing social and economic stratifications. As a city, we must no longer tolerate segregated and stratified educational systems. We must also refuse to accept public policy decisions that reinforce existing class distinctions and allow institutionalized educational inequalities to persist. It is time to reunite the two educational cities of Chicago. We must provide equal access and opportunities for learning to everyone: rich and poor, white and minority. Chicago's separate and increasingly unequal system of education at all levels cannot be allowed to continue.

NOTES

1. "A Portrait of Segregation in New York City's Schools." 2013. *New York Times*, May 11. www.nytimes.com/interactive/2012/05/11/nyregion/segregation-in-new-york-city-public-schools.html?_r=0
2. Jordan, Reed. 2014. "America's public schools remain highly segregated." *Urban Wire*, August 27. www.urban.org/urban-wire/americas-public-schools-remain-highly-segregated
3. "Stats and Facts." 2015. Chicago Public Schools, February. http://cps.edu/About_CPS/At-a-glance/Pages/Stats_and_facts.aspx
4. "Stats and Facts." 2015. Chicago Public Schools, February. http://cps.edu/About_CPS/At-a-glance/Pages/Stats_and_facts.aspx
5. Bogira, Steve. 2013. "Three families tell us why they ditched CPS." *Chicago Reader*, September 24. www.chicagoreader.com/chicago/cps-alternatives-suburbs-magnet-selective-enrollment-lowincome/Content?oid=11046489
6. Bogira, Steve. 2013. "Three families tell us why they ditched CPS." *Chicago Reader*, September 24. www.chicagoreader.com/chicago/cps-alternatives-suburbs-magnet-selective-enrollment-lowincome/Content?oid=11046489
7. Francisco, Tonya, and WGN Web Desk. 2014. "The competitive world of selective enrollment school admission in Chicago." WGN, June 24, 2014. http://wgntv.com/2014/05/23/a-look-at-the-competitive-world-of-selective-enrollment-school-admission-in-chicago/
8. Wong, Alia. 2014. "The Cutthroat World of Elite Public Schools." *Atlantic*, December 4.
9. Francisco, Tonya, and WGN Web Desk. 2014. "The competitive world of selective enrollment school admission in Chicago." WGN, June 24, 2014. http://wgntv.com/2014/05/23/a-look-at-the-competitive-world-of-selective-enrollment-school-admission-in-chicago/
10. Nitkin, Alex. 2016. "CPS Selective-Enrollment High School Letters Are Being Sent Friday." *DNAInfo*, February 18. www.dnainfo.com/chicago/20160218/downtown/when-will-cps-selective-enrollment-high-school-acceptance-letters-be-sent
11. Chicago Community Trust. *Generation All*. www.generationallchicago.org/about-us/
12. "Best High Schools in Illinois." 2015. *U.S. News & World Report*. www.usnews.com/education/best-high-schools/illinois
13. Chicago Public Schools. http://cps.edu/Schools/Find_a_school/Pages/findaschool.aspx
14. Ibid.
15. Perez, Juan Jr. 2014. "CPS gives schools new ratings to judge success and trouble." *Chicago Tribune*, December 3. www.chicagotribune.com/news/local/breaking/chicago-school-rating-update-met-20141203-story.html
16. "How CPS schools stack up under new rating system." 2014. *Chicago Tribune*, December 3. www.chicagotribune.com/chi-new-chicago-school-rating-infographic-20141203-htmlstory.html

17. Chicago Public Schools. http://cps.edu/Schools/Find_a_school/Pages/findaschool.aspx

18. Chicago Public Schools. http://cps.edu/Schools/Find_a_school/Pages/findaschool.aspx

19. Ibid.

20. Ibid.

21. Chicago Public Schools. http://cps.edu/Schools/Find_a_school/Pages/findaschool.aspx

22. Keefe, Alex. 2013. "Emanuel: CPS school closures 'not taken lightly,' but must be done." *WBEZ*, March 23. www.wbez.org/news/emanuel-cps-school-closures-not-taken-lightly-must-be-done-106253

23. "Chicago board votes to close 50 schools." 2013. *CNN*, May 22. www.cnn.com/2013/05/22/us/illinois-chicago-school-closures/

24. Lutz, B.J., and Michelle Relerford. 2013. "CPS to Shutter 54 Schools in Closure Plan." NBC, March 21. www.nbcchicago.com/blogs/ward-room/chicago-public-school-closures-199247301.html

25. Austen, Ben. 2013. "The Death and Life of Chicago." *New York Magazine*, May 29.

26. Keefe, Alex. 2013. "Emanuel: CPS school closures 'not taken lightly,' but must be done." *WBEZ*, March 23. www.wbez.org/news/emanuel-cps-school-closures-not-taken-lightly-must-be-done-106253

27. "Did Chicago make the right decision to close 50 schools?" 2013. Race Matters Institute, June 5. www.racemattersinstitute.org/blog/chicago-schools

28. Coen, Jeff, David Heinzmann, and John Chase. 2012. "Emanuel's push for more charter schools is in full swing." *Chicago Tribune*, September 24. http://articles.chicagotribune.com/2012-09-24/news/ct-met-charter-schools-chicago-strike-20120924_1_charter-schools-charter-networks-resources-from-neighborhood-schools

29. Hinz, Greg. 2014. "Chicago's charter-schools experiment flops." *Crain's Chicago Business*, October 13. www.chicagobusiness.com/article/20141013/BLOGS02/141019962?template=printart

30. Chicago Public Schools. http://cps.edu/Schools/Find_a_school/Pages/findaschool.aspx

31. Strauss, Valerie. 2014. "Where Gates money is going in education world this year." *Washington Post*, May 16. www.washingtonpost.com/blogs/answer-sheet/wp/2014/05/16/where-gates-money-is-going-in-education-world-this-year/

32. Perez, Juan Jr. 2015. "CPS charter debate smoldering in Chicago and Springfield." *Chicago Tribune*, May 21. www.chicagotribune.com/news/local/breaking/ct-chicago-charter-school-debate-met-20150522-story.html

33. Institute on Metropolitan Opportunity at the University of Minnesota Law School. 2014. *Charter schools in Chicago: No model for education*, p. 1.

34. Fitzpatrick, L. 2014. "Study: Charter schools have worsened school segregation." *Chicago Sun-Times*, October 13. http://breakingnews.suntimes.com/chicago/study-charter-schools-have-worsened-school-segregation/

35. Lipman, Pauline. 2012. "A Battle Between Education and Business Goals." *New York Times*, September 12.

36. Perez, Juan Jr. 2015. "Study looks at aftermath of Chicago school closings in 2013." *Chicago Tribune*, January 22. www.chicagotribune.com/news/local/breaking/ct-chicago-school-closings-study-met-20150122-story.html

37. V.V.B. 2015. "The scandal at the top of America's third-largest school system." *Economist*, October 15.

38. V.V.B. 2015. "The scandal at the top of America's third-largest school system." *Economist*, October 15.

39. V.V.B. 2015. "The scandal at the top of America's third-largest school system." *Economist*, October 15.

40. Eaton, Fran, and Dennis LaComb. 2015. "Chicago Public School Superintendent indicted thanks to mother with a blog." *Watchdog*, October 13. http://watchdog.org/242143/chicago-public-school-superintendent-indicted/

41. Perez, Juan Jr. 2016. "Chicago Public Schools debt further downgraded by Standard and Poor's." *Chicago Tribune*, January 16. www.chicagotribune.com/news/local/breaking/ct-chicago-schools-bond-rating-downgrade-met-0116-20160116-story.html

42. Sawchuk, Stephen, and Denisa R. Superville. 2016. "Long Building, Chicago Schools' Fiscal Crisis Reaches Boiling Point." *Education Week*, May 16.

43. Perez, Juan Jr. 2016. "State says CPS doesn't warrant financial intervention." *Chicago Tribune*, May 6. www.chicagotribune.com/news/local/breaking/ct-cps-state-financial-investigation-met-20160506-story.html

44. The Education Trust. 2015. Press Release: Students Who Need the Most Continue to Get the Least, March 25. https://edtrust.org/press_release/students-who-need-the-most-continue-to-get-the-least/

45. CPS Office of Communication. 2015. Press Release: *CPS Calls For Springfield to Provide "20 for 20,"* November 17. http://cps.edu/News/Press_releases/Pages/PR1_11_17_2015.aspx

46. Perez, Juan Jr., Grace Wong, and Tyler Davis. 2016. "Chicago Teachers Union, police reform group rally for tax hike, elected oversight." *Chicago Tribune*, June 22. www.chicagotribune.com/news/local/politics/ct-chicago-school-board-teacher-rally-met-20160622-story.html

47. Biasco, Paul. 2016. "Aldermen Push To Use TIF Surplus Money to Prevent CPS Cuts," January 20, *DNAChicago*. www.dnainfo.com/chicago/20160120/logan-square/aldermen-push-use-tif-surplus-money-prevent-cps-cuts

48. Florida, Richard. 2014. "Class-Divided Cities: Chicago Edition." *Atlantic: CityLab*, February 4. www.citylab.com/housing/2013/02/class-divided-cities-chicago-edition/4306/

49. Ibid.

50. "The Global Edge: An Agenda for Chicago's Future." 2007. The Chicago Council on Global Affairs, p. 43.

51. "The Global Edge: An Agenda for Chicago's Future." 2007. The Chicago Council on Global Affairs, p. 43.

52. "High School Teaching for the Twenty-First Century: Preparing Students for College." 2007. Alliance for Excellent Education, September.

53. Ibid.

54. Friedman, Thomas L. 2005. "It's a Flat World, After All," *New York Times*, April 3.

55. "Fiscal Year 2013: Statistical Digest," 2013. City Colleges of Chicago. www.ccc.edu/menu/Documents/CCC-FYStatisticalDigest2013.pdf

56. Fain, P. 2012. "Price of success." *Inside Higher Education*, January 16.

57. Strahler, Steven. 2015. "How City Colleges inflates graduation rates." *Crain's Chicago Business*, October 17. www.chicagobusiness.com/article/20151017/issue01/310179995/how-city-colleges-inflates-graduation-rates

58. Ibid.

59. Ibid.

60. Emanuel, Rahm. 2011. Chicago's plan to match education with jobs. *Wall Street Journal*, December 19.

61. City Colleges of Chicago. N.D. *About City Colleges of Chicago.* ttp://www.ccc.edu/menu/Pages/About-City-Colleges.aspx

62. Ylisela, J. 2012. "Is City Colleges doing the right thing?" *Crain's Chicago Business*, October 20.

63. Ylisela, J. 2012. "Is City Colleges doing the right thing?" *Crain's Chicago Business*, October 20.

64. Gonzalez, J. 2011. "Chancellor seeks to transform institution that changed her life." *Chronicle of Higher Education*, April 10.

65. Goodman, Larry. 2012. Quoted in Ylisela, J. 2012. "Is City Colleges doing the right thing?" *Crain's Chicago Business*, October 20.

66. Strahler, Steven. 2015. "How City Colleges inflates graduation rates." *Crain's Chicago Business*, October 17. www.chicagobusiness.com/article/20151017/issue01/310179995/how-city-colleges-inflates-graduation-rates

67. Reyes, Hector. 2012. Quoted in Ylisela, J. 2012. "Is City Colleges doing the right thing?" *Crain's Chicago Business*, October 20.

68. Hampton, Branden. 2016. "South Side students face long commutes as Chicago City Colleges consolidate programs." *Chicago Mosaic*. http://chicago-mosaic.medill.northwestern.edu/city-colleges-race/

69. Smith, Ashley A. 2016. "Completion and Controversy." *Inside Higher Ed*, February 16. www.insidehighered.com/news/2016/02/16/despite-improved-graduation-rates-city-colleges-chicago-chancellor-faces-faculty

Tourism Policy and Chicago's Urban Identity

By Costas Spirou

In the context of the new economy and the role amenities play as drivers of growth, Chicago competes with other cities to advance its urban tourism infrastructure. Chicago's substantial tourist infrastructure in the form of museums, parks, stadiums, and convention centers produce a multitude of other related amenity services. This paper examines the role of structure and agency as it relates to the creation of the tourism industry. Investment in Chicago's tourist infrastructure has been shaped by political forces, civic groups, corporations and social/cultural trends.

INTRODUCTION

Urban tourism and policies that advance its promotion, as well as cultural planning that affirm past heritage and construct new destinations are increasingly becoming commonly used strategies in urban centers across the world. Cities pursue the creation and maintenance of comprehensive visions to assess current resources, induce the rebirth of existing cultural assets, develop new ones, invest in physical infrastructure and commit to related policies; all actions occurring within complex social, political and economic milieus.

In this article, I present the current development of urban tourism in Chicago and conclude with some reflections on the role of structure and agency, as well as the unique issues that arise within this new economy. I do not subscribe to the position that the role of the consumer is the key factor in the tourism production process, almost singe-handedly determining the creation of this industry. While the consumer plays an important role, just as critical is the investment and creation of the infrastructure that occurs within a complicated set of circumstances, shaped by political forces, civic groups, corporate interests and general social trends. These, I believe, serve as the fundamental elements in the making of the tourism industry. The tourist experience is thus informed by an appropriate infrastructure and a positive perception of the need to visit the "tourist bubble" is predetermined by the process of producing that desire.[1]

A NEW ERA OF TOURISM: INFRASTRUCTURAL DEVELOPMENT ALONG THE LAKEFRONT

Following his election as mayor in 1989, Richard M. Daley brought an intense commitment to advancing culture and tourism in Chicago. Since then, the city has experienced a considerable construction boom of amenities along the lakefront, extensive efforts toward beautification and numerous festivals and related programming aiming to help grow the local economy. Daley's commitment can be drawn from the fact that during his first decade in office (1989-2000) twelve from a total of twenty events managed by the Mayor's Office of Special Events (now part of the Chicago Department of Cultural Affairs & Special Events) were instituted. In addition, during the last ten years of his tenure, additional events as well as multi-billion dollar construction projects adorned the lakefront including Navy Pier, Millennium Park, Soldier Field, the Museum Campus and the conversion of Meigs Field.

In 1989 the city embarked on a plan that would redevelop its 3,300-foot pier just north of Grant Park. Completed in 1995, Navy Pier cost over $200 million and presented the public with many new attractions including the Chicago Children's Museum, a 32,000 square foot indoor botanical garden, a 15 story Ferris Wheel, street entertainment areas with outdoor stages, an IMAX theatre, retail concessions, restaurants, food courts, a skyline stage, a festival hall, a huge ballroom, and 50 acres of parks and promenades. The project had a considerable impact on the nearby communities including the revitalization of housing in the adjacent neighborhood of Streeterville.[2] In the Fall of 1999, the complex was the recipient of a $27 million, 900 seat Chicago Shakespeare Theatre, significantly diversifying its overall use.[3] The Pier renovations were so extensive that the location was unable to maintain its prior status on the National Register of Historic Places.[4]

The Pier is the most popular attraction in the City of Chicago. According to the Chicago Office of Tourism and the Chicago Convention and Tourism Bureau, its attendance exceeded 7 million in 1997. By 2003, 8.7 million visited the pier generating $45.8 million and by 2012, the pier attracted 9.2 million.

According to recent data from the Office of Marketing and Business Partnerships at Navy Pier, 65 percent of the visitors reside in the Chicagoland area with an average household income of $84,000.[5] The majority (82 percent), are between the ages of 21-54 and more than 80 percent stay on the grounds for three hours or more. The most popular events include the Fireworks during the summer months (1.4 million visitors) and the Winter WonderFest every December (600,000 visitors). Navy Pier is currently undergoing a significant redevelopment which is expected to cost $115 million. It is viewed by Chicagoans and tourists alike as a center of entertainment and recreation and it generates substantial tax revenue for the city.

The Lakefront Millennium Project is the most recent, culturally-based development effort of the Richard M. Daley administration. Mayor Daley announced in 1998 his plan for a major expansion of the park system along the lakefront. The new park was constructed on rail yard land and was originally estimated to cost $150 million with over $120 million to be generated from revenue bonds. The remaining funds were to be derived from corporate sponsors and private donations. On 16.5 acres, the new space was to include an outdoor performance stage, an indoor theatre, a skating rink, gardens, and concession stands. The Grant Park Symphony would perform at this new location and the city would utilize the amenities for other musical festivals. Proceeds from the two-level, 2,500 space parking garage, scheduled to be constructed underneath the park, would be used to pay off the bonds and the project would open in the summer of 2000.[6]

Within a year, the plan was substantially expanded to include additional amenities such as a warming house and a restaurant for an ice skating rink, an increase of the planned indoor theatre seating from 500 to a 1,500-seat auditorium, a commuter bicycle center, a glass green house hall and an improved music pavilion design with good sight lines. This new plan also resulted in expanding the park to 24.6 acres. According to Ed Uhlir, Millennium Park Project Director: "Grant Park is Chicago's front yard. Sadly this 16-acre corner of the park has been a blight for too long. Millennium Park will remedy that with a plan that brings Chicagoans together on a year-round basis."[7]

The Millennium Park Project was hampered by cost overruns and delays. For example, initially scheduled to be completed in 2000, Frank Gehry's band shell opened in the summer of 2004. While early cost estimates required $17.8 million for the structure, the actual cost ballooned to $50 million. Initial projections for the flowing stainless steel bridge were around $8 million but surpassed the $13 million mark.[8] The cost of the entire park development reached $500 million when it finally opened in 2004. While earlier, Mayor Daley in a letter to the people of Chicago described the Millennium Park as "an exciting new cultural destination for families and children, and an economic magnet for visitors and conventioneers" he later, indirectly acknowledging its development challenges, placed the project in a historical context by indicating that this is a "...civic project [that] marks the new Millennium as no other project ever before undertaken in the history of Chicago."[9]

Millennium Park attracted 1.5 million visitors during its first year and attendance reached 5 million ten years later in 2014. More interestingly, though the opening of the park has brought about changes both in the surrounding area as well as in the public policy front. Aqua tower, a new 82 story skyscraper to the north of the park, was completed in 2010. According to Gerard Kenny, a Chicago real estate developer "The opening of Millennium Park made this [skyscraper project] thing go."[10] Similarly, the nearby Streeterville neighborhood experienced an unprecedented residential boom that included the construction of 13 new high-rises. That increased by one third the influx of new apartments and condominiums to the neighborhood, totaling 12,523 units.[11]

Local government officials also realized that the world class park positively impacted the property values across the Loop. As a result, in the Fall of 2005 the city considered a new tax on the downtown area. The funds from this special property tax district, estimated at about $18 million annually, would support the $7 million operating and maintenance park budget. According to a city spokeswoman "This is a way of looking at keeping the downtown vital and making sure that it continues to be the attraction and destination that it is right now."[12] In early October of 2005, following vocal opposition by business leaders and property owners,

Mayor Daley withdrew support of the tax proposal. The growth of the surrounding area has been extensive and real estate capital investment has been significant. In 2015, plans are underway for the Wanda Vista tower. Designed by Studio Gang Architects, this $950 million project would be completed in 2019 and become the third tallest building in the city's skyline. At 93 stories tall, the structure would provide more than 400 residential units and a 169 room hotel.[13]

To the southern edge of Grant Park, the development of the Museum Campus can be viewed as one of the most aggressive plans of Mayor Daley's culturally-driven redevelopment agenda during the last decade. The vision to join the grounds of the Field Museum of Natural History, the Shedd Aquarium and the Adler Planetarium and thus create a museum campus, required the re-routing of northbound, five traffic lane, Lake Shore Drive, which cut through and separated these cultural institutions. With the approval of a bond in 1994 for the expansion of nearby McCormick Place (Chicago's major convention center) funds were allocated for the South Lake Shore Drive project. At a cost of more than $120 million, the Metropolitan Pier and Exposition Authority carried out the project with city and state financial resources.[14]

After the completion of the relocation of Lake Shore Drive to the west, additional work was conducted to add 57 more area acres, including expansive greenways, massive landscaping, raised terraces, sidewalks and land bridges designed to cover the old multilane thoroughfare. To put into perspective the size of this project, consider that more than 120,000 cubic yards of dirt were displaced and the ground was lowered by as much as 22 feet to create a tiered lawn.[15] The purpose of the Museum Campus has been to create a destination place and increase the attendance of Chicagoans and tourists at the three museums.

Meigs Field and Soldier Field have also added to the infrastructural development and amenities necessary for further developing Chicago as a city of tourism. Meigs Field was a small airport along the lakefront providing business leaders with easy access to downtown Chicago. Following the end of a 50 year airport lease in 1996 with the Chicago Park District, Mayor Daley put forth a proposal to create a 91-acre park at a projected cost of $27.2 million. The plan would link the park to the Museum Campus and would include botanical gardens, playgrounds, wetlands, a nature center and a sensory garden for the visually or hearing impaired. The island would be accessible by a ferry and a rubber-wheeled trolley. According to city projections the "superpark" would generate over $30 million a year in revenue from parking, concessions, souvenirs and other fees and it would draw more than 350,000 visitors annually. This environmental park would be fully accessible to the disabled as ramps would extend to the lake, fully accommodating those using strollers and wheelchairs.[16]

The plan faced political opposition by then Governor Jim Edgar, who argued that closing Meigs would negatively affect the transportation of the region. The state filed a lawsuit to take control of the property, eventually resulting in a compromise that would allow the airfield to remain open for an additional five years. Following that operation term the city would proceed with its plans to create a park on Northerly Island. In 2001 the State and the City agreed to keep Meigs Field open until 2006. Yet, the federal portion of the agreement did not pass, setting the stage for the March 2003, middle-of-the-night destruction of the runway. Large X-shaped markings were carved out in the center of the runway by city equipment, ending the history of the Field as an airport, and giving complete control of the space to the mayor.

In the summer of 2005 the Charter One Pavilion opened at Northerly Island, a 7,500-seat venue offering outdoor concerts and live entertainment to music fans.[17] Renamed FirstMerit Bank Pavilion, the structure was expanded in 2013 to accommodate 30,000 spectators. Nearby Soldier Field, home of the Chicago Bears of the National Football League (NFL), has also become part of this culturally-based image advanced by Mayor Daley. Located adjacent to the Museum Campus to the south, Soldier Field opened in 1924 and since then it has been identified as an integral part of the city. The facility is owned and operated by the Chicago Park District and its major tenants, the Bears, have been leasing the stadium. The relationship between the city and the ownership of the team has been contentious, especially after 1986 when the team won the Super Bowl and began to argue against the antiquated Soldier Field, advancing pressure for a brand new facility with a large number of luxury skyboxes.

As the team explored multiple options both in the city, the suburbs and even in neighboring Indiana, Mayor Daley continued to support the Soldier Field choice. Stadium development has proven capable of reshaping urban space even at the neighborhood/community level.[18] Because of its lakefront location and its proximity to the Museum Campus a new facility would complement the city of culture theme.

In the summer of 2000, following many years of "battles" over locations and financing, Bears officials and Mayor Daley settled old differences and jointly began to promote an ambitious proposal for a new stadium that included substantial redevelopment of the surrounding areas. Daley also took another step in his campaign "to restore the Lakefront", a central piece of his administration's ongoing effort to improve Chicago's downtown and near downtown public spaces.[19]

The cost of the Soldier Field renovation surpassed the $680 million mark, with the Bears contributing $200 million, and the remaining financed by Chicago's two percent hotel-motel tax. The Illinois Sports Facilities Authority (ISFA), an agency created to oversee construction of another Chicago stadium, the New Comiskey Park in the late 1980's, issued bonds to cover the city's share of stadium construction costs. The physical plan specified a new football stadium set within, though also rising substantially above, the classical colonnades crowning Soldier Field's east and west facades. Extensive underground parking was added and surface parking areas to the south of the stadium were landscaped, adding more that fifteen acres of green space to the lakefront.

Overall, 1,300 trees of 45 different species were planted, a sledding hill was configured and a children's garden was created.[20] The new facility opened in 2003, and is in concert with the city's larger vision of keeping Soldier Field as part of the lakefront, positioning it as an additional piece to the available entertainment venues along Chicago's front yard.[21]

Daley's commitment to advancing the tourism industry persisted over the years through these infrastructural developments. In his 2003 inaugural address, he reaffirmed this position, charting the future of this sector of the economy: "And we must continue to enhance the competitive advantage of our tourism and convention industry, which attracts thirty million visitors to Chicago each year, pumping some $8 billion a year into the Chicago economy."[22]

THE CYCLICAL NATURE OF TOURISM: TURNING THE CORNER AFTER SEPTEMBER 11TH?

In his 2000 State of the City address, Mayor Daley proudly exclaimed: "And with tourism numbers at an all time high, the rest of the world is finally discovering what we have known for a long time: Chicago is a beautiful, diverse, welcoming and culturally rich city-on a par with the greatest cities in the world.[23] A few months later, at a speech during the opening of the annual meeting of the Chicago Convention and Tourism Bureau, the Mayor proclaimed his vision, asserting that he wants Chicago to be "on the leading edge of tourism and travel."[24] By that time the city had invested enormous resources in infrastructure and had promoted itself in a way capable of realizing this vision.

Following the September 11 attacks, Chicago tourism experienced a decline that lasted close to three years. But all of these efforts referenced in the previous section altered Chicago's image as Mayor Daley explained in a speech at the Massachusetts Institute of Technology: "Visitors are often surprised at Chicago's beauty. Some of them come to Chicago expecting Carl Sandburg or Nelson Algren. Instead, they find Martha Stewart."[25]

Since his election into office, current Mayor Rahm Emanuel has approached the development of the tourist industry with the same zeal as his predecessor. In 2014 Emanuel announced that his administration set a new goal of 55 million visitors to the city by 2020. This would be the outcome of an ambitious plan that would involve an ambitious marketing campaign with the theme "Be Part of Something Epic: Chicago." The goal of the campaign is to attract tourists from California, Denver and the East Coast. Internationally, the focus would be placed on Canada, Mexico and China. Emanuel noted ""At every level, this is a great place, a very affordable place to have a world-class experience, and you don't have to go to New York to do that."[26]

The most recent data available from Choose Chicago, the official destination marketing organization for Chicago reveals considerable success. In 2013, an all-time record in room occupancy and other areas were achieved (See Table 1). Similarly, the monthly occupancy and average daily rates between January 2014 and March 2015 continue to improve (Table 2). Finally, as Table 3 shows, visitation rates for domestic and overseas visitors are at record highs.

Table 1. Drivers of Chicago's Tourism

	2007	2008	2009	2010	2011	2012	2013
Occupancy Rate (%)	75.18	71.50	67.24	69.78	72.14	75.16	75.28
Average Daily Rate	$198.23	$201.24	$164.28	$169.55	$177.25	$187.18	$191.95
Supply (million)	11.214	11.745	12.158	12.492	12.749	12.862	13.136
Demand (million)	8.431	8.397	8.175	8.716	9.197	9.666	9.889

Source: Choose Chicago

Table 2. Monthly Occupancy and Average Daily Rate (ADR) January 2014 to March 2015

Month	Average Daily Rate	Occupancy
March '15	$170.61	71.2%
February '15	$140.99	57.1%
January '15	$139.20	51.1%
December '14	$165.15	65.6%
November '14	$215.32	77.1%
October '14	$233.51	84.4%
September '14	$234.20	86.9%
August '14	$197.39	88.1%
July '14	$202.61	87.4%
June '14	$237.07	88.1%
May '14	$277.59	85.2%
April '14	$174.62	76.6%
March '14	$158.35	68.2%
February '14	$136.29	55.2%
January '14	$124.70	44.1%

Source: STR, Inc

Table 3. Visitation Rates, 2007-2013

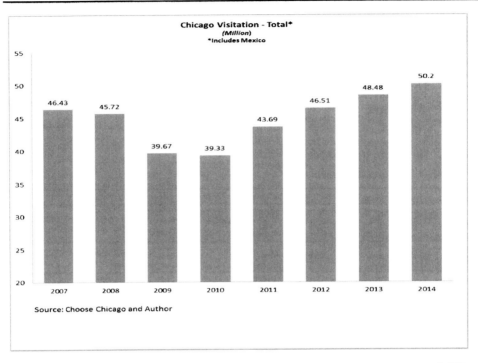

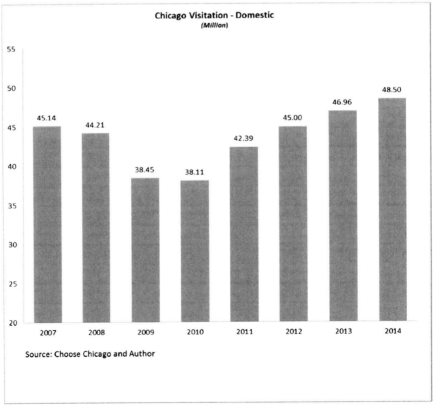

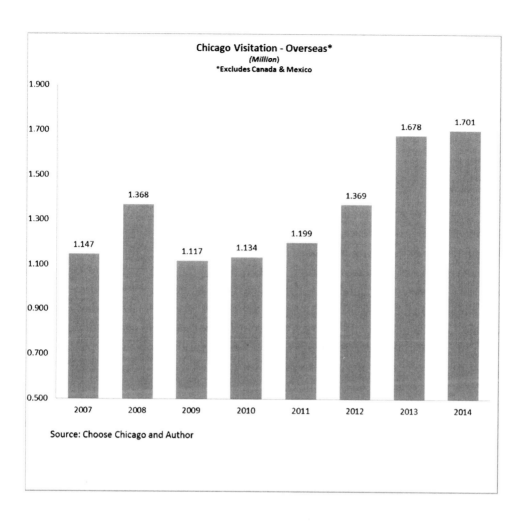

Chicago Visitation - Overseas*
(Million)
*Excludes Canada & Mexico

Source: Choose Chicago and Author

THE CHICAGO METROPOLITAN REGIONAL TOURISM DEVELOPMENT

But it is also other cities, on the periphery of the metropolitan area, that have invested in the development of their downtown via tourism. For example, the City of Aurora, located about 35 miles west of downtown Chicago, on the banks of the Fox River. Following its incorporation in 1845, Aurora slowly evolved into a manufacturing center. In the mid-1850s, the Chicago, Burlington and Quincy Railroad Company, which operated from 1849 to 1970, placed its railcar factory and maintenance facilities within Aurora's borders. The facility closed down in 1974, largely due to the completion of the Eisenhower Expressway, which allowed commuters to bypass the city on their way from the western suburbs to the Loop.[27]

The recession of the 1970s put more pressure on the local economy, forcing many of the factories and businesses to shut down. The large suburban malls that opened close by lured shoppers away from an increasingly dilapidated downtown. For example, the 1975 development of the Fox Valley Center, adjacent to the city's eastern Naperville border, introduced a sea of trendy, new stores. A bit further east, the self-enclosed Oakbrook Center opened in 1962. The Oakbrook mega mall complex saw successive expansions in 1973 and in 1981, affecting the economic future of many downtowns in the western suburbs.

During the late 1980s the Aurora City Council recognized that resurrecting its core was vital if the community was to rebound from its economic malaise. Downtown historic preservation has received special attention. Riverboat gambling and a casino located in the downtown in 1993, which created the resources and energy for a downtown renaissance. Façade restoration of existing historic structures and concern with the architectural detail of new developments gained momentum.[28] Between 1999 and 2004 more than 500 projects came under review and 60 building owners utilized special finance opportunities provided by the city to aid in the rehabilitation of the city center. In 2003, the first Downtown Heritage Tour and Cell-Phone Guided Walking Tour formally marketed the history of downtown Aurora to tourists.[29] Parades and children's activities, musicals and theater productions, outdoor performances, a popular Farmers Market and street vendors, have focused Aurora on a strategy that utilizes its developing downtown identity as a magnet to also entice businesses. Many of the city's recent promotional material reference the downtown area as a "Neighborhood," and broadly describe the city as "the Midwest's Newest Urban Lifestyle Community."

The addition of specialty restaurants and attention to formal gathering spaces like the Millennium Plaza, Rotary Park, Tivoli Plaza and the Sesquicentennial Park, have helped attract a housing development program that is expected to further fuel the vibrancy of the core. In addition to a major condominium complex, a 14-story hotel and an adjacent 100,000 square foot convention center have been proposed.[30] The key element making all this work is image. Aurora has bet its future on the motto of its celebrated son and local icon, Bud Meyer, a business leader and philanthropist who often publicly explained that "The image of the city is its downtown."[31]

Recent development in downtown Aurora included support for a burgeoning restaurant row, which has been linked to the demolition of several blocks of downtown dilapidated structures. The outcome has been the establishment of a number of new dining venues just west of the Hollywood Casino on New York Street. According to Sherman Jenkins, executive director of the Aurora Economic Development Commission. "And as the economy continues to inch its way back, we'll be ready as more developers and investors look to us."[32]

CONCLUSION

It is apparent that structural changes have impacted Chicago over the last five decades. De-industrialization, population decentralization and globalization have played a critical role, leaving the urban core subjected to disinvestment, decline and widespread social problems in housing and education amongst others. Within this rapidly evolving socioeconomic environment, cities are fiscally strained to provide needed social services to their residents. They increasingly identify urban tourism and its potential revenue capability as a viable response and a key economic development strategy to provide recreation and revenue.

The recent emergence of a new economy of leisure, amenities, and quality of life considerations have similarly shifted the interplay between structure and agency as cities not only view urban tourism as an economic development tool, but also as a recruiting mechanism capable of attracting new economy entrepreneurs and workers. In the last twenty-five years Chicago has made a deliberate effort to physically reorganize its lakefront and embrace the advancement of urban tourism as an economic development tool. However, the success of this strategy, hinges on a continuously concerted effort to maintain the needed organizational capacity in marketing and image building, while balancing that against the competitive desires of other cities that have also intensified their efforts to attract visitors to their locales.

NOTES

1. Judd, D. R. "Constructing the Tourist Bubble" in *The Tourist City*. D. R. Judd and Feinstein, S. S., Editors. New Haven: Yale University Press, 1999. Pages 35-53.
2. Kaiser, R. "Blazing a Trial Through Lost Chicago." *Chicago Tribune*. August 5, 1997; McCarron, J. "Downtown Unchained? The Building Boom is Back." *Chicago Tribune*, August 11, 1997; Bernstein, D. "Just a Quite Night at Home." *Crain's Chicago Business*, May 3, 2004.
3. Jones, C. "The Location is the Thing Chicago's Shakespeare Rep Poised for Move to Navy Pier, and Perhaps for Wider Recognition." *Chicago Tribune*, February 1, 1998.
4. Reardon, P. "Navy Pier off US Historic List. *Chicago Tribune*, February 18, 1992.
5. Muno, J. Sponsorship Overview. Office of Marketing and Business Partnerships, Navy Pier. 2014.
6. Shields, Y. "Chicago plans to issue for park expansion." Bond Buyer, April 324 (30364) (1998): 3, 6; Spirou, C. "Urban Beautification and the Construction of a New Municipal Identity in Chicago" in *The New Chicago: A Social and Cultural Analysis*, ed. by J. Koval, L. Bennett, F. Demissie and Bennett, M. Philadelphia: Temple University Press, 2006. Pages 294-303.
7. City of Chicago. New Millenium Plans Unveiled to Chicago Plan Commission on March 11, 1999. *Department of Transportation*, March 1999.
8. Kamin, B. "Reinventing the Lakefront: To Shape the Shoreline." *Chicago Tribune*, October 26, 1998.
9. City of Chicago. Chicago's Millennium Park. *Office of Tourism*, May 2003.
10. Corfman, T. "Mandarin Oriental Hotel Will Check In. *Chicago Tribune*, June 8, 2005.

11. Bergen, K., and Handley, J. "High-Speed High-Rises Stagger Streeterville." *Chicago Tribune*, July 17, 2005.

12. Gallun, A. and Heinz, G. "City Floats Tax Hike for Loop." *Crain's Chicago Business*, August 29, 2005.

13. Kamin, B. "Proposed Skyscraper Could be Third Tallest—or Fifth Tallest—in Chicago." *Chicago Tribune*, April 14, 2015.

14. Lake Shore Drive. *Planning*. February 61 (2) (1995): 42.

15. Kamin, B. "Reinventing the Lakefront: To Shape the Shoreline." *ChicagoTribune*, October 26, 1998.

16. Hill, J. and Borsky, D. "City Lifts Veil in Hopes for Meigs Wetlands, Botanical Gardens are included. *Chicago Tribune*, July 2, 1996.

17. Kot, G. "Stunning Skyline." *Chicago Tribune*, June 27, 2005.

18. Spirou, C. and Bennett, L. *It's Hardly Sportin': Stadiums, Neighborhoods and the New Chicago*. DeKalb: Northern Illinois University Press, 2003; Spirou, C. "Die Expansion von Stadien als kulturelle Strategie der Stadtplanung und Stadterneuerung in den USA" in *Das Stadion. Geschichte, Architektur, Politik, Oekonomie*. M. Marschik, R. Muellner, G. Spitaler and Zinganel, M., editors. Vienna: Turia & Kant, 2005. Pages 413-445.

19. Osnos, E. and Pearson, R. "Bears, City Says This Maybe Teal Deal for Soldier Field." *Chicago Tribune*. August 16, 2000.

20. Ford, L. "Soldier Field Landscaping Takes Shape." *Chicago Tribune*, April 26, 2004.

21. Spirou, C. and Bennett, L. "Revamped Stadium … New Neighborhood?" *Urban Affairs Review* 37 (2002): 675-702.

22. Daley, R. M. Inaugural Address. *Journal of the Proceedings*, City Council, May 5, 2003.

23. Daley, R. M. *State of the City Address*. January 19, 2000.

24. Daley, R.M. *Speech at the annual meeting of the Chicago Conventions and Tourism Bureau*, March 24, 2000.

25. Daley, R.M. *Richard M. Daley Remarks at MIT*, April 7, 2005.

26. Spielman, F. "Mayor Launches Plan to Boost Tourism Without Mentioning 'City Lights.'" *Chicago Sun-Times*. 2015.

27. City of Aurora. Alderman's Information Guide, Alderman's Office. June, 19, 2005.

28. Seigenthaler, K. "3 Paths Converge on Aurora's Downtown." *Chicago Tribune*. February 26, 1987.

29. City of Aurora. 2003/2004 Annual Report. Aurora Economic Development Commission. Aurora, IL, 2004.

30. Garbe, D. "Hotel, Convention Center in Works for Aurora." *Chicago Sun-Times*. July 7, 2005.

31. Christensen, K. Downtown Aurora Newsletter. May 1, 2003.

32. McCarthy, J. "Aurora Downtown Vitality on the Menu: City Sees Restaurant Row's Growth as an Appetizer for Development." *Chicago Tribune*. April 9, 2010.

PART VI

Metropolitan Chicago

Introduction

At the beginning of the twentieth century, social scientists at the University of Chicago on the city's South Side sought descriptively and "scientifically" to capture urban land use growth patterns. The most famous was a model of concentric rings of growth. This model was used to describe Chicago at the turn of the twentieth century. As depicted in Figure 1, at the center was downtown Chicago: "the Loop," named after the original loop of the Chicago River, and later the Chicago Elevated tracks. Factories and slums surrounded this downtown area in the next circle out from the Loop. Further out were the working-class neighborhoods, and residential and commuter zones, each following the other.

Ernest Burgess (1925), who developed the concentric circle model, argued that there was a correlation between the distance from the downtown area of a city and the wealth of an area; wealthier families with the desire and means to escape the dirt, grime, and crime of the city tended to live further away from the downtown area. After World War II, wealthy families and the middle class moved even further away from the central city, into the emerging sprawl of the suburbs. Since 1950, more than 90 percent of growth in

Figure 1. Concentric Rings of Growth for Chicago.

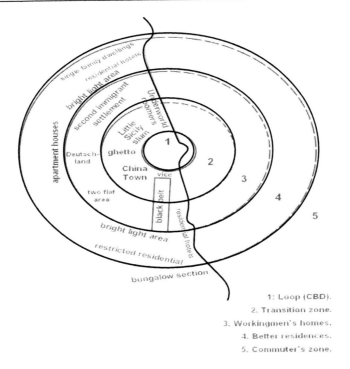

1: Loop (CBD).
2. Transition zone.
3. Workingmen's homes.
4. Better residences.
5. Commuter's zone.

Source: Adapted from Burgess, Ernest. 1925. *The City*. University of Chicago Press.

US metropolitan areas has occurred far away from central downtowns, in the suburbs. This mass migration to the suburbs was made possible by various federal public policies, like the 1944 Servicemen's Readjustment Act and the 1956 Interstate and Defense Highways Act. As shown Figure 2, in the decades following World War II, the Chicago metropolitan region continued its unsustainable sprawl, further and further away from the city.

Although the concentric ring model was never a perfect fit, it is even less so today. Chicago is no longer a compact urban area, surrounded by wealthy and white suburbs. Chicago is now part of a much larger metropolitan region with over 12 million people, spanning three states. Today, metropolitan areas are no longer neat concentric rings of growth like rings on a tree, but rather complicated systems, more like a human body with a heart and brain still in the downtown area, and networks of arteries, veins, nerves, and appendages stretching for many miles.

Today, a new migration is taking place. As described by many of the articles in this section, a demographic inversion is occurring throughout the Chicago region. Driven out of the city by global market forces and gentrification, lower-income and working-class families, along with new immigrants, are dispersing to the suburbs in search of cheaper housing and jobs. Inner-rung suburbs, once favored for their proximity to the central city

Figure 2. Developed Area, 1900–2005.

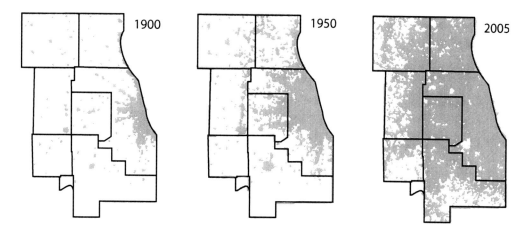

Source: U.S. Environmental Protection Agency and CMAP.

Figure 3. Share of the Region's Poor in Suburbs (Chicago Metropolitan Region), 2000–2013.

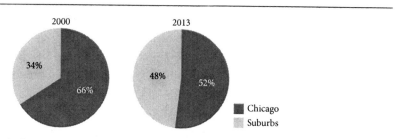

Adapted from: Heartland Alliance, 2016: "Poor By Comparison: Report on Illinois Poverty." Data from U.S. Census Bureau's 2000 decennial census and 2013 American Community Survey 1-year estimates program

and access to public transportation, are also being abandoned in favor of newer suburbs further away and accessible only by highways and interstates. As a result, our suburbs are becoming more diverse, both racially and economically.

Poverty in Chicago is no longer confined to the inner city. Cook County and Chicago now have a declining proportion of the regional poverty population, and our suburban communities now have an increasing proportion. As detailed in Figure 3, the Heartland Alliance has reported that the share of poverty between the city and the suburbs in the Chicago region is nearly an even 50/50, up from a 66/34 split between the city and suburbs in 2000. In DuPage County, one of the wealthiest counties in the United States, poverty has been growing at an alarming 63.3 percent.

Unfortunately, most suburban areas are ill prepared to deal with the increasing needs of the growing poor. One of the greatest challenges of suburban poverty is geography. Safety net programs for the poor have traditionally and more easily been provided in central cities. Public hospitals, nutrition assistance programs, child-care programs, and food banks are few and far between in sprawling suburban areas. The lack of adequate public transportation in the suburbs usually means that those who may benefit most from the sparse programs simply cannot get to them. Detailed by Chuck Sudo in this section, our region's lack of attention and investment in public transportation is also hampering economic development.

Suburban municipalities are facing their own financial challenges. Many still are reeling from the housing bubble burst of 2008, as prices for home sales are just now reaching what they were in 2005. Tumbling values and a glut of foreclosures and short sales in the past decade have resulted in lower property tax revenues. The impact of the 2008 recession also hit commercial and retail establishments, meaning less sales tax revenue for municipalities. Thus, municipalities that relied heavily on property and sales taxes and could not raise money any other way have been trying to make up revenue through federal and state grants. Yet, the state, also dealing with its own financial crisis, has been less able and unwilling to send money back to municipalities to fund local government services. As many Chicagoland suburbs face mounting debt, their problems are exacerbated by severely underfunded pension funds.

One of the greatest challenges facing the Chicago metropolitan region is the spatial mismatch between jobs and affordable housing. Increasingly, low- and moderate-income workers must move further from their jobs to find affordable housing, incurring greater commuter costs. Where the metropolitan job supply is growing, there is little affordable housing; and where the metropolitan job supply is decreasing, there is affordable housing.

The solution to this spatial mismatch between jobs and affordable housing is either better public transportation for reverse commuting, new low-cost housing in the suburbs, or some combination of the two. Land-use zoning policies which encourage high-density, mixed-use developments in the suburbs (as opposed to single-family homes on large lots) is needed. Unfortunately, exclusionary zoning laws, found in many suburban communities, make it nearly impossible for affordable housing to be built. Without regional planning and agreement, there is little incentive for well-to-do suburbs to become more inclusive. This metropolitan disconnect is exacerbated by the lack of a regional identity. City residents are loath to aid the suburbs, and vice versa. There is no metropolitan identity and no incentive to cooperate in the short term.

Created in 2006, the Chicago Metropolitan Agency for Planning (CMAP) serves as the region's official agency for comprehensive planning of land use and transportation. Although CMAP does not have taxing or enforcement powers, it has developed a regional "long-range comprehensive plan to link transportation, land use, the natural environment, economic prosperity, housing, and human and community development."[2] Listed below is a summary of some of the CMAP 2040 recommendations:

- Livable Communities

- Achieve Greater Livability through Land Use and Housing
- Manage and Conserve Water and Energy Resources
- Expand and Improve Parks and Open Space
- Promote Sustainable Local Food
- Human Capital
  - Improve Education and Workforce Development
  - Support Economic Innovation
- Efficient Governance
  - Reform State and Local Tax Policies
  - Improve Access to Information
  - Pursue Coordinated Investments
- Regional Mobility
  - Invest Strategically in Transportation
  - Increase Commitment to Public Transit
  - Create a More Efficient Freight Network

Some suburbs have taken these recommendations and written them directly into their development plans, but it has not been enough. Despite the efforts of CMAP and other regional organizations, politics and government in the Chicago metropolitan region remain in flux. Governmentally, the region remains fragmented, with some efforts at coordination occurring but no move to a regional government. As detailed in the articles which follow, mayors in suburban municipalities have come together with the mayor of Chicago in councils of government and mayoral organizations, but they have yet to reach agreement on controversial issues like affordable housing and creating a third airport.

NOTES

1. See http://www.ilpovertyreport.org/sites/default/files/uploads/PR15_Report_FINAL.pdf
2. Chicago Metropolitan Agency for Planning. 2014. "2040 Comprehensive Plan." www.cmap.illinois.gov/about/2040

Planning Chicago

By Carl Abbott

In this article, written for the Encyclopedia of Chicago, Carl Abbott traces the history of urban planning in Chicago and the "continuing challenge ... to craft political alliances and civic institutions to support physical efficiency and social equity across the entire metropolitan area."

Everyone plans. Businesses contemplate markets and products, social service agencies seek to improve service to their clients, workers think about retirement, politicians calculate their chances for reelection. In the language of urban history and policy, however, "planning" refers to efforts to shape the physical form and distribution of activities within a city. The objects of planning are sites and systems—the neighborhoods and places within which we carry on our lives and the networks that link the parts of a metropolitan area into a functioning whole. Planning shaped everything from Pullman and Hyde Park to the Chicago park system and the web of highways that knit together the metropolitan region.

* * *

Chicago's planning history offers a lesson that can be generalized to other American cities: efficiency is an easier goal than equity. Residents have found it relatively easy to agree and act on community needs that invite engineering solutions, for it has been possible to argue convincingly that canals, roads, sewers, and parks serve the entire population. Chicagoans have been less ambitious and less successful in shaping ideal communities that combine physical quality with social purpose. They have tried repeatedly to improve on the typical

Carl Abbott, "Planning Chicago," *The Encyclopedia of Chicago*, ed. James R. Grossman, Ann Durkin Keating, and Janice L. Reiff. Copyright © 2004 by Newberry Library. http://www.encyclopedia.chicagohistory.org. Reprinted with permission.

products of the real-estate market, but their experiments have faced often intractable issues of class and race. Success has usually required planning for narrowly defined segments of the middle class, while planning for socially inclusive communities at any large scale has built social conflict into the community fabric.

METROPOLITAN PLANNING

In the decades around the turn of the [20th] century, a widely shared metropolitan vision coalesced around the planning of systems to integrate the sprawling Chicago region. New York and Chicago epitomized the urban crisis of fin de siècle America, whose institutions seemed to be overwhelmed by waves of European immigration, increasing polarization of wealth, and the sheer complexity and congestion of the giant city. These challenges of headlong metropolitan growth called forth similar responses in both cities. Some Americans reacted with sweeping utopian or dystopian visions of the national future. Others searched for practical technological fixes such as electric lighting, improved sanitation, or electric streetcars and subways. Still others constructed ameliorative institutions such as settlement houses and began to lay the foundations of a modern welfare state with the social and economic reforms of Progressivism. And a significant minority worked to systematize the future growth of their cities, consolidating separate local governments into vast regional cities and developing regional plans for the extension of public services.

This story began in Chicago with the park system of the late nineteenth century. Although separate South, West, and Lincoln Park commissions (1869) served the three geographic divisions of the city, their investments and improvements worked together as a unified whole. Large semi-pastoral parks in the zone of the fastest residential growth allowed the poor and middle classes to enjoy temporary respite from the city. Broad boulevards connected the parks in a great chain from Lincoln Park to Jackson Park.

The annexation of 1889 tripled the area of the city; it took in established suburban communities and vast tracts of undeveloped land and set the stage for large public expenditures for water supply and sanitation. The Sanitary District of Chicago (1889) covered 185 square miles; its impressive regional accomplishment was construction of the Sanitary and Ship Canal (1900) and the reversal of the Chicago River to carry the city's waste into the Illinois and Mississippi Rivers. Annexation also paved the way for a metropolitan vision that achieved full expression in Daniel Burnham and Edward Bennett's *Plan of Chicago* of 1909. Promoted by a civic-minded business elite and widely embraced by middle-class Chicagoans, the "Burnham Plan" was an effort to frame the market (and the work of city builders) with a regional infrastructure of rationalized railroads, new highways, and regional parks to anticipate population growth. The plan knit downtown and neighborhoods, city and suburbs and surroundings, to a distance of 60 miles. It was to be implemented with public investments that would order and constrain the private market. The plan took the regional booster vision of the nineteenth century and transformed it into a concrete form and format for shaping a vast but functional cityscape.

Economically comprehensive as well as spatially unifying, the plan envisioned a Chicago that located management functions, production, and transportation in their most appropriate places. It assumed that the city would continue to be the fountainhead of industrial employment.

* * *

The commercial-civic elite mounted a vigorous campaign to put the Burnham Plan into action. The city established a unique City Plan Commission—a miniature city parliament of 328 businessmen, politicians, and civic leaders—to monitor and promote implementation. Advocates tirelessly preached the gospel of urban efficiency with newspaper and magazine stories (575 in 1912 alone), illustrated lectures, a motion picture, and *Wacker's Manual of the Plan of Chicago,* a summary text that introduced the Burnham Plan to tens of thousands of Chicago schoolchildren.

Chicagoans acted in accord with many of Burnham's prescriptions. The city acquired lakefront land for Grant Park, a stately open space to set off and contrast with the growing skyline. Creation of the Cook County Forest Preserve system implemented another set of recommendations. So did the extension of Roosevelt Road, improvement of terminals for railroad freight and passengers, movement of harbor facilities to Lake Calumet, and widening of North Michigan Avenue to allow expansion of the downtown office core.

As growth moved beyond the city limits, civic leaders in 1923 organized the semipublic Chicago Regional Planning Association. This effort to keep alive the planning vision of the 1910s was a forum for the voluntary coordination of local government plans outside the direct control of Chicago. Involving municipalities from three states, it had substantial success in coordinating park expansion and highways. However, the growing scale of the metropolitan area also introduced the erosive problem of suburban independence and competition for growth that would dominate regional planning in the United States in remaining decades of the century.

The Burnham Plan was certainly not perfect—it spoke to social issues indirectly at best—but it did place the question of good urban form at the center of the public agenda and held up Chicago as a model for wide-ranging thought about metropolitan futures. A publication entitled *Chicago's World-Wide Influence* (1913) trumpeted the importance of Chicago planning. Burnham and Bennett had tried out their ideas in San Francisco and followed with consulting work in other cities. The *Plan of Chicago* was also a template for more "practical" comprehensive planning in the 1920s.

* * *

Since the 1920s, the civic ideal has eroded in the face of racial conflict, suburban self-sufficiency, industrial transition, and the daunting complexity of a huge metropolitan region. Like every other large American metropolis, Chicago has fragmented by race and place. At the same time, urban planning as a field of work began to splinter into poorly connected subfields. Advocates of public housing worked in the 1920s and 1930s for specific state and federal legislation. Proponents of improved social services became social workers and bureaucrats of the incipient welfare state. Engineers and builders of physical infrastructure concentrated on adapting a rail-based circulation system to automobiles, as with Chicago's Wacker Drive, Congress Expressway, and hundreds of miles of newly paved or widened thoroughfares. In Chicago and elsewhere, New Deal work relief programs reinforced the transmutation of comprehensive planning into a set of public works projects. City planners were left to effect incremental changes in private land uses by administering zoning regulations.

Chicagoans returned to the intentional creation of "better" communities with the help of the federal government after World War II. The Housing Acts of 1949 and 1954, the bases for an urban renewal program lasting until 1974, were intended as federal-local partnerships to rescue blighted city districts with exemplary reconstruction. But the politics of planning required that new or newly improved neighborhoods be homogeneous communities for single races or classes. This generation of neighborhood planning found it possible to bridge the chasms of class or race, but not both. The results were not necessarily bad, but they were neither as comprehensive nor as socially integrative as planning idealists might have hoped.

A central postwar imperative was how to keep white Chicagoans on the South Side in a time of heavy black migration and ghetto expansion. The city in the 1950s used urban renewal to clear low-rent real estate, attract new investment in middle-class housing, and buffer large civic institutions. A key example was the city's partnership with Michael Reese Hospital and Illinois Institute of Technology to create the new neighborhoods of Lake Meadows and Prairie Shores. High-rise apartments integrated middle-class whites and middle-class African Americans while displacing an economically diversified black neighborhood. The city and the University of Chicago worked together on a similar makeover of Hyde Park that preserved the university and a university-oriented neighborhood while building economic fences against lower-income African Americans. Federal funds also financed arrays of public housing towers, such as the Robert Taylor Homes, to hold black Chicagoans within the established ghetto.

Oak Park since the 1960s has offered an alternative approach to middle-class integration. Oak Park residents have used social engineering rather than land redevelopment to manage integration and harmonize some of the tensions of race and place. Working through private organization rather than municipal government, Oak Parkers have directly faced the problem of racial balance and quotas, marketing their town to white families and selected black families and steering other blacks to alternative communities.

The planned suburb of Park Forest (1948) tried to be inclusive by class (at least the range of the middle class). In so doing, however, it was solving a problem of the last century rather than directly addressing the issues of race and suburban isolation. The Park Forest plat reflected the best of midcentury suburban design, using superblocks to reduce the impact of automobiles and assembling the blocks into neighborhood units with neighborhood parks and schools. It also mixed single-family homes and two-story garden apartments so that upward mobility was possible within the same community. Park Forest has nonetheless gained increasing racial variety, emerging in the 1980s as another example of successful integration.

Park Forest, like Riverside, Evanston, and Pullman in the previous century, also assumed that men and women operated in separate spheres. Such communities turned inward on home and neighborhood for women and children while opening out to the workplace for men. This social vision would prove fragile as social customs changed and a majority of American women entered the workforce by the 1970s.

Chicago's South Shore neighborhood offers a twist on the Park Forest story. Efforts to replicate the Hyde Park experience of racial integration failed in the 1960s and 1970s, in part because of the contrast between middle-class whites and working-class blacks. Instead, it has gained as a broadly based African American neighborhood with the help of development efforts orchestrated by the community-oriented South Shore Bank (now ShoreBank).

In a less progressive variation on the Oak Park and South Shore examples, the private sector has increasingly controlled downtown redevelopment in the interests of business corporations and their professional and managerial employees. Through the 1960s, redevelopment initiative remained with the city because urban renewal put local governments in control of land acquisition. The University of Illinois campus in Chicago was built on lands acquired through urban renewal. In a variation on the Hyde Park / University of Chicago story, it transformed tracts originally intended for replacement housing into a pioneering public campus. As federal urban renewal funds dried up with the Housing and Community Development Act (1974) and the Reagan administration, however, the public sector lost most of its capacity to act directly. Efforts to leverage mixed-use development have met with success outside the Loop but left a gaping hole in the center of downtown during the 1990s.

Planning for regional systems, in contrast, has been more successful. Infrastructure planners can fall back on the rhetoric of technically sound proposals and sidestep direct confrontation with racial conflict. The Chicago Regional Plan Association issued *Planning for the Region of Chicago* in 1956. The Northeastern Illinois Planning Commission (NIPC) began work for a six-county region in 1957; it has issued and updated regional plans for water, open space, recreation, and land development. The 1962 plan of the Chicago Area Transportation Study (CATS) was a national model for transportation demand forecasting. CATS (now a federally recognized transportation planning organization) and NIPC have had the practical success of framing a regional road/rail system that reflects Burnham and Bennett's ideas and has kept the vast metropolis together.

Nevertheless, regional growth frameworks cannot themselves stem intraregional competition for jobs and upper-income residents. Mayor Richard M. Daley might admonish his suburban counterparts in 1997 that "we have to think of mass transit as a regional issue," point proudly to the continuing importance of downtown Chicago jobs, and convene meetings to discuss regional cooperation. Only the federal courts, however, have been able to override local isolationism on issues such as low-income housing.

CONCLUSION

In the civic moment of the late nineteenth and early twentieth centuries, business interest and "civic" interest converged around the physical redesign of the metropolis. Much of the private sector was self-consciously public in rhetoric and often in reality. Middle-class women as well as men shared a vision of a reformed city that was implicitly assimilationist. The well-oiled economic machinery of the metropolis would have a place for everyone; improved housing and public services would help to integrate newcomers into the social fabric.

Even as the imposing *Plan of Chicago* was being so vigorously promoted, however, Chicago's growing black population was posing a challenge that lay outside the intellectual framework of physical planning. The congratulatory report *Ten Years Work of the Chicago Plan Commission* (1920) made no reference to the bloody race riot of the previous year. In the second half of the century, planning fractured into technical specialties and efforts to improve pieces of the metropolis—downtown, historic districts, new suburbs, and the occasional integrated neighborhood. In a time when everyone acknowledges the economic unity of city regions, the continuing challenge is to reinvigorate the civic-mindedness that has served Chicago well in the past and to craft political alliances and civic institutions to support physical efficiency and social equity across the entire metropolitan area.

Remarks by the President at the Urban and Metropolitan Policy Roundtable on July 13, 2009

By President Barack Obama

I went to college in LA and New York, and law school across the river from Boston, I received my greatest education on Chicago's South Side, working at the local level to bring about change in those communities and opportunities to people's lives ...

And that experience also gave me an understanding of some of the challenges facing city halls all across the country. And I know that those challenges are particularly severe today because of this recession. Four in five cities have had to cut services, just when folks need it the most, and 48 states face the prospects of budget deficits in the coming fiscal year.

And that's one reason why we took swift and aggressive action in the first months of my administration to pull our economy back from the brink, including the largest and most sweeping economic recovery plan in our nation's history. If we had not taken that step, our cities would be in an even deeper hole, and state budget deficits would be nearly twice as large as they are right now, and tens of thousands of police officers and firefighters and teachers would be out of a job as we speak. And I think that all of you are aware of that.

But what's also clear is we're going to need to do more than just help our cities weather the current economic storm. We've got to figure out ways to rebuild them on a newer, firmer, stronger foundation for our future. And that requires new strategies for our cities and metropolitan areas that focus on advancing opportunity through competitive, sustainable, and inclusive growth ...

Now, the first thing we need to recognize is that this is not just a time of challenge for America's cities; it's also a time of great change. Even as we've seen many of our central cities continuing to grow in recent years, we've seen their suburbs and exurbs grow roughly twice as fast—that spreads homes and jobs and businesses to a broader geographic area. And this transformation is creating new pressures and problems, of course, but it's also opening up new opportunities, because it's not just our cities that are hotbeds of innovation anymore, it's our growing metropolitan areas.

And when I spoke to the U.S. Conference of Mayors last year, I tried to hone in on this point that what I think traditionally had been seen as this divide between city and suburb, that in some ways you've seen both city and suburb now come together and recognize they can't solve their problems in isolation; they've got to be paying attention to each other. And these metropolitan areas, they're home to 85 percent of our jobs and 90 percent of our economic output.

Now, that doesn't mean investing in America comes at the expense of rural America; quite the opposite. Investing in mass transit and high-speed rail, for example, doesn't just make our downtowns more livable; it helps our regional economies grow. Investing in renewable energy doesn't just make our cities cleaner; it boosts rural areas that harness that energy. Our urban and rural communities are not independent; they are interdependent.

So what's needed now is a new, imaginative, bold vision tailored to this reality that brings opportunity to every corner of our growing metropolitan areas—a new strategy that's about Southern Florida as much as Miami; that's about Mesa and Scottsdale as much as it's about Phoenix; that's about Aurora and Boulder and Northglenn as much as about Denver.

An early step was to appoint Adolfo Carrion as our first White House Director of Urban Affairs. And his team and he share my belief that our cities need more than just a partner—they need a partner who knows that the old ways of looking at our cities just won't do. And that's why I've directed the Office of Management and Budget, the Domestic Policy Council, the National Economic Council, and the Office of Urban Affairs to conduct the first comprehensive interagency review in 30 years of how the federal government approaches and funds urban and metropolitan areas so that we can start having a concentrated, focused, strategic approach to federal efforts to revitalize our metropolitan areas.

And we're also going to take a hard look at how Washington helps or hinders our cities and metro areas—from infrastructure to transportation; from housing to energy; from sustainable development to education. And we're going to make sure federal policies aren't hostile to good ideas or best practices on the local levels. We're going to put an end to throwing money at what doesn't work—and we're going to start investing in what does work and make sure that we're encouraging that.

Now, we began to do just that with my budget proposal, which included two investments in innovative and proven strategies. I just want to mention these briefly. The first, Promise Neighborhoods, is modeled on Geoffrey Canada's successful Harlem Children's Zone. It's an all-encompassing, all-hands-on-deck effort that's turning around the lives of New York City's children, block by block. And what we want to do is to make grants available for communities in other cities to jumpstart their own neighborhood-level interventions that change the odds for our kids.

The second proposal we call Choice Neighborhoods—focuses on new ideas for housing in our cities by recognizing that different communities need different solutions. So instead of isolated and monolithic public housing projects that too often trap residents in a cycle of poverty and isolate them further, we want to invest in proven strategies that actually transform communities and enhance opportunity for residents and businesses alike.

But we also need to fundamentally change the way we look at metropolitan development. For too long, federal policy has actually encouraged sprawl and congestion and pollution, rather than quality public transportation and smart, sustainable development. And we've been keeping communities isolated when we should have been bringing them together.

And that's why we've created a new interagency partnership on sustainable communities, led by Shaun Donovan, as well as Ray LaHood and Lisa Jackson. And by working together, their agencies can make sure that when it comes to development—housing, transportation, energy efficiency—these things aren't mutually exclusive; they go hand in hand. And that means making sure that affordable housing exists in close proximity to jobs and transportation. That means encouraging shorter travel times and lower travel costs. It means safer, greener, more livable communities.

So we're off to a good start. But the truth is, that Washington can't solve all of these problems that face our cities, and frankly, I know that cities don't expect Washington to solve all these problems. Instead of waiting for Washington, a lot of cities have already gone ahead and become their own laboratories for change and innovation, some leading the world in coming up with new ways to solve the problems of our time.

So you take an example like Denver. Their metropolitan area is projected to grow by one million residents over the next 15 years or so. But rather than wait for a congestion crisis, they're already at work on plans to build and operate a public transit system up to the challenge, and to surround that system with smart new housing, retail, and office development near each stop.

Philadelphia is an example of what's been called "urban agriculture." It may sound like an oxymoron, but one proposal is trying to make a situation where fresh, local food supplies are within a short walk for most city residents, which will have a direct impact not only on the economy and on the environment, but also make an immeasurable difference in the health of Americans.

Or Kansas City. One idea there focuses on transforming a low-income community into a national model of sustainability by weatherizing homes and building a green local transit system.

Three different cities with three unique ideas for the future. And that's why they're three of the cities that members of my Cabinet and Office of Urban Affairs will visit this summer as part of an ongoing national conversation to lift up best practices from around the country, to look at innovations for the metropolitan areas of tomorrow. Forward-looking cities shouldn't be succeeding despite Washington; they should be succeeding with a hand from Washington. We want to hear directly from them, and we want to hear directly from all of you, on fresh ideas and successful solutions that you've devised, and then figure out what the federal government should do or shouldn't do to help reinvent cities and metropolitan areas for the 21st century.

So I know that this change is possible. After all, I'm from a city that knows a little something about reinventing itself. In the 19th century, after a cataclysmic fire, Chicagoans rebuilt stronger than before. In the last century, they led the world upward in steel and glass. And in this century, under my friend Mayor Daley's leadership, they're helping to lead the world forward in newer, greener, more livable ways.

Daniel Burnam said, "Make no little plans." And that's the spirit behind his bold and ambitious designs unveiled 100 years ago this month that helped transform Chicago into a world-class city. That's the same spirit which we have to approach the reinvention of all America's cities and metropolitan areas—a vision of vibrant, sustainable places that provide our children with every chance to learn and to grow, and that allow our businesses and workers the best opportunity to innovate and succeed, and that let our older Americans live out their best years in the midst of all that metropolitan life can offer. Now is the time to seize that moment of possibility, and I am absolutely confident that, starting today with this conversation, you and I together, we're going to be able to make this happen.

The Metro Moment

By Bruce Katz

The following excerpts are from a 2010 commencement speech at the University of Illinois at Chicago, College of Urban Planning and Public Affairs. The speech was delivered by Bruce Katz who serves as the Director of the Metropolitan Policy Program at the Brookings Institution.

Y ou begin your professional career at what can only be described as a Metro Moment, in the United States and throughout the world. Metropolitan areas, cities and their surrounding suburbs, exurbs and rural communities, are the world's essential communities. These places are the engines of national prosperity. They are on the front lines of demographic transformation. They are the vehicles for environmental sustainability. They are the vanguards of innovation … in technology, in business, in government policy, and practice.

If this is a Metro Moment, then it is also a time for individuals who are engaged in building strong cities and suburbs. Professionals who plan, design, finance, develop, retrofit, manage, implement in ways that affect the lives of metro citizens every day. Like metros, your profession is on the front lines, of a revolution in thinking and practice.

The traditional ways of specialized disciplines and siloed bureaucracies are giving way to holistic thinking and integrated solutions. This, in turn, is fuelling a burst of creativity and imagination. These are not your parents' metros and this is not your parents' urban planning profession.

So let me situate your work in the complex dynamics of metropolitan America. Broad forces have positioned metropolitan areas as the engines of national prosperity.

Thomas Friedman has famously taught us that the world is "flat." But the spatial reality of modern economies is that they concentrate intensely in a relatively small number of places. Strictly speaking, there is no single American economy, but rather a network of highly connected, hyperlinked, and economically integrated metros.

The real heart of the American economy lies in the top 100 metropolitan areas that take up only 12 percent of our land mass, but harbor two-thirds of our population and generate 75 percent of our gross domestic product. These metropolitan areas dominate the economy because they gather and strengthen the assets—innovation, human capital, and infrastructure—that drive economic growth and productivity. The Chicago metropolis, for example, is home to 67 percent of the population of Illinois, but contributes 78 percent of that state's GDP.

Metros punch above their weight. The true economic geography, here and abroad, is a metropolitan one, enveloping city and suburb, exurb and rural town. Goods, people, capital and energy flow seamlessly across the metropolitan landscape. Labor markets are metropolitan as are housing markets and commuter-sheds. Sports teams, cultural institutions, and media all exist in metropolitan space.

As we emerge from this devastating recession, metropolitan economies will undergo a radical shift. They are likely to become more export oriented, less consumption oriented. They are likely to make a slow but critical transition to lower carbon, through renewable energy sources, the manufacture of sustainable infrastructure and sustainable products, and changes in buildings and the built environment. And they are likely to be even more dependent on innovation as the catalyst for growth and more reliant on educated and skilled workers.

For today's graduates, the point is this: The U.S. economy is going through a substantial restructuring with enormous implications for every aspect of the work you are about to do. If metros are the engines of national prosperity, then they are also on the front lines of demographic transformation.

* * *

We are a growing nation. Our population exceeded 300 million back in 2006 and we are now on our way to hit 350 million around 2025. We are a diversifying nation. An incredible 83 percent of our growth this decade was driven by racial and ethnic minorities. We are an aging nation. The number of seniors and boomers exceeded 100 million this decade.

We are a nation riven by educational disparities. Whites and Asians are now more than twice as likely to hold a bachelors degree as blacks and Hispanics.

We are a nation divided by income inequities and a growing gap between rich and poor. Low wage workers saw hourly earnings decline by 8 percent this decade; high wage workers saw wages rise by 3 percent.

America's top 100 metropolitan areas are on the front lines of our nation's demographic transformation. The trends I've identified—growth, diversity, aging, educational disparities, income inequities—are happening at a faster pace, a greater scale, and a higher level of intensity in our major metropolitan areas.

Let's take diversity and immigration as an example of the leading role of metropolitan areas.

Racial and ethnic minorities accounted for an astonishing 83 percent of national population growth this decade. As a result, Hispanics now make up roughly 15 percent of the nation's population. African Americans comprise a little over 12 percent of the nation's population. Racial and ethnic minorities make up an even larger share of the population in the top 100 metros: nearly 19 percent of metro populations are Hispanic; nearly 14 percent African American.

We are well on the path to becoming a majority-minority nation and metros are leading the way. Seventeen metropolitan areas are now majority minority, compared to 14 in 2000 and just five in 1990. Thirty-one metropolitan areas have children populations that are majority minority.

The growing diversity of America owes primarily to the natural increase in racial and ethnic populations that were already present in the U.S. in 2000. But new immigrants continued to come to America this decade, accounting for roughly 30 percent of national population growth. In metro America, the pace and volume of immigration was faster, with the share of growth approaching one third. As a result, one in every six metropolitan residents is now foreign born compared to one in eight Americans in total. This share is larger than the share experienced during the other great wave of international migration in the early 20th century.

Like that earlier period, immigration is one of the most contentious issues in our nation, best illustrated by Arizona's recent actions. Yet the benefits of immigration—and diversity more broadly—are immense: New markets; new ideas; new workers to replace those that retire; new connections to emerging markets outside the U.S.

So we have a central challenge: How do we embrace diversity and adapt to being a majority–minority nation? How do we particularly focus on educating and training the future, diverse workforce of Americans, so that they can compete and succeed globally?

Metros are not only engines of prosperity and on the front lines of demographic transformation … they are also vehicles for delivering environmental sustainability. The low-carbon economy, like the export-oriented economy, will be primarily invented, financed, produced and delivered in the top 100 metros.

The investment base for the green economy is intensely concentrated; 94 percent of venture capital comes from the top 100 metro areas.

The most innovative aspects of the green economy will cluster around major, largely metro-based, research institutions. Fifteen of the 21 national labs run by the Department of Energy are located within the top 100 metropolitan areas. Making our old and new homes, office, retail, and commercial facilities energy efficient will primarily be a metropolitan act, given the heavy concentration of our population, buildings, and businesses.

As metros move forward, they will need to make some hard choices about development. Despite the resurgence of many cities and urban cores, sprawl remains alive and well in the United States, which helps explain why the U.S. has double the per capita carbon dioxide emissions of other modern economies like Germany and the United Kingdom.

During this decade, cities and high density suburbs grew a little under 5 percent while less developed counties grew at more than three times that rate. By 2008, more than 40 percent of metropolitan population lived in spread out areas, creating a distended "autoscape" in place of the traditional landscape of human habitation.

One of the most difficult challenges before us, for both environmental and economic reasons, is to move away from a sprawling, distended landscape to communities that connect jobs, housing, and transport for people and firms.

America's metros are confronting the super-sized challenges of our new global order with energy, invention, and creativity. Challenged by continuous economic restructuring, metros are finding new ways to bolster innovation whether by financing wind energy and fuel cells in struggling, industrial metros like Cleveland or by connecting new entrepreneurs to money, markets, partners, management, and other resources in prosperous metros like San Diego.

Confronted with a diverse, less educated workforce, metros are laboring to elevate human capital by preparing disadvantaged workers to excel in such global hotbeds of employment as logistics in Louisville, life sciences in the Bay Area, and health care in both.

Burdened by concentrated poverty, a new wave of housing developers are producing mixed income housing in America's poorest neighborhoods—in Pittsburgh, in Chicago, in St. Louis—as a catalyst for modernizing and improving neighborhood schools. The result is not just quality, distinctive housing but, more importantly, neighborhood schools that work and sharp improvements in student performance.

Faced with rising congestion, exploding gas prices and aging systems, metros are designing and implementing market-shaping infrastructure investments to reconfigure freeways in Milwaukee, modernize water and sewer systems in Atlanta, build out region wide transit in Denver, and install fiber optic networks in Scranton.

And, confronted with what Strobe Talbott calls the "existential threat of global warming," metros like Seattle and Chicago are taking ambitious steps to create quality, sustainable places by promoting green building, transit oriented development, urban regeneration, and renewable sources of energy.

What knits these policy efforts? It's their embrace of a new style of governance that brings together city and suburban leaders around common purpose, cuts across conventional lines of government, business, university and philanthropy and deploys systemic market and environment shaping investments and interventions.

* * *

The Metro Moment has meaning and import far beyond those few of us who observe metros or build metros or govern metros. This is truly a call to this generation to build a different world of metro opportunity and possibility.

A Metro Moment requires that we act, with vision, imagination, and confidence. Will we seize the possibilities before us?

Trading Places

The Demographic Inversion of the American City

By Alan Ehrenhalt

Throughout the United States, a demographic inversion is taking place. The affluent are now choosing city life over life in the suburbs. Immigrants and those with lesser means have little choice but to settle in the suburbs. Chicago is gradually coming to resemble a traditional European city—with more of the rich living downtown and many of the poor in the suburbs.

Thirty years ago, the mayor of Chicago was unseated by a snowstorm. A blizzard in January of 1979 dumped some 20 inches on the ground, causing, among other problems, a curtailment of transit service. The few available trains coming downtown from the northwest side filled up with middle-class white riders near the far end of the line, leaving no room for poorer people trying to board on inner-city platforms. African Americans and Hispanics blamed this on Mayor Michael Bilandic, and he lost the Democratic primary to Jane Byrne a few weeks later.

Today, this could never happen. Not because of climate change, or because the Chicago Transit Authority now runs flawlessly. It couldn't happen because the trains would fill up with minorities and immigrants on the outskirts of the city, and the passengers left stranded at the inner-city stations would be members of the affluent professional class.

* * *

We are not witnessing the abandonment of the suburbs or a movement of millions of people back to the city all at once. But we are living at a moment in which the massive outward migration of the affluent that characterized the second half of the twentieth century is coming to an end. For several decades now, cities in the United States have wished for a "24/7" downtown, a place where people live as well as work, and keep the streets busy, interesting, and safe at all times of day. This is what urbanist Jane Jacobs preached in the 1960s, and it has long since become the accepted goal of urban planners. Only when significant numbers of people lived downtown, planners believed, could central cities regain their historic role as magnets for culture and as a source of identity and pride for the metropolitan areas they served. Now that's starting to happen, fueled by the changing mores of the young and by gasoline prices fast approaching $5-per-gallon. In many of its urbanized regions, an America that seemed destined for ever increasing individualization and sprawl is experimenting with new versions of community and sociability.

Why has demographic inversion begun? For one thing, the deindustrialization of the central city, for all the tragic human dislocations it caused, has eliminated many of the things that made affluent people want to move away from it. Nothing much is manufactured downtown anymore (or anywhere near it), and that means that the noise and grime that prevailed for most of the twentieth century have gone away. Manhattan may seem like a loud and gritty place now, but it is nothing like the city of tenement manufacturing, rumbling elevated trains, and horses and coal dust in the streets that confronted inhabitants in the early 1900s. Third-floor factory lofts, whether in Soho or in St. Louis, can be marketed as attractive and stylish places to live. The urban historian Robert Bruegmann goes so far as to claim that deindustrialization has, on the whole, been good for downtowns because it has permitted so many opportunities for creative reuse of the buildings. I wouldn't go quite that far, and, given the massive job losses of recent years, I doubt most of the residents of Detroit would, either. But it is true that the environmental factors that made middle-class people leave the central city for streetcar suburbs in the 1900s and for station-wagon suburbs in the 1950s do not apply any more.

Nor, in general, does the scourge of urban life in the 1970s and '80s: random street violence. True, the murder rates in cities like Chicago, Philadelphia, and Cleveland have climbed in the last few years, but this increase has been propelled in large part by gang- and drug-related violence. For the most part, middle-class people of all colors began to feel safe on the streets of urban America in the 1990s, and they still feel that way. The paralyzing fear that anyone of middle age can still recall vividly from the 1970s—that the shadowy figure passing by on a dark city street at night stands a good chance of being a mugger—is rare these days, and almost nonexistent among young people. Walk around the neighborhood of 14th and U streets in Washington, D.C. on a Saturday night, and you will find it perhaps the liveliest part of the city, at least for those under 25. This is a neighborhood where the riots of 1968 left physical scars that still have not disappeared, and where outsiders were afraid to venture for more than 30 years.

The young newcomers who have rejuvenated 14th and U believe that this recovering slum is the sort of place where they want to spend time and, increasingly, where they want to live. This is the generation that grew up watching "Seinfeld," "Friends," and "Sex and the City," mostly from the comfort of suburban sofas. We have gone from a sitcom world defined by "Leave It to Beaver" and "Father Knows Best" to one that offers a whole range of urban experiences and enticements. I do not claim that a handful of TV shows has somehow produced a new urbanist generation, but it is striking how pervasive the pro-city sensibility is within this generation, particularly among its elite. In recent years, teaching undergraduates at the University of Richmond, the majority of them from affluent suburban backgrounds, I made a point of asking where they would prefer to live in 15 years—in a suburb or in a neighborhood close to the center of the city. Few ever voted for suburban life.

I can't say that they had necessarily devoted a great deal of thought to the question: When I asked them whether they would want to live in an urban neighborhood without a car, many seemed puzzled and said no. Clearly, we are a long way from producing a generation for whom urban life and automobile ownership are mutually exclusive. In downtown Charlotte, a luxury condominium is scheduled for construction this year that will allow residents to drive their cars into a garage elevator, ride up to the floor they live on, and park right next to their front door. I have a hard time figuring out whether that is a triumph for urbanism or a defeat. But my guess is that, except in Manhattan, the carless life has yet to achieve any significant traction in the affluent new enclaves of urban America.

Not that cars and the demographic inversion aren't closely related; they are. In Atlanta, where the middle-class return to the city is occurring with more suddenness than perhaps anywhere in the United States, the most frequently cited reason is traffic. People who did not object to a 20-mile commute from the suburbs a decade ago are objecting to it now in part because the same commute takes quite a bit longer. To this, we can add the prospect of $5-per-gallon gasoline. It's impossible at this point to say with any certainty just what energy costs will do to American living patterns over the next decade. Urbanists predicted a return to the city during previous spikes in the cost of gasoline, notably during shortages in the 1970s. They were wrong. Gas prices came down, and the suburbs expanded dramatically. But today's prices at the pump are not the result of political pressures by angry sheiks in the Persian Gulf. They are the result of increased worldwide demand that is only going to continue to increase. Some suburbanites will simply stay where they are and accept the cost. But many will decide to stop paying $100 every few days for a tank of gasoline that will allow them to commute 40 or 50 miles a day, round-trip.

Ultimately, though, the current inversion is less the result of middle-aged people changing their minds than of young adults expressing different values, habits, and living preferences than their parents. The demographic changes that have taken place in America over the past generation—the increased propensity to remain single, the rise of cohabitation, the much later age at first marriage for those who do marry, the smaller size of families for those who have children, and, at the other end, the rapidly growing number of healthy and active adults in their sixties, seventies, and eighties—have combined virtually all of the significant elements that make a demographic inversion not only possible but likely. We are moving toward a society in which millions of people with substantial earning power or ample savings can live wherever they want, and many will choose central cities over distant suburbs. As they do this, others will find themselves forced to live in less desirable places—now defined as those further from the center of the metropolis. And, as this happens, suburbs that never dreamed of being entry points for immigrants will have to cope with new realities. It should come as no surprise that the most intense arguments about hiring and educating the undocumented have occurred in the relatively distant reaches of American suburbia, such as Prince William County, Virginia.

The reality of demographic inversion strikes me every time I return to Chicago, the city in which I was born and grew up. My grandfather arrived there in 1889, found his way to the Near West Side, and opened a tailor shop that remained in business for 50 years. During that time, the neighborhood was a compact and somewhat culturally isolated enclave of Jewish and Italian families. (It was also the location of Hull House and the original home of the Chicago Cubs.) The building that housed my grandfather's store was torn down in the 1960s when the University of Illinois built its Chicago campus in the neighborhood. The street corner where the store stood now houses part of the university science complex.

The UIC campus is, to my eyes, one of the ugliest in America. But I have made my peace with that. What interests me is what is going on all around that neighborhood, now called University Village. For a while after the school was built, its environs were a sort of residential no-man's-land, dangerous at night and unattractive to the young academics who taught there. Today, assistant professors at UIC generally don't live there either, but for a different reason: They can't afford it. Demand for the townhouses and condominiums on the Near West Side has priced junior faculty out of the market. One can walk a couple of blocks down the street from where my grandfather's shop once stood and order a steak for $24.

You might respond that there is nothing especially noteworthy in this. A college setting, liberal academics, houses close to the city's cultural attractions: That's garden-variety gentrification. What else would you expect?

If you feel that way, you might want to ride an elevated train going northwest, to the lesser-known Logan Square, a few miles beyond the Loop. Whatever Logan Square might be, it is not downtown chic. It is a moderately close-in nineteenth-century neighborhood with a history fairly typical for a city that A.J. Liebling once called "an endless succession of factory-town main streets." Logan Square was developed primarily by Scandinavian manufacturers, who lived on the tree-lined boulevards while their workers, many of them Polish, rented the cottages on the side streets. By the 1970s, nearly all the Poles had decamped for suburbia, and they were replaced by an influx of Puerto Ricans. The area became a haven for gangs and gang violence, and most of the retail shopping that held the community together disappeared.

Logan Square is still not the safest neighborhood in Chicago. There are armed robberies and some killings on its western fringe, and, even on the quiet residential streets, mothers tell their children to be home before dark. But that hasn't prevented Logan Square from changing dramatically again—not over the past generation, or the past decade, but in the past five years. The big stone houses built by the factory owners on Logan Boulevard are selling for nearly $1 million, despite the housing recession. The restaurant that sits on the square itself sells goat cheese quesadillas and fettuccine with octopus, and attracts long lines of customers who drive in from the suburbs on weekend evenings. To describe what has happened virtually overnight in Logan Square as gentrification is to miss the point. Chicago, like much of America, is rearranging itself, and the result is an entire metropolitan area that looks considerably different from what it looked like when this decade started.

Of course, demographic inversion cannot be a one-way street. If some people are coming inside, some people have to be going out. And so they are—in Chicago as in much of the rest of the country. During the past ten years, with relatively little fanfare and surprisingly little press attention, the great high-rise public housing projects that defined squalor in urban America for half a century have essentially disappeared. In Chicago, the infamous Robert Taylor Homes are gone, and the equally infamous Cabrini-Green is all but gone. This has meant the removal of tens of thousands of people, who have taken their Section 8 federal housing subsidies and moved to struggling African American neighborhoods elsewhere in the city. Some have moved to the city's southern suburbs—small suburbs such as Dixmoor, Robbins, and Harvey, which have been among the poorest communities in metropolitan Chicago. At the same time, tens of thousands of immigrants are coming to Chicago every year, mostly from various parts of Latin America. Where are they settling? Not in University Village. Some in Logan Square, but fewer every year. They are living in suburban or exurban territory that, until a decade ago, was almost exclusively English-speaking, middle-class, and white.

There are responsible critics who look at all this and see a lot being made out of very little. They argue that, in absolute numbers, the return to the urban center remains a minor demographic event. They have a point. In most metropolitan areas, in the first few years of the twenty-first century, many more people have moved to the suburbs than have moved downtown. A city of half a million that can report a downtown residential population of 25,000—5 percent of the total—can claim that it is doing relatively well. …

Even if the vast majority of cities never see a downtown residential boom of massive proportions—there is no doubt that a demographic inversion, in which the rich are moving inside and the poor are moving outside, is taking place. The crucial issue is not the number of people living downtown, although that matters. The crucial issue is who they are, and the ways in which urban life is changing as a result.

What would a post-inversion American city look like? In the most extreme scenario, it would look like many of the European capitals of the 1890s. Take Vienna, for example. In the mid-nineteenth century, the medieval wall that had surrounded the city's central core for hundreds of years was torn down. In its place there appeared the Ringstrasse, the circle of fashionable boulevards where opera was sung and plays performed, where rich merchants and minor noblemen lived in spacious apartments, where gentlemen and ladies promenaded in the evening under the gaslights, where Freud, Mahler, and their friends held long conversations about death over coffee and pastry in sidewalk cafes. By contrast, if you were part of the servant class, odds were you lived far beyond the center, in a neighborhood called Ottakring, a concentration of more than 30, 000 cramped one- and two-bedroom apartments, whose residents—largely immigrant Czechs, Slovaks, and Slovenes—endured a long horse-car ride to get to work in the heart of the city.

* * *

[Finally, there is] the vision of Jane Jacobs, who idealized the Greenwich Village of the 1950s and the casual everyday relationships that made living there comfortable, stimulating, and safe. Much of what Jacobs loved and wrote about will not reappear: The era of the mom-and-pop grocer, the shoemaker, and the candy store has ended for good. We live in a big-box, big-chain century. But I think the youthful urban elites of the twenty-first-century are looking in some sense for the things Jacobs valued, whether they have heard of her or not. They are drawn to the densely packed urban life that they saw on television and found vastly more interesting than the cul-de-sac world they grew up in. And, by and large, I believe central cities will give it to them. Not only that, but much of suburbia, in an effort to stay afloat, will seek to urbanize itself to some extent. That reinvention is already taking place: Look at all the car-created suburbs built in the 1970s and '80s that have created "town centers" in the past five years, with sidewalks and as much of a street grid as they can manage to impose on a faded strip-mall landscape. None of these retrofit efforts look much like a real city. But they are a clue to the direction in which we are heading.

In the 1990s, a flurry of academics and journalists (me among them) wrote books lamenting the decline of community and predicting that it would reappear in some fashion in the new century. I think that is beginning to happen now in the downtowns of America, and I believe, for all its imperfections and inequalities, that the demographic inversion ultimately will do more good than harm. We will never return—nor would most of us want to return—to the close-knit but frequently constricting form of community life that prevailed 50 years ago. But, as we rearrange ourselves in and around many of our big cities, we are groping toward the new communities of the twenty-first century.

Poverty in DuPage County

By Barbara Rose

The number of suburban poor is growing in metropolitan areas across the country. In DuPage County, which is one of the most affluent counties in the country, over 56,000 residents live at or below the poverty level. One in every five households in DuPage County has an annual income below $35,000. Although suburban poverty is less concentrated, and therefore less visible, than in the more blighted areas of Chicago—it is here and it is growing. As poverty disperses to the suburbs, policymakers must recognize that the interests of suburbanites and city dwellers are no longer diametrically opposed.

A tourism guide depicts DuPage County, eight miles west of Chicago, as "the magnificent miles," a playground of upscale hotels and shopping centers, manicured golf courses and pristine prairie paths. One of the nation's wealthiest counties—with a median household income exceeding $77,000 a year—it's a place where leafy older neighborhoods and historic downtowns alternate with new tracts of super-sized houses, landscaped corporate campuses and clusters of boxy industrial buildings.

By all appearances, John Moore, a corporate finance and strategy professional, enjoys the good life in a new subdivision on the western edge of the county, where homes sold for $490,000 when his was built in 2006. But appearances are deceiving. Two years ago, Moore lost his six-figure job at an international software company. He has nearly exhausted his savings paying his mortgage. Unable to find work or to sell his home in a market glutted with foreclosures, he visits food pantries to stock his fancy four-year-old kitchen. He gets medical care through a network that donates services to the low-income uninsured.

The same network helps Francisca, who asked that her last name be withheld. Francisca lives with her husband Julio and their four teenage sons in a two-bedroom apartment less than a mile from Village Hall in Addison. Julio makes $8.50 per hour working seven days a week, sometimes two shifts a day, cleaning warehouses, a church and a movie theater. Francisca tried to supplement the family's meager income by buying discounted goods in Chicago and selling them to her neighbors at a profit. But lately, because of the bad economy, her customers can't afford to pay for the winter coats they bought on installment.

In Glen Ellyn, where the median household income is nearly $90,000, Laura Davidson gets home from an overnight shift at Target to her family's ground-floor apartment in time to take a two-hour nap before getting her six-year-old off to school. She will get another chance to sleep when her toddler naps at noon. Their middle-class life crumbled after her husband, a 31-year-old machinist, became disabled. Even with food stamps and help from charities, they aren't making it.

These are not the comfortable lifestyles that lure families to the suburbs. Yet venture into any corner of DuPage County's 334 square miles and you discover people in need. They include the newly impoverished, hit by illness or unemployment or both, and the marginally employed, whose payday-to-payday struggle gets harder in bad times.

The number of suburban poor is growing in metropolitan areas across the country. Their neighborhoods little resemble the graffiti-scarred pockets of hopelessness common to big cities; but their situation is no less debilitating. The suburban poor subsist, often all but invisible to the more-fortunate majority, in high-cost areas where their income doesn't begin to cover basic needs.

"DuPage County has changed," says Rita Gonzalez, a member of the DuPage County Board. "The demographics have changed. People's financial situations have changed." Today, nearly 6 percent of DuPage's population of 930,000 lives below the federal poverty level of $22,050 for a family of four. A much larger segment struggles to make ends meet. These so-called "working poor" live at twice the poverty level, a common proxy for low income.

Together with poverty-level residents, they make up 15.8 percent of the county's population, or about one in six residents. Their number grew steadily even during the boom years of the 1990s, more than doubling to about 145,000 by 2008.

"It's a challenge to leadership to take the demographic shift that's been going on for decades and make sure it is a positive for our community," says Candace King, executive director of DuPage Federation on Human Services Reform, an umbrella group that coordinates responses to families in need.

A STUDY IN CONTRASTS

The changes in DuPage mirror powerful trends across the country, where poor families in search of jobs and affordable rents move farther from city centers, even as affluent empty nesters and young professionals gravitate downtown. The United States marked a watershed in 2005 when the number of poor living in suburbs outnumbered those in cities for the first time, according to a Brookings Institution study of 100 metropolitan areas. Urban poverty is more concentrated; but in absolute numbers, the suburban poor population is larger.

"We are more of a suburban nation. Our suburbs are growing faster than the cities," says Elizabeth Kneebone, a Brookings Institution senior analyst. "As that population has grown, it also has diversified."

The result is sharp contrasts. In central Wheaton, across the street from luxury condominiums, people wait in line at a nonprofit for free food and clothing. In Lisle during evening rush hour, men and women with backpacks and rolling suitcases cross a busy six-lane highway on foot, making their way from a bus stop to an overnight shelter in a church. A meat market in Addison features goat legs for $2.79 per pound within a short drive from a Lombard butcher selling boneless prime rib for $12.99 per pound.

In a suburban land of plenty, the poor remain isolated and often overlooked. Immigrants such as Francisca, who came from Mexico 13 years ago to join her husband in Bensenville, increasingly bypass the city to settle in the suburbs, where they often find little support to help them assimilate.

Today, immigrants and low-income families displaced from gentrifying city neighborhoods crowd into older suburban apartments and tract homes. At the same time, many of the manufacturing jobs that once helped newcomers get a financial foothold have disappeared, replaced by low-paying service work. More recently, the collapse of the real estate market eliminated hundreds of local construction jobs.

Fernando Ibarra is feeling the impact. He stood shivering in line on a chilly evening last October, a clean-shaven 28-year-old in a gray sweatshirt, waiting for a food pantry to open at People's Resource Center in downtown Wheaton. A bricklayer and union member, he and his brothers found good-paying jobs when they moved to West Chicago from Mexico six years ago, but the work dried up two years ago. Now he struggles to support his wife and two-year-old daughter on an $11 hourly wage assembling cabinetry. Of the construction market, he says simply, "It's bad."

Poverty rates inevitably increase during downturns, but suburban areas paid a heavier toll during this recession than in previous ones. Among the hardest hit are communities on the metropolitan fringe, where the torrid building boom fueled a false prosperity.

"Suburbs are feeling the brunt," Kneebone says. "This downturn is only going to contribute to the suburbanization of poverty. Many areas are unprepared. There's less of a safety net in these communities."

In DuPage, both public and private providers of social services are feeling the strain. "All of the agencies are feeling a little bit overwhelmed," says Joan Rickard, human services manager at DuPage County Community Services.

"I DON'T KNOW WHERE WE WOULD BE"

At the nonprofit People's Resource Center, a 35-year-old multiservice agency that operates one of the county's largest food pantries, demand surged by nearly 30 percent in the second half of 2009 compared with the same period a year earlier. The pantry distributed nearly 21,000 grocery carts of food. Recipients are allowed one visit per month.

"It's the most dramatic increase in our history," says Development Director Karen Hill. "We're seeing a lot of families that have never had to use a food pantry before, people who never in a million years thought they'd use a food pantry."

"They're desperately looking for any service," says Food Services Director Melissa Travis. "We all have this image there's this huge welfare state." But many struggling people, she adds, "don't qualify for any kind of government help. They can't afford medical insurance, medicine for their kids, mortgage payments. They come in here much more stressed, much more afraid."

Many of the pantry's patrons are unemployed. But 56 percent report at least one family member working. They were getting by until their hours got cut or, like Ibarra, they were forced to take lower-paying jobs.

On the evening when Ibarra stood in line, the waiting area filled to standing room only with dozens of people, each with a different story. An Iraqi family had fled Baghdad's violence for Wheaton. A 62-year-old Wood Dale woman quit her job to care for her frail husband. A mother of three could no longer make ends meet on her factory wages. A shy Sudanese refugee from Carol Stream lost her job as a nursing assistant.

Among the first-time visitors was Paula Marcum, a single mom with four children who works as an assistant facilities manager for a local bank. "Things have gotten a little tight," says the Warrenville resident, explaining that she fell behind in her rent when a roommate moved out without warning.

Davidson, the Target employee, began visiting the pantry last year when she and her disabled husband, George, exhausted their savings. In better times, their combined household income had inched above $60,000. Then she was laid off from her job as an administrative assistant and her husband's health deteriorated. The Social Security Administration denied him permanent disability payments for a degenerative spine condition that has left him unable to work or even to care reliably for their youngest, an active curly-haired blond toddler, Zachary.

* * *

"AT THIS POINT I NEED MIRACLES"

Access DuPage member Estella Rodriguez, 61, spends part of her days keeping the linoleum floors shining in the spotless basement apartment she shares with her husband in Glendale Heights. They pay rent to a family that owns the split-level house, where an American flag decal decorates the front door. She also takes an English class at the College of DuPage and looks for work. Her husband, who is treated for cancer by Access DuPage, earns $7.75 per hour as a commercial mover. (The minimum wage in Illinois is $8.25 per hour.)

A grandmother now, Rodriguez raised two sons alone while working in an airplane-parts factory after emigrating from Mexico to California in 1985. One son is a registered nurse; the other works in medical records. "I'm very happy about my sons; they have a good life," she says. "I love America."

For Francisca's four teenage sons, a similar upwardly mobile path seems less certain. Isolated from support that could help her improve her prospects, she encounters barriers even when she tries to access basic safety-net services at the food pantry near her apartment in Addison.

On one visit to the pantry, Francisca brought one of her sons—a polite and fluently bilingual high school senior—to help her communicate in English. The pantry's paid coordinator sent the pair away to get copies of their birth certificates, a requirement to be placed on a list for holiday baskets. When they returned with the copies, he asked them for a letter proving the family's need. When she returned with the letter, hoping to take home food, he allowed her to take some bread off a front table, then motioned her to an exit.

On a cold evening in Francisca's small living room, an image of Mary Magdalene flickered on a votive candle. Her family turned on the kitchen's oven to warm the apartment. She recalled a time when both she and Julio were sick and unable to work, when the family ate for a week on $34 they had saved for emergencies.

Then Julio spoke about his dream of a better future for his sons: good jobs, a home. What would it take to realize his dream? "At this point I need miracles," he says.

Chicagoland's Metropolitan Mayors Caucus

By Bonnie Lindstrom

The Mayors Caucus began as a forum to foster cooperation among the municipalities in the Chicago metropolitan region. This article presents a case study of the development of the Mayors Caucus as a new institution established to overcome the region's extreme government fragmentation and decades of city-suburban hostility. The article concludes with the argument that "in the twenty-first century, developing new capacities to solve regional problems will depend on developing new institutional arrangements, on a shared vision of the region's challenges, and on strong leadership."

In *Exploring Ad Hoc Regionalism* (2002), Douglas Porter and Allan Wallis argue that the nation is in a time of invention and experiment aimed to develop governance capacity to address regional challenges.[1] They suggest that one of the ways to develop governance capacity is to enhance existing institutional arrangements such as councils of governments (COGs). The Metropolitan Mayors Caucus is an example of an institutional arrangement that emerged from the Chicago metropolitan region's suburban COGs.

The Mayors Caucus was first established so that the mayors in the six-county region could work together on issues of mutual concern. The Mayors Caucus established an agenda and set up task forces to address issues specific to their municipalities. After it was formally designated a nonprofit organization, the Mayors Caucus joined the region's civic and nonprofit advocacy organizations in ad hoc coalitions to promote its regional agenda.

Bonnie Lindstrom, from "The Metropolitan Mayors Caucus: Institution Building in a Political Fragmented Metropolitan Region," *Urban Affairs Review*, vol. 46, no. 1, pp. 37-45, 47-62. Copyright © 2010 by Sage Publications. Reprinted with permission.

This is a case study of how Chicago's suburban COGs developed into the Mayors Caucus, and the impact the Caucus has had on regional governance.

POLITICAL FRAGMENTATION

The Chicago metropolitan region is one of the most politically fragmented in the nation. The six counties in northeastern Illinois (Cook, DuPage, Kane, Lake, McHenry, and Will) are the core of the Chicago metropolitan region. By 2010, the metropolitan region had over 1,200 units of local government, composed of 273 municipalities (including the city of Chicago); county and township governments, special purpose districts,[2] and joint action water agencies.[3] The political fragmentation is the result of Illinois laws that limit municipal indebtedness and revenues, encouraging the creation of special purpose districts with their own bonding power and taxing authority.[4]

The political fragmentation is also the result of a historic city-suburban hostility dating to the late nineteenth century. From 1870 to 1893, the city of Chicago expanded from 35 square miles to approximately 185 square miles by annexing adjacent townships whose residents voted to join the city to be able to utilize city services, primarily Lake Michigan water. Chicago's rapid annexation of its adjacent townships, the possible threat that the city would cut off Lake Michigan water, and the influx of immigrants from Southern and Eastern Europe to work in Chicago's heavy industries contributed to suburban distrust of Chicago before World War I. After World War II, the city of Chicago experienced the in-migration of African-Americans from the South and White flight from city neighborhoods. Chicago Democrat versus suburban Republican competition for control of the Illinois General Assembly intensified city-suburban hostility in the 1980s and 1990s.

METROPOLITAN MAYORS CAUCUS

Given a political culture of local autonomy and a historic pattern of city–suburban hostility, what explains the establishment of a new regional institution such as the Metropolitan Mayors Caucus in 1997? The primary answer is that the mayor of Chicago [then Richard M. Daley] and the leaders of the suburban COGs agreed to work together based on their awareness that they shared the same concerns on maintaining the region's economic vitality and promoting sustainable development.

Their willingness to cooperate was also based on the successes of the suburban COGs. Beginning in the 1950s, mayors in different subregions began meeting in voluntary municipal leagues to find ways to cooperate to meet the challenges they faced. In the 1970s the municipal leagues were established as legally constituted councils of mayors to meet federal requirements for local consultation in programming their allotted surface transportation funds. As the councils of mayors became institutionalized stakeholders in surface transportation planning, the COGs became regional stakeholders. At the same time, their collaboration in programming federal funds established a pattern of resolving common challenges.

COALITION PARTNERS

The Mayors Caucus worked first with its membership on air pollution and relations with Commonwealth Edison. For its initiatives on housing, education funding reform, freight rail and ground transportation, and regional growth, the Mayors Caucus needed coalition partners to achieve its goals. In the 1980s, the region's business leadership (represented by civic organizations) became actively engaged in a regional dialogue on how to remain competitive in a global economy. The Commercial Club of Chicago, whose members included the CEOs of the major corporations in the region, established the Civic Committee to pursue policies that would improve education and workforce development in Chicago and make Chicago and the region more attractive for new businesses. The two major regional initiatives of the Civic Committee were the establishment of World Business Chicago, a public-private partnership with Chicago, and adding new runways at O'Hare International Airport.

After the Civic Committee issued a report calling for the region to unite to solve its transportation, education, and inequitable tax problems, the committee established Chicago Metropolis 2020 to pursue this agenda.[5] The Civic Committee and Chicago Metropolis 2020 were joined by two other civic organizations: the Chicagoland Chamber of Commerce and the Metropolitan Planning Council (MPC). The civic organizations were joined in their initiatives by public-interest advocacy organizations originally founded to promote an agenda of social justice and reinvestment in lower-income Chicago neighborhoods. Concerned about job creation on the exurban fringe at the expense of inner-city poverty and job loss, Business and Professional People for the Public Interest and the Center for Neighborhood Technology have agendas supporting sustainable regional development.

From Republican to Democratic Hegemony

During the 1990s, the Republican leadership in the General Assembly, James "Pate" Philip and Lee Daniels, were both from DuPage County, the most Republican county in Illinois. Pate Philip was the president of the Illinois Senate throughout the 1990s. Lee Daniels was the house speaker for two years and minority leader for the other eight. The two leaders promoted a partisan legislative agenda that favored the Republican suburbs over Chicago interests. Pate Philip, in particular, articulated a political philosophy strongly antagonistic to Chicago and its minority residents.

The sweep by Democrats in the 2002 election altered the balance of political power in the state. For the first time in 26 years, the Democrats controlled the Governorship and had a majority in both houses of the Illinois General Assembly. The Democratic leadership in the General Assembly, Emil Jones and Michael Madigan, represented south and southwest Cook suburbs and neighborhoods in south and southwest Chicago. Political power had moved from the economically prosperous suburbs in northwest Cook and northeast DuPage Counties to the city of Chicago and the suburbs in south and southwest Cook County. With a Democratic majority in the Illinois General Assembly and a newly elected Democratic governor, members of the legislature supported the new measures proposed by the civic organizations, advocacy groups, and the Mayors Caucus.

REGIONAL COOPERATION

The Mayors Caucus and the civic organizations worked cooperatively on policies in which they had a common agenda. All of the civic organizations, including the Chicagoland Chamber of Commerce, supported Mayor Daley's initiatives for regional economic development. The Civic Committee, Chicago Metropolis 2020, and the Mayors Caucus supported initiatives on surface transportation and freight rail. The Mayors Caucus worked with Chicago Metropolis 2020 and the Metropolitan Planning Council on initiatives to increase the supply of affordable housing in the region and to promote sustainable development.

World Business Chicago and the CREATE Program

The city of Chicago, Chicago Metropolis 2020, and the Chicagoland Chamber of Commerce established World Business Chicago as a public-private partnership to attract new and retain existing businesses. Founded in 1998 as an outgrowth of an initiative of the Civic Committee of the Commercial Club of Chicago, World Business Chicago's mission is to heighten the region's profile as a destination for global investment and talent. The organization was originally chaired by Chicago Mayor Richard M. Daley, its current members are appointed by Mayor Emanuel, and the city funds more than half of World Business Chicago's $3.2 million annual operating budget.

Since 1974, the mayors had worked cooperatively in each suburban council of mayors to prioritize their allocation of surface transportation funds. The federal legislative priorities of the Mayors Caucus for 2005 reflected this long-standing involvement in regional transportation issues. The Mayors Caucus strongly supported the reauthorization of federal funding for transit, highway, and safety programs. In addition, they recommended funding support for the Chicago Region Environmental and Transportation Efficiency Project (CREATE), a public-private partnership proposed by Mayor Richard M. Daley to resolve the freight rail gridlock in the region.

Housing

In the late 1990s, the major civic organizations and planning agencies began working with local governments and state housing officials to address the region's serious housing-jobs mismatch and the lack of affordable housing. The Metropolitan Planning Council had issued "For Rent: Housing Options in the Chicago Region" in 1999. The report, funded by HUD, detailed the affordable housing crisis in the Chicago region. The problems identified were increasing housing costs, increasing traffic congestion, and a decreasing supply of rental housing.

Working with the Metropolitan Planning Council, the first housing initiatives of the caucus were to develop a set of housing endorsement criteria designed "to promote housing and mixed-use developments that meet community needs while also addressing broader regional sensible growth goals."[6] The caucus approved the nonbinding Housing Action Agenda on February 28, 2002.

Many of the suburbs have moved beyond a nonbinding acceptance of the housing endorsement criteria proposed in 2002 in planning for transit-oriented development in their downtowns. In 2009, the Housing Committee and the MPC worked with inter-jurisdictional housing collaboratives in south and west Cook County to find solutions to the foreclosed and vacant properties in their areas.

REGIONAL CONFLICT

Regional cooperation broke down when the Mayors Caucus and the civic leadership addressed three critical transportation issues: expanding regional airport capacity, restructuring the region's two planning agencies, and restructuring and refinancing the RTA. These three issues were of critical importance to the business community. When the Mayors Caucus was established, the mayors knew that there was no consensus among its membership on the question of expanding airport capacity and so initially agreed to keep the issue off the table. In 2001 they established a Regional Air Capacity Task Force to discuss the issues of expanding O'Hare and building a third airport. Not only was the question of how to restructure the two planning agencies and the RTA not on, its agenda, but also the membership of the Mayors Caucus was unhappy with legislation initially proposed by the civic community.

Expanding Regional Airport Capacity

One of the most contentious issues in regional decision making was whether to add new runways at O'Hare International Airport or build a new regional airport in southeast Will County on a greenfield site near Peotone. Throughout the 1990s, proposals to add new runways at O'Hare were stopped by a coalition of Republicans from DuPage County and suburbs adjacent to the airport. The suburbs adjacent to O'Hare in northwest Cook and northeast DuPage counties had established the Suburban O'Hare Commission (SOC) in 1981. They were financially supported by the DuPage County Board. In the 1990s, the suburbs in SOC formed a coalition with the South Suburban Mayors and Managers Association to push for the new Peotone airport. The mayors in the South Suburban Mayors and Managers Association were proactive in promoting the Peotone airport as a way to revitalize the south Cook suburbs that had suffered from deindustrialization in the 1960s and 1970s.

By the late 1990s, expanding O'Hare had become the top priority for the regional business community. The Civic Committee of the Commercial Club took the lead in pressing for expanded capacity at O'Hare. Mayor Richard M. Daley and the airline industry supported adding new runways. The Cook County Board never took a position regarding new runways at O'Hare, nor did the Metropolitan Planning Council and the other advocacy organizations.

Consistent with its mandate, the Mayors Caucus took no official position on expanding O'Hare International Airport. The Regional Air Capacity Task Force provided the opportunity for participants to present their positions and listen to other positions. The task force was not asked to find a consensus or make recommendations on the issue. The Mayors Caucus, representing SOC municipalities vehemently opposed to any expansion of O'Hare Airport as well as those municipalities strongly in favor, remained neutral. The Mayors Caucus also remained neutral on the equally contentious question of building the Peotone airport.

The Northeastern Illinois Regional Transportation Task Force

After Democrats won the governorship and control of the Illinois General Assembly in 2002, the region's business community pressed for a resolution of the contentious issues regarding restructuring the region's transportation and land-use agencies. In late 2003 the Illinois General Assembly established the Northeastern Illinois Regional Transportation Task Force chaired by Congressman Lipinski (D-Chicago) to make recommendations regarding whether restructuring the transportation agencies into a single agency was viable.

The task force voted down the super agency proposed by Chicago Metropolis 2020 at its meeting in February 2004. The members argued that it would be a step to regional government without local input. The Transportation Task Force returned with five revised resolutions on April 12. The resolutions were to restructure NIPC and CATS, restructure the RTA with the chairman appointed by the governor, combine Metra and Pace, increase the number of directors on the RTA, and establish a universal fare card. The Regional Transportation Task Force resolutions were sent to the Illinois General Assembly.

The Chicago Metropolitan Agency for Planning

The Mayors Caucus began its own hearings over the summer of 2004 to determine whether it would be best to reinvent the two planning agencies or merge them. Their recommendations would then be submitted to the General Assembly. The Mayors Caucus established a CATS/NIPC Coordinating Committee composed of the officers of the two agencies with oversight by the caucus and the region's county board chairmen. The recommendations of the coordinating committee were to have an oversight board for the two agencies, but the agencies themselves would still have final authority over any plans they submitted to the oversight board. The mayors would maintain control over land-use and zoning issues and would continue to control the local surface transportation allocation projects through the Councils of Mayors process.

In 2005, after consultation with all of the stakeholders, legislation was introduced to consolidate the two agencies. In May, the Illinois General Assembly unanimously approved the legislation (110-0). The Regional Planning Board was established as a municipal corporation with a 15-member board. The Mayors Caucus coordinated the transition of CATS and NIPC into the Regional Planning Board with funding assistance from the MacArthur Foundation. The Regional Planning Board was renamed the Chicago Metropolitan Agency for Planning (CMAP)

CMAP reflects the new political and population balance of the region. One-third of its members represent Chicago, one-third of its members represent suburban Cook County, and one-third of its members represent the collar counties. THE MPO policy committee is the federally designated metropolitan planning organization for the region. The mayors of the suburban regional councils continue to control their allocation of surface transportation funding. The new agency has no authority over the local zoning, land-use, and annexation decisions made by the region's municipalities.

For the first time, the Chicago metropolitan region has a planning agency whose decision-making board is appointed by elected officials in the region. The oversight board is entirely composed of members selected by the county board presidents and the mayors, giving regional stakeholders, including the county board chairmen, the final say in the decisions.

Restructuring and Refinancing the RTA

The Illinois General Assembly did not act on the recommendations of the Northeastern Illinois Regional Transportation Task Force regarding the RTA. In October 2004, a bipartisan committee of the Illinois House was established to consider the recommendations of the task force and began a series of hearings in Springfield and Chicago. In the fall of 2007, the Special Committee on Mass Transit had developed comprehensive legislation for long-term funding for operations designed to achieve a better coordinated, more efficient, and more accountable regional transit system. The bill included long-term financing through an increase in the regional sales tax and a Chicago real estate transfer tax and the requirement that the allocation of federal and state funds to the three service boards be modified to reflect new regional reality. The bill passed the legislature on January 2008 and was signed into law.

ANALYSIS

The Mayors Caucus has proven successful in advancing its policy agenda and working with state legislators and government agencies to achieve its goals. As a regional stakeholder, the Mayors Caucus has worked with the civic organizations in ad hoc coalitions in regional task forces. The mayors knew when they established the caucus that they would not have a consensus on the question of how to expand airport capacity. The question of restructuring NIPC and CATS and restructuring and refinancing the RTA, however, presented new challenges for a caucus based on consensus building.

Mayors Caucus: Membership Agenda

The region's mayors originally agreed to work together on initiatives dealing with global competitiveness, noncompliance with the Clean Air Act standards on ozone, electric deregulation, and regional economic development. The "The Greenest Region Compact" of Metropolitan Chicago states their continuing focus:

> We, the undersigned Mayors will strive to improve the environment in the Chicago region by taking actions in our own operations and communities. Through our leadership we will demonstrate the economic and social viability of sustainable and environmentally-friendly practices.[7]

Their original priorities have expanded. The Critical Infrastructure Committee, begun because of the earlier problems with Commonwealth Edison, now has expanded to ensure the protection of natural gas, potable water, and telecommunications as well as electric power. The most recent initiative in providing information and technical services to the membership is the task force on service delivery for police and fire services.

The legislative agenda of the Mayors Caucus similarly centers on those items that the membership supports: unfunded personnel and pension mandates, the cable and video competition law, protecting state-shared revenues, and protecting the Chicago region's share of state transportation funding. The education reform legislation remains one of the Mayors Caucus's main legislative objectives.

Mayors Caucus: Regional Stakeholder

The Mayors Caucus was a regional stakeholder in reorganizing the two planning agencies and efforts to restructure the RTA. The Mayors Caucus, representing the 273 municipalities including Chicago, was a participant in the final legislation that merged NIPC and CATS into the Chicago Metropolitan Agency for Planning. The approval of the Mayors Caucus membership was critical for restructuring the two planning agencies: reauthorization of CATS would require a two-thirds agreement on the part of the region's mayors.

Refinancing the RTA and the STAR Line

The proposals regarding restructuring and refinancing the RTA generated the most controversy and were harder to resolve. Before the Northeastern Illinois Regional Transportation Task Force met, the Mayors Caucus had drafted legislation for restructuring the RTA, which became part of the final bill. The Mayors Caucus did not reach a consensus on increasing the sales tax in the collar counties. One tension underlying the proposal to increase the sales tax in the collar counties was that there was no agreement between the mayors from the south and southwest Cook suburbs and those from the northwest Cook and collar counties. The Republican members of the General Assembly had sent a letter to Congressman Lipinski as chair of the Task Force arguing that

> an attempt to restructure our transportation governance system may jeopardize the collaborative balance that exists between the City of Chicago and the rapidly developing suburban region. ... The governance system is balanced regionally and politically.[8]

Their argument was based on the historic hostility between the city of Chicago and the Republican suburbs. The flaw in their argument was that restructuring and refinancing the RTA was no longer a simple city-suburban issue. In the new regional context, the RTA, and Metra in particular, had become identified with transportation policies that advantaged northwest Cook, DuPage, and Will County residents and seriously disadvantaged residents in the south and southwest Cook suburbs.

One of the most contentious issues was Metra's planned Suburban Transit Access Route (STAR) line. The proposed STAR line would run from Joliet north to Hoffman Estates (using the Elgin, Joliet & Eastern railroad line) and then in the median strip of Interstate 90 to O'Hare International Airport. When the RTA supported Metra's proposed $1 billion suburb-to-suburb commuter rail system, the municipalities in the South Suburban Mayors and Managers Association were outraged.

In a letter to Metra Chairman Jeff Ladd, the South Suburban Mayors and Managers Association argued that the new STAR line would "perpetuate the economic disparity between the northern region of the metropolitan area and the south suburbs."[9] Rep. Jesse Jackson Jr. (D-2nd) who represents the suburbs in south Cook County argued that the

STAR line would mainly serve a White area rich in jobs and not dependent on transit. The needs of his constituents, minority populations with long commutes to jobs in the northwest suburbs or downtown, were ignored.

In an interview with the *Daily Southtown,* Metra's chairman Jeff Ladd responded to the criticism that Metra was unconcerned about the commuter rail needs of the south and southwest suburbs. He said,

> "Metra is not a social service agency ... and it is not looking to solve the unemployment issue. What good does it do to start a rail service that nobody rides?"[10]

His argument ignored the fact that the Metra Electric Line to the south suburbs has the 4th highest ridership of the 11 lines.[11]

The other contentious issue was Metra's serious neglect of the Electric Line itself. Commuters complained of unfair ticketing practices, the lack of on-train restrooms, and poorly maintained stations. The Randolph Street terminal, gutted in 1996 for planned restoration, had not been repaired. After a series of hearings were held, Metra ordered new cars with on-train restrooms, removed the turnstiles, upgraded its stations, and completed the Randolph Street terminal and began planning for the SouthEast line, a new commuter line east of the Metra Electric line that would serve the south suburbs.

Regional Political Culture: Local Government Autonomy

The conflict surrounding the recommendations of the Northeastern Illinois Transportation Task Force to merge NIPC and CATS and restructure and refinance the RTA highlights the historical support in the region for the benefits of fragmented government. The statements made by Republican mayors, who did not represent the Mayors Caucus, against consolidating the planning agencies, centralized transportation planning, and making the governor more responsible for the agencies reflect a long-standing opposition to the establishment of a regional government.

The resolutions proposed by the Northeastern Illinois Regional Transportation Task Force reflected the changing socio-demographic and political landscape in the region. The Republicans on the task force attempted to categorize the resolutions as exemplifying the older city-suburban split and a Democratic power grab. Labeling the outcome of the task force as a city-suburb conflict or a Democratic power grab deliberately obscured the critical fact that the task force proposed a shift to address the inequities in service to the inner-ring suburbs and suburbs in south and southwest Cook.

One of the underlying concerns of the Republican legislators was that any attempt to merge NIPC and CATS and restructure the RTA would create new bureaucracies and "[usurp] the authority granted to local units of governments in Article VII of the Illinois Constitution"[12] Their concerns regarding the merger of NIPC and CATS into CMAP and the restructuring of the RTA have proven unfounded. The region's political culture remains based on local government autonomy and a reluctance to establish autonomous public authorities.

In the years since the resolutions proposed by the Northeastern Illinois Regional Transportation Task Force to restructure and refinance the Regional Transportation Authority, reforms have not been implemented. The RTA had not changed the older, formula-based process for allocating funding between the CTA and Metra nor had the RTA initiated a universal fare card linking all three transit agencies. The CTA and Pace have established an integrated fare system utilizing credit and debit cards and tickets from fare vending machines. Metra, continuing with its own system of paper tickets that conductors punch individually, initiated its own system of online ticket sales in 2009. Anticipation that restructuring and refinancing the RTA would lead to a "seamless" regional transportation system that would coordinate fare collection and services has not been achieved. The failure to implement the reforms proposed by the Transportation Task Force underscores how difficult it is to change an institution when individual members have already established territory and historic patterns of interaction.

INSTITUTION BUILDING AND REGIONAL GOVERNANCE

In his analysis of the emergence of global city regions, Allen J. Scott (2000) argues that a new form of governance has emerged, involving a set of complex institutional responses in reaction to the emerging global-local system.[13] He argues that the development of a policy agenda committed to institution building is critical for regional stability and economic growth. These institutions are needed to overcome the fragmentation characteristic of local governments and to work toward collective decision-making. In *Regions and the World Economy*, Scott (1998) underscores that as global city regions develop more capacity for collective decision making, intraregional conflict will emerge.[14] Both greater intraregional collaboration and increased intraregional conflict have occurred in the Chicago metropolitan region

The formation of the Metropolitan Mayors Caucus was the way to overcome the extreme government fragmentation and decades of city-suburban hostility. The Mayors Caucus serves as a regional forum and a regional stakeholder. Its institutional antecedents were the suburban councils of mayors, the suburban COGs, and the intralocal agreements for service delivery negotiated by the municipalities. The catalyst for Mayor Daley's overture to the suburban COGs was the potential consequences of noncompliance with the Clean Air Act on the economic well-being of the region and the quality of life of its residents. The success of the Mayors Caucus with Commonwealth Edison and the Clean Air Campaign firmly established the caucus as a new institution representing the region's mayors.

The Mayors Caucus also serves as a model for collaboration and cooperation in the region. Although the RTA reforms have not been instituted, the three transit agencies are now consulting and cooperating with the COGs and other stakeholders. This change in approach was facilitated by the resignations of Jeff Ladd as chairman of Metra in 2006 and Frank Kruesi, President of the CTA, in 2007. Their successors are not polarizing, choosing instead to cooperate with each other and other stakeholders.

In the twenty-first century, developing new capacities to solve regional problems will depend on developing new institutional arrangements, on a shared vision of the region's challenges, and on strong leadership. Denver's Metro Mayors Caucus, a cooperative alliance of the 39 mayors in the Denver metropolitan region, has the same commitment to decision making by consensus as Chicago's Mayors Caucus. Its agenda is focused on those issues of greatest importance to the Denver metropolitan region: growth management, multimodal transportation, affordable housing, and intergovernmental cooperation. The Pittsburgh Renaissance is the result of the organizational capacity of a public-private partnership (the Allegheny Conference on Community Development) and the enduring commitment of the region's corporate elite to expand and diversify the regional economy.[15]

Los Angeles and New York City face different challenges. Both global city regions have multiple governments with independent financial resources. The conflict over restructuring and refinancing the RTA highlights the problems in restructuring a public authority with its legally established funding formulas and institutionalized patterns of interaction. Global city regions with entrenched public authorities and strong county governments may have more difficulty in developing a vision and a consensus on how to achieve that vision. Metropolitan New York City spans three states and has three public transportation authorities. The Port Authority of New York and New Jersey as the regional planning agency has not been able to overcome the intense economic rivalry among the political jurisdictions in the tristate area.[16] Metropolitan Los Angeles has strong city and county governments with little incentive to develop coordinated regional policies.[17]

Regional governance is not regional government. Regionalism, to cite Savitch and Vogel (1996), is "an incremental and evolutionary process."[18] Regional governance in the twenty-first century is also an incremental and evolutionary process, one that necessitates building new institutional capacity for collective decision making.

NOTES

1. Porter, D. R., and A. D. Wallis. 2002. *Exploring Ad Hot Regionalism.* Cambridge, MA: Lincoln Institute of Land Policy.
2. These special purpose districts include park and recreation districts, school districts, fire protection districts, mosquito abatement districts, sewage districts, water supply districts, drainage districts, cemetery districts, irrigation and water conservation districts, and soil conservation districts.
3. This pattern is statewide. The state of Illinois has more units of local taxing bodies than any other state (Lawrence 2009).

4. Ford, J. 1980. Intergovernmentalism and regional governance in the 1980s. Paper presented at the Conference on Illinois Government and Politics, Springfield.

5. Chicago Metropolis 2020 and the Metropolitan Mayors Caucus. 2002. Recommendations for developing attainable workforce housing in the Chicago region. Chicago.

6. Metropolitan Mayors Caucus. 2002. Housing action agenda. Chicago.

7. Metropolitan Mayors Caucus. 2009b. Greenest region compact of metropolitan Chicago. Chicago.

8. Letter to the Honorable William Lipinski, Chairman, March 23, 2014.

9. Diversity, Inc. 2003. Letter to Jeffrey Ladd, Metra Chairman.

10. *Daily Southtown*. 2003. Time for new blood on Metra board. June 12.

11. Metra. 2009. Ridership reports-System facts. http://metrarail.com/metralenlhome/about_metraplanningrecords reports/ridership report.

12. Letter to the Honorable William Lipinski, chairman, March 23, 2004.

13. Scott, A. 1. 2000. Global city-regions: Economic planning and policy dilemmas in a neoliberal world. In *Urban-suburban interdependencies,* edited by R. Greenstein and W. Wiewel, 119-40. Cambridge, MA: Lincoln Institute *of* Land Policy.

14. Scott, A J. 1998. *Regions and the world economy: The coming shape of global production, competition, and political order.* Oxford, UK: Oxford Univ. Press.

15. Jezierski, L. 1996. Pittsburgh: "Partnerships in a regional city." In *Regional politics: America in a post-city age,* edited by H. V. Savitch and R. K. Vogel, 159-81. Thousand Oaks, CA: Sage.

16. Berg, B., and P. Kantor. 1996. New York: The politics of conflict and avoidance. In *Regional politics: America in a post-city age,* edited by H. V. Savitch and R. K. Vogel, 25-50. Thousand Oaks, CA: Sage.

17. Saltzstein, A. L. 1996. Los Angeles: Politics without governance. In *Regional politics: America in a post-city age,* edited by H. V Savitch and R. K. Vogel, 51-71. Thousand Oaks, CA: Sage.

18. Savitch, H. V, and R. K. Vogel, eds. 1996. *Regional politics: America in a post-city age.* Thousand Oaks, CA: Sage.p. 294.

International Study Finds Chicago Public Transit Lacking, Dysfunctional

By Chuck Sudo

The Organization for Economic Cooperation and Development found that public transportation in Chicago lags behind other major cities. In addition to a lack of coordination between RTA, CTA, Pace and Metra, our public transportation infrastructure is in dire need of upgrading. Lack of attention, cooperation and dwindling public investment in transit is hampering economic development around the region.

There are several issues preventing Chicago area public transit from being truly worthy of a city that sees itself as world class. Among those issues: funding; overlapping bureaucracies; and a lack of coordination between RTA, CTA, Pace Suburban Bus and Metra. Example: there is absolutely no reason Metra should be implementing Ventra more than a year after CTA and Pace went through headaches to do so. All three should be on board with the shared-fare payment system *now* [Ventra is the name of the joint fare system for CTA and Pace, launched system-wide in July of 2014. The Ventra rollout was widely criticized and viewed as a systemic failure].

This lack of coordination and the transit agencies acting independent of each other are among the reasons an international economic group found Chicago's transportation infrastructure to be lacking and, by extension, hampering economic development around the region. The study by the Paris-based think tank, the Organization for Economic Cooperation and Development found insufficient accountability among the four transit agency groups to be another issue ... The group called Chicago public transit "relatively depressing."

The report offers very little new information for those paying attention to the area's public transit network, but it is a blow to Mayor Rahm Emanuel and others who continue to use "public transit system" and "world class" in the same sentence so frequently it appears they may be wishing it so. Olaf Merk, the author of the report, told the Tribune, "My own impression of the Chicago transit system would be that it is surely below the best urban transit systems in the world."

The report lends credence to a recommendation earlier this year [2014] by the Northeastern Illinois Transit Task Force that the separate operational structures of CTA, Metra and Pace be combined into one larger agency. RTA recommended last year that planning departments at the three agencies be consolidated. Merk and his team relied heavily on previous reports by the Metropolitan Planning Council and Metropolis Strategies (formerly Chicago Metropolis 2020) that found ridership on CTA and Metra has declined since 1980, and that the agencies are more concerned with protecting their turf than addressing ridership needs.

Funding is another critical issue broached in the report. Chicago spends less on transit capital needs than it did 20 years ago, and Chicago's per capita transit spending is falling behind other cities in the U.S. and internationally … London spends five times more on transit per capita than Chicago, while New York spends three times more, the report found. Both New York and Philadelphia have a single board that oversees and appoints managers of transit operations … Outdated transit funding was also a target of the report.

The lack of accountability may be the most damning issue cited in the report. It lists a supermajority voting requirement at RTA, where 75 percent of board members have to vote in favor of anything, and the five Chicago-based appointees that block many decisions at RTA. "The current governance structure of public transport allows agencies to point fingers at each other when there are problems," the report said. "In addition, the sheer number of board members (47) creates a heavy management structure … as all of these are political appointees, not elected by the general public like in some other U.S. metropolitan areas" … The report concluded, "Public transit in Chicago is organized such that it is difficult to identify the main actor to hold accountable for underperformance."

The Municipal Government Debt Crisis

By John Nothdurft and Sheila Weinberg

The economic recession that began in 2007 exposed and aggravated a government debt crisis that had been brewing for many years. Slow and negative economic growth, plummeting housing values, and rising costs for social safety-net programs, came together at one time, making it impossible to hide the extent to which municipal governments were borrowing to pay for current operations, while at the same time, shortchanging their workers' pension funds.

For this project we analyzed the financial condition of 518 primary taxing districts within Cook County, the second-most populous county in the United States and home to the City of Chicago. Data were derived from the most recent financial reports published on the Cook County Treasurer's Web site on June 30, 2012. The 518 taxing districts have a combined "financial burden" of almost $34 billion. The Institute for Truth in Accounting (IFTA) determined the "financial burden" by subtracting liabilities the taxing districts have accumulated to date, including unfunded retirement liabilities, from the assets available to pay those liabilities.[2]

Specifically, we found the following:

- Unfunded pension liability, $31.07 billion
- Unfunded retirees' health care benefits liability, $7.18 billion
- Other debts and liabilities, $24.88 billion
- Total amount of bills, $63.13 billion
- Assets available to pay bills, $29.41 billion
- Financial burden (total bills minus assets), $33.72 billion

There are 1,966,356 households in Cook County.3 Simple division produces the following average per-household amounts:

- Unfunded pension liability, $15,799
- Unfunded retirees' health care benefits liability, $3,651
- Other debts and liabilities, $12,655
- Total amount of bills, $32,105
- Assets available to pay bills, $14,957
- Financial burden (total bills minus assets), $17,147

The financial burden created by the federal government is $574,042 per household,[4] while the financial burden of the Illinois government is $32,905 per household. When added together, the total federal, state, and local financial burden on the average household in Cook County is a staggering $624,094.

These numbers, even the per-household numbers, may be meaningless to many readers. What does it mean to say an average household has a "financial burden" of $32,905 from the state of Illinois plus an additional $17,147 from local governments? Will it ever have to be paid? When, and how quickly? What could be the consequences if the debt comes due and it can't be paid?

Here, briefly, are the answers to these important questions:

- Taxpayers may pay higher taxes due to lower bond ratings (requiring higher interest payments on debts)…
- Residents may suffer as mandatory payments to pension funds crowd out spending on necessary public services such as fire, police and sanitation. Longer response times to fire alarms and calls for police, less frequent garbage collection, and less maintenance of roads and parks are inevitable
- Unless retirees' pension and health care benefits are renegotiated or government services are cut, future taxpayers will be forced to pay these benefits as they come due, but they will receive no corresponding government services.
- Higher property tax rates cause property values to fall and businesses to flee, leading to a spiral of even higher tax rates on those who remain to raise the needed funds.

- Population and business flee communities and states that are raising taxes relative to other communities and states or that appear to be heading toward a debt crisis. Residents suffer higher rates of unemployment and lower incomes as a result. States such as Indiana and Wisconsin already are benefitting from Illinois' pending crisis.
- Finally, a debt crisis occurs when a government entity cannot afford to make scheduled or negotiated principal and interest payments on debt, plus pensions and health benefits owed to retired workers. The result, as we are witnessing in Detroit, is municipal or county bankruptcy or its equivalent, control over day-to-day operations given to a state or court-appointed trustee or emergency manager.[5] Dramatic cuts in services, defaults on bonds, and higher taxes are invariably parts of the workout.

* * *

At the heart of local debt problems are personnel costs, which make up the majority of county and municipal expenditures. According to the U.S. Census Bureau, "Local governments—which include counties, cities, townships, special districts and school districts—accounted for 12.2 million full-time equivalent employees in 2010."[6]

The average total compensation (wages and benefits) for government employees according to the Bureau of Labor Statistics stands at $39.83 an hour. In comparison, the average private-sector worker receives $29.40 an hour in compensation.[7] This equates to an average compensation of $83,000 a year for a government worker while the typical private-sector worker's compensation is about $61,000.

In addition to the high personnel costs, rampant borrowing from pension funds has contributed to making governments' long-term commitments to public workers fiscally unsound...

There is a growing and legitimate fear that Cook County could be heading over a financial cliff, not in 10 or 20 years but in the next three to five years. If this were to happen to either Cook County or the City of Chicago, it would easily be the largest government bankruptcy (or its equivalent, if formal bankruptcy is not a legal option) in the nation's history...

The increasing debt levels of Cook County's 553 taxing districts corresponds closely with the rise in tax burdens, the biggest of which are property and sales taxes. An analysis by the Treasurer's Office found an average increase of 121 percent for the top 50 residential property tax amounts in each municipality form 1996 to 2009.[8] This rapid increase in taxes has fueled a significant migration of population and businesses out of Cook County. According to the U.S. Census Bureau, Cook County was the only county in the top ten in population to lose population since 2000...

This study found that 70 percent of promised retirement benefits have not been reported on the taxing districts' balance sheets. In addition, government officials have not included all of the government's current costs, such as those related to pension and retiree health care benefits, in their annual budgets. This lack of truth and transparency in government budgeting and accounting makes it impossible for even the most sophisticated user of such reporting to independently determine a judge a public-sector entity's financial condition...

Because of the lack of truth and transparency in budget processes, the public has not been aware that 181 taxing districts in Cook County have been accumulating debt at alarming rates. Research conducted for this report found the taxing districts have accumulated a total "financial burden" of $33.7 billion...Financial burdens often exist because costs, especially those for employees' retirement benefits, were incurred by the taxing districts in prior years but responsibility for paying these costs was shifted onto future taxpayers. This practice violates public accountability principles that stress the current generation of citizens should pay for current-year services and not shift to future-year taxpayers.

State and local governments are not held to the same accounting standards as most business and even publicly traded companies. Under outdated government accounting policies, citizens and even elected officials have been left in the dark as their governments were accumulating unsustainable retirement liabilities. This is because the government accounting standards have required governments to **not report** the majority of their unfunded retirement liabilities on their balance sheets.

* * *

Municipalities are in such precarious financial shape primarily because their police and firefighters pension plans are greatly underfunded. Not enough assets have been set aside to fund promised benefits. More than half of these plans have unfunded liabilities of more than 300 percent of covered payroll.

The unfunded liability for the Village of Forestview's Firefighters Pension Plan, for example, is more than 10 times the amount of related payroll. In other words, to pay off this plan's unfunded liability, the village would have to lay off all of the covered employees for more than 10 years and divert the payroll dollars they would have received solely to paying for the promised pension. Three other municipalities' unfunded liabilities are more than nine times the amount of covered payroll...

Over the years municipalities have not contributed enough to properly fund the pension plans. In non-home rule communities the ability to fund the plans is restricted because state tax caps limit how much tax levies can increase. While the plans' assets are managed by the municipalities, local elected officials are, for the most part, not in control of benefits provided. For the most part state laws determine the amount of benefits employees will receive.

* * *

Drivers of underfunded retirement plans include benefit enrichments, employees living longer than expected, lower-than-assumed investment returns, and government officials promising benefits without providing adequate funding.

* * *

States, counties and municipalities can adopt policies that address the decisions that have created the crisis and hid it from the public's view for many years...We offer this brief list... as a guide to concerned taxpayers and policymakers alike.

1. Adopt accounting practices that provide maximum transparency...
2. Create an accurate and complete accounting of all the new missions and obligations the municipality has adopted over time...
3. Fully count pension...obligations as expenses and insist they be fully funded...
4. Acknowledge more employees will be retiring and living longer after retirement than previous budgets assumed, and increase projected liability...Reduce forecasts of the return on investment of pension funds to more realistic levels.
5. Carefully manage the use of tax increment financing to ensure that TIF districts are not diverting needed public funds from other services and that taxpayers are not subject to the risk of having to pay off loans if the expected increase in tax revenues doesn't appear.
6. Above all, elected officials need to avoid the twin temptations of providing new services without asking taxpayers to pay for them and putting the demands of special-interest groups above the taxpaying public.

* * *

Like all governments, the taxing districts of Cook County derive their just powers from the consent of the governed. Therefore each taxing district has a special responsibility to report on its actions and the results of those actions. These reports must provide useful information that enables the citizens and their elected representatives to make informed decisions. Governments must change how they prepare their budgets and financial reports to provide this information.

NOTES

1. John Nothdurft is director of government relations for The Heartland Institute. Sheila Weinberg is founder and CEO of the Institute for Truth in Accounting...The authors would like to especially thank Cook County Treasurer Maria Pappas and Mr. Patrick O'Meara for assistance with data and valuable advice and insights throughout the development of this paper.
2. Capital assets and debt related to capital assets are not included in these calculations.
3. The number of households represents the occupied households in 2010 according to the United States Census Bureau, http://www.census.gov/popfinder/. The United States Census Bureau defines a household as including "all persons who occupy a housing unit as their usual place of residence." The average number of people per household in the U.S. is 2.59, in Illinois is 2.63, and in Cook County is 2.63, http://quickfacts.census.gov/gfd/states/17/17031.html.

4. The number of households represents the occupied households in 2010 according to the United States Census Bureau, http://census.gov/prod/cen2010/briefs/c2010br-07.pdf.

5. Eric Scorsone, Ph.D. and Nicolette Bateson, CPA, "Evaluating a Chapter 9 Bankruptcy for City of Detroit: Reality Check or Turnaround Solution?" Department of Agricultural, Food and Resource Economics, Michigan State University, February 1, 2012, http://news.msu.edu/media/documents/2012/02/c763d393-5bad-4864-815b-4f8ff501f289.pdf.

6. "State and Local Governments Employ 16.6 million Full-Time Equivalent Employees in 2010," U.S. Census Bureau, August 30, 2011, http://www.census.gov/newsroom/releases/archives/governments/cb11-146.html/

7. Eli Lehrer and Steve Stanek, "The State Public Pension Crisis: A 50-State Report Card," The Heartland Institute, April 2010, http://heartland.org/sites/all/modules/custom/heartland_migration/files/pdfs/27578.pdf.

8. "Pappas Details Impact of Local Government Debt," Cook County Treasurer's Office, June 21, 2011, http://www.cookcountytreasurer.com/newsdetail.aspx?ntopicid=434.

PART VII

A New Chicago

Introduction

To borrow the words of a Biblical prophet, "without a vision, a people perish. With vision, faith and commitment a people flourish." In past decades Chicago has faced major crises as old social, economic, and political systems have partially collapsed and have partially been reformed. The Old Chicago is passing away so a New Chicago can be born.

The two terms of Mayor Harold Washington were a watershed, a major turning point. But he left an uncompleted reform agenda for us to implement. Some reforms were adopted under Mayor Richard M. Daley but the list of reforms needed under reelected Mayor Rahm Emmanuel and a new city council remains very long. Racial and political machine forces continue to reassert themselves in the city council, in elections, and in local governments throughout the metropolitan region. The political future of Chicago is still to be determined.

Locally, the connection between race and poverty has led to unprecedented homicides despite new policing strategies. The most impoverished, struggling neighborhoods on the city's south and west sides, which are overwhelmingly African American, have suffered the most. While crime in Chicago as a whole has remained steady, neighborhoods like Auburn-Gresham and Englewood have seen a complicated web of gang warfare emerge from what used to be just a handful of dominant gangs. Gang factions now number in the hundreds, making it hard for even gang members themselves to keep track.

Since 2012 there have been over 500 homicides nearly every year in Chicago, far more than New York or Los Angeles, cities with two and three times the population. Mayor Emanuel decided to send more police officers to the streets to combat this—taking officers off administrative duties to walk beats. While the impact of an increased police presence remains to be seen, it doesn't address the fundamental causes of violence and thus can only be seen as part of the solution. Even hiring more police officers is unlikely to stem the tide of violence. And while Chicago has so far avoided the riots of cities like Ferguson, Missouri and Baltimore, Maryland, relations between minority communities and the police remain tense.

The Chicago Public Schools (CPS) in 2012 was downsized as Mayor Emanuel, who argued they were underutilized, closed over 50 schools. As thousands of students were displaced, parents and teachers cited safety concerns for children who were forced to walk further, often crossing different gang territories, to attend new schools. Closing neighborhood schools according to Catalyst Chicago is "also a bad omen for communities. The last thing Englewood, Austin or any of the neighborhoods—most of them poor and black—that stand to lose schools need is another boarded-up vacant building."[1] Despite closings and an increase in the number of charter schools in Chicago, CPS still faces a billion-dollar deficit and its test scores while slowly improving, remain unacceptably low.

Nationally, the election and reelection of President Barack Obama brought about changes in Washington and the promise of more positive urban policies. But because we are still recovering from the Great Recession of 2008 and two foreign wars, a gridlocked Congress has prioritized cutting the budget and reducing deficit spending. State cutbacks in local government and school funding are even greater. If there is to be improvement in our metropolitan region, we will probably have to depend primarily upon ourselves. In the years immediately ahead, we must strengthen our local economy and fortify our role in the global economy. To do this, we must compete as a metropolitan region and while we have many advantages, which include our diverse economy, we have yet to develop a coherent focus in either the private or public sectors. Job gains in the tech sector and in downtown businesses are not enough to sustain the entire regional economy.

In a period of austerity, new projects provide a symbol of hope. The new Lucas Museum and the DePaul sports arena are being created in the south loop. The new Obama Presidential Library will anchor and boost parts of the south side, while the Maggie Daley Park and remodeled Navy Pier will bring more residents and tourists to these downtown attractions. The housing market has improved as the number of foreclosed homes begins to drop. Yet, challenges remain in making a new and better Chicago.

Ultimately, progress depends upon our collective vision for our city's future. Our vision must transcend the machine/reform and Republican/Democrat divisions of local and national politics. Our vision must transcend city and suburban divisions and public and private sector divides. Our vision of a New Chicago must be drawn from deeper wellsprings. We need to reassert the biblical vision of a just city in which old inequities, hatreds, and injustices are dissolved.

Let us work to create a New Chicago characterized by joy rather than by suffering. Let us cut our high rate of infant mortality and improve the health of everyone. Let the homeless be housed, the hungry fed, and the unemployed and underemployed provided meaningful and rewarding work. Let crime, which has characterized our city for so long, be eliminated. Let everyone walk freely on our streets unafraid. Let traditional hatreds as well as racial, religious, and sexual discrimination disappear.

Let our metropolitan region be an example of how to resolve the problems that now plague our planet. Let us end pollution and create a more energy-efficient green city. Let us order our economy and our education system so that the underclass is fully integrated back into society. No more shall we be a metropolitan region that is half rich and half poor.

The struggle for the future of Chicago and our region occurs at many levels. It takes place in elections that dominate the political arena. It takes place in governmental struggles to implement reforms. It occurs in the marketplace as new firms arise, as old companies create new products, and as some enterprises die. It takes place in each of our neighborhoods and communities. It requires a sustained commitment by many individuals to create a new and more just Chicago.

We are engaged in a struggle of hope against despair. It is our task to uphold the vision of a New Chicago and to convince Chicagoans and their leaders to embrace it. This is a task for a lifetime, as the final article attests.

NOTES

1. Forte, Lorraine. 2013. "For Smooth School Closings, CPS Has a Lot of Promises to Keep." *Catalyst Chicago*. April 3. http://www.catalyst-chicago.org/news/2013/04/03/20939/smooth-school-closings-cps-has-many-promises-keep

How Long Is Your Anger?

By Mary Scott Simpson

In this article, Mary Scott Simpson argues that we have not sustained our anger at an unjust political system. Instead we have turned "toward acceptance of the failures of our political system" and turned "toward private amusements and away from public action."

One of my favorite moments in modern drama occurs in Bertolt Brecht's *Mother Courage*. The title character waits with a young-soldier outside an army officer's tent; both are there to protest unjust treatment by an army captain. Courage listens with scant patience to the tirade of the young soldier (he won't "stand for injustice"), then asks: "But how long? How long won't you stand for injustice? One Hour? Two?" She sings for him "The Song of the Great Capitulation," an account of the series of small failures, accommodations, compromises through which she has come "to march in lockstep with the rest." At last she advises him, "You should stay here with your sword drawn if you're set on it and your anger is big enough ... but if your anger is a short one, you'd better go." And then she takes her own advice. She leaves, "I've thought better of it. I'm not complaining."

I think of this scene often as I consider the turns of events in the city and the country over the past few years—turnings toward acceptance of the failures of our political system, turnings toward private amusements and away from public action. "Curses," I say to myself, "that was a most remarkably short anger." And I'm inclined to think that more than just a cause or two may be lost in the shuffle. For me, cultivating a long anger and, thus, keeping faith with that belief in democracy which, when offended, gives rise to anger has come to be a matter of personal and cultural survival.

Courage, like many another Brechtian protagonists, knows both that she is given to lapses in virtue and that the system that surrounds her nudges her toward those lapses: it makes survival so desperate an undertaking that only the advantaged few can afford sustained virtue. I, too, see the system that surrounds us as one reason why so many, once angry, have thought better of it and aren't complaining. Our trouble, however, is not so much a matter of survival amid scarcity as it is a matter of surviving plenitude.

As a people we are governed by a restless urge to consume—food, clothes, gadgets, relationships, news, ideologies, causes. I regularly find myself awash in impressions: a whirl of polyester, electric woks, sunshine laws, punk rock, T-groups, protein diets; boycotts, catastrophes and intimations of apocalypse. The buzz is ubiquitous. In such circumstances, to sustain anger, to sustain a thought requires Promethean powers of concentration.

Our system teaches us to live like those pigeons that congregate on El platforms—scurrying frantically from one bright flash to the next, hoping for grain and finding (worse luck) discarded gum wrappers. Allowing ourselves to follow that pattern has consequences for our character—individually and corporately. It means, at least, that we may be allowing the erosion of some capacities that make us human: the capacity for fidelity, for instance, to other persons, to our own beliefs, to carefully considered goals. I wonder, too, what we do to our capacity for hard thought when we subject our minds daily to the impressionistic patterns of the six o'clock news: fragments and facts, uninterrupted, unexamined. And I wonder what difference it will someday make that we consistently prefer intense, ephemeral pleasures to the others—longer, slower, substantial satisfactions that come from solving problems, making things, keeping promises.

These are habits we can't afford to lose.

Choosing a goal (the political reformation of Chicago, for instance), then pursuing it steadily—testing, refining ourselves and our ideas through experience: these things take years, not months of our time. But those who give themselves to that long endeavor learn that there are goods of a personal sort to be taken from it—growth in skill and understanding, certainly, but perhaps even more important, the sense that one has said, "Here I stand," and meant it to a world that is forever telling us, "Move along, there."

To sustain one's anger is to secure one's humanity.

Index

S

Segregation, racial 35–37, 43, 83
Shakman Decree 91, 92, 93
Shakman, Michael 87, 88, 91, 93
Sorich, Robert 81, 93
Special Districts 269
Suburbs, Suburban 125, 126

T

Tax Increment Finance Districts (TIFs)
        139–143
Transparency 75, 76, 132, 133, 139

U

Unemployment 183, 269
Urban Renewal 30, 226, 227

V

Voorhees Center 57

W

Ward 24, 25, 32
Washington, Harold 82, 85
White flight 252

CPSIA information can be obtained
at www.ICGtesting.com
Printed in the USA
LVOW09s2223060317
526315LV00004B/7/P